Schmidt Ink, Inc.

Creating Universes with

Business Objects Designer XI V3

SAP Business Objects XI V3 - CBT

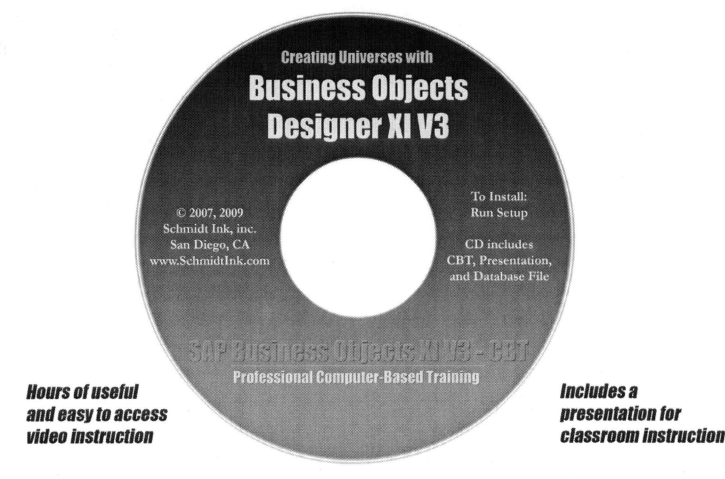

Creating Universes with
Business Objects Designer XI V3

© 2007, 2009
Schmidt Ink, inc.
San Diego, CA
www.SchmidtInk.com

To Install:
Run Setup

CD includes
CBT, Presentation,
and Database File

SAP Business Objects XI V3 - CBT
Professional Computer-Based Training

Hours of useful and easy to access video instruction

Includes a presentation for classroom instruction

Robert D. Schmidt
Independent Business Objects Trainer, Consultant, and Author for Over 15 Years

Schmidt Ink, Inc.
Creating Universes with Business Objects Designer XI V3

Published by
Schmidt Ink, Inc.
San Diego, CA 92122

Printed in USA

Schmidt Ink, Inc.
Phone: (858) 405-9317
www.schmidtink.com

Other Schmidt Ink, Inc. Publications:
Creating Documents with BusinessObjects: Desktop Intelligence XI R2 (978-0972263672)
Creating Documents with BusinessObjects XI R2 - CBT (978-0972263641)
Creating Universes with Designer XI R2 - CBT (978-0972263634)

0-9722636-2-4 (978-0-9722636-2-7)

I dedicate this book to my family. I also dedicate it to all the readers who trust my books to help further their knowledge and careers. I appreciate your trust and thank you for the motivation that you give me.

Introduction

Thank you for purchasing Creating Universes with Business Objects Designer XI V3. I hope that this book provides you with the reference and training that will help you to become a Business Objects professional. In this book we will examine many topics on creating universes. Most of these topics will reference a database called SI Data V3.

The SI Data V3 database is delivered on the accompanying CD in a Microsoft Access database. You may use this database directly, or import it into SQL Server. Importing it to SQL Server is recommended, because some of the functions in this book are SQL Server specific. There are also Oracle versions of the formulas. The database contains data from an investment company that had a one-year portfolio fund. In this fund there were six portfolios that traded stocks from their respective industries. The data also includes calls to clients and the daily prices of included stocks.

It is also better if you can export your universe into a Business Objects repository, as we will create a linked universe in this course. Link universes require a repository for security (CMS). If you do not have a repository set up, you will still be able to do most of the examples in the book.

The CD does not contain a demo version of Business Objects software. It is assumed that you have the product and that it is set up and running.

The CD does contain a PDF presentation file. This presentation can be used to present the material to your fellow employees. You may not print this PDF and distribute it to anybody other than yourself, as this is a copyright violation. However, you may purchase the books directly from the distributor at a discounted price so that everybody viewing the presentation has a book. You may call 1-800-247-6553 for more information.

The CD also contains a CBT (Computer-Based Training) application. To install the CBT, run the SetUp.exe file. If the application runs, but no videos are visible, then install the Flash player from Adobe.com. This CBT is copyrighted and only the purchaser of the book has rights to use it. I include the CBT to help readers better understand the examples and material in the book. If you desire to place it on a corporate intranet, then please contact me to obtain the rights to do so. You should get the contact information on my website: www.SchmidtInk.com.

If your company has many people to train in Business Objects Designer, Web Intelligence, and/or Desktop Intelligence, then you may be interested in the Corporate Training Package. This package gives a company limited rights to reproduce the manuals in order to train their employees. Please contact us at RSchmidt@SchmidtInk.com for more information. You may also contact me at this address, if you have any questions on any of the exercises in the book. Please also send any comments and suggestions that you may have.

Sincerely,
Robert D. Schmidt
www.SchmidtInk.com

Table of Contects

Chapter 2: Conditions in Our Universe 75

Chapter 3: Inserting Tables and Joins 99

Chapter 4: Working with Multiple Fact Tables 151

Introduction

After years of training and consulting Business Objects, I decided to write a book that truly teaches how to create Business Objects Universes. The first book was very successful, but the readers had lots of comments and suggestions. With this edition, I tried to address their concerns, which has made this version a really great book. One thing that you will notice about my book, is that there is no advanced user section. The reason for this is simple - If you are going to use Business Objects professionally, then what's the point to not being advanced. This does not mean that the book is difficult to understand, because we usually start with simple topics, and then complicate it by adding new complexities. For example, the first two chapters only deal with a single table. With this table, we create objects and conditions independently of any data complications that may be introduced by adding additional tables. Then, as the course goes on, we add tables to our universe. These tables make the universe more complicated by introducing more elements, including Fan-traps and Chasm-traps. Since we proceed in this manner, we are able to discuss solutions as they are introduced.

The book always has the graphics on the left (top) side of the open book, and the text is always on the right (bottom). The book is formatted this way, so that we can have many large graphics that help readers to understand the topics. There are also many exercises that help readers to create the universe that is used throughout the book. This continuity should help the reader evolve into a professional level universe designer. The database used to create the universe is on the CD that accompanies this book. It will probably be in a Microsoft Access database and/or in flat files. This data should be imported into Oracle, SQL Server or some other database. The book has both SQL Server and Oracle examples, but you should be able to convert the examples into your database's format. For example, the book has a First of Year example for both Oracle and SQL Server. To best understand Universe Design, a reader should know SQL. It is very important to understand that the universe is creating SQL to retrieve data, and the reader should understand exactly what this SQL is doing. This doesn't mean that you should be an expert at SQL, but you should know basic queries and subqueries.

To start universe design, we will need to have access to the database where the data resides. To do this, we will need to create an ODBC data source, which is the first topic in the first chapter. ODBC data sources are not part of Business Objects, but are necessary for universe design with relational databases. There are other types of connections, such as OLE connections, and if you are comfortable with this type of connection, then you can use it instead. Also, Oracle can use an Oracle connection, which is also okay. Once the connection is established, then the course is much less difficult, because the remaining of the course is concerned with the Business Objects Designer application.

One last note, it is best if readers of this book have used or plan on using one of the Business Objects reporting applications, as this will help you to understand how the universe is being used. This understanding is essential for logical design and testing.

Universe Definition

Deep Space View of our Universe

Courtesy of NASA and the Hubble Space Telescope

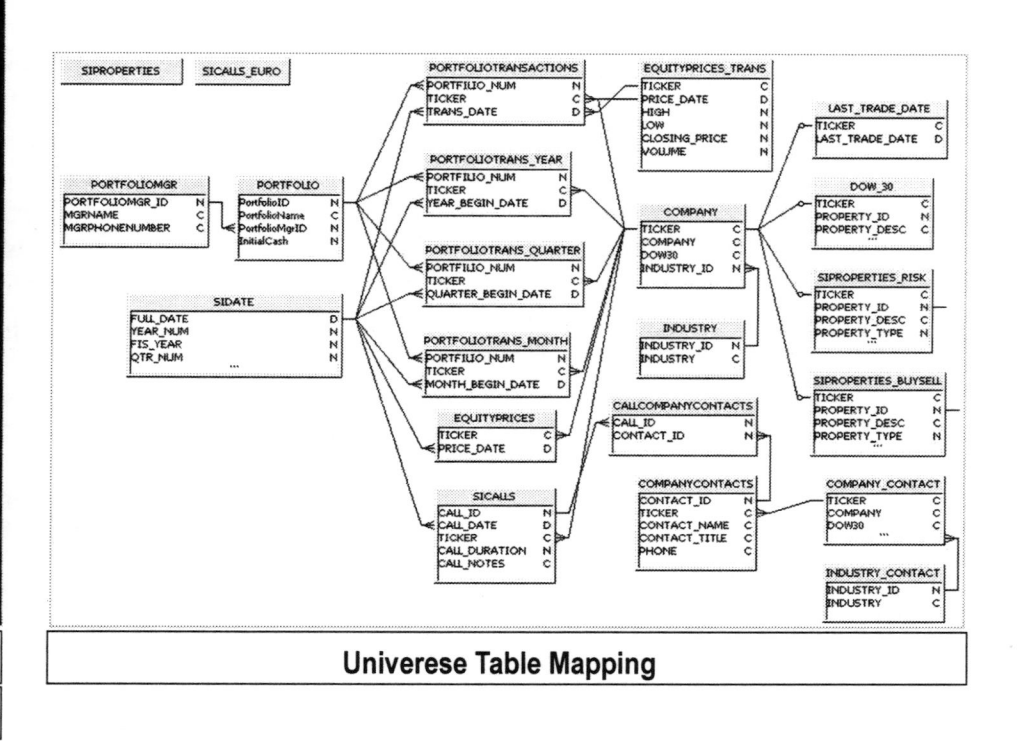

Univerese Table Mapping

Universe Definition

The real Universe contains all matter and energy. It contains everything. A Business Objects universe contains what it needs to contain to create the reports that it needs to support. The entire universe is very large and difficult to understand. A Business Objects universe should not be too large and difficult to understand. The real universe was created for its purpose, one that people have always argued about. A Business Objects universe needs to be created for a specific purpose, and there should be no arguments as to what it is for.

With these contrasts between the real universe and a Business Objects universe, one has to wonder why Business Objects universes are called universes. The universe contains galaxies, solar systems, and planets. It may have been better to call a Business Objects universe a galaxy, because a business can be divided into different functional groups - Sales, Support, Manufacturing, Financials, Inventory, and so forth. This means that a company should have several universes, probably at least one for each function of the business.

With this in mind, we need to focus our universes on specific needs of the company. This will make them both easier to develop and easier to understand.

Notes

Universe Contexts

Portfolio Transactions

Equity Prices

Calls

Photos Courtesy of NASA and the Hubble Space Telescope

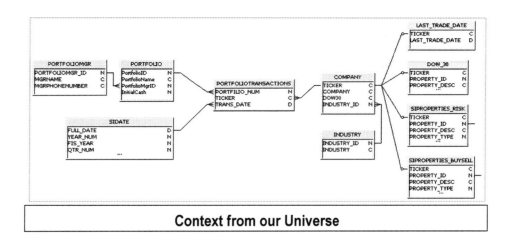

Context from our Universe

Universe Contexts

So, now we know that universes are usually assigned to specific businesses within a company. For example, the Sales universe. Within the Sales universe, we should find Orders and Invoices. If we want to know information about orders, then we will go to the orders section. However, if we want to know which orders have been invoiced, then we should go to the invoice area.

Usually, when an order is placed within a company that order gets stored in a transaction table, we'll call this table Orders. This transaction table has all of the orders placed with the business. The Orders table will use other tables, such as customer and product. So information on orders can be retrieved from this collection of tables. If we wanted to continue the Universe analogy, then we can call this collection of tables a solar system. If there were only one solar system in the galaxy, then we would not worry too much about naming it or how it relates to other solar systems, because there is only one.

However, in the Sales universe, we may also have the Invoice section. The invoice section gets data every time an order is invoiced. The Invoice table is also a transaction table. By the way, we also know these transaction tables as Fact Tables. The invoice table probably also uses the Customer and Product tables. Now, we have two different tables, both using the same supporting tables, which are also known as Dimension tables.

So, now that we have two systems within our one universe, we need to identify these systems, Business Objects does this with Contexts. This means that universes can contain no contexts - only one system, or multiple contexts - multiple systems.

In the universe that we are going to create, we will end up with three contexts - Portfolio Transactions, Equity Prices, and Calls. Our universe allows us to report on a business that started a one-year trading company. This company began in 2000 and liquidated in 2001. During its existence it bought and sold stock through six different departments- DOW 30, Technology, Media, Finance, Biotechnology, and Alternative Energy. In this class we will build a universe that allows report developers to create reports on this business. By the way, it is really of no matter what the type of data is that we are reporting on. It could be Manufacturing, Clinical Testing, Engineering, Biotechnology, Warehousing, Human Resources, and so on. This is the beauty of Business Objects, since we are only organizing the data into an accessible form. Granted, there are industry specific formulas that a designer will have to know and understand, but every industry will have Fact tables, Dimension tables, Dimensions, Measures, and Conditions.

Notes

Universe Objects

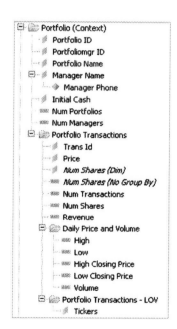

Portfolio (Context)
- Portfolio ID
- Portfoliomgr ID
- Portfolio Name
- Manager Name
  - Manager Phone
- Initial Cash
- Num Portfolios
- Num Managers
- Portfolio Transactions
  - Trans Id
  - Price
  - *Num Shares (Dim)*
  - **Num Shares (No Group By)**
  - Num Transactions
  - Num Shares
  - Revenue
- Daily Price and Volume
  - High
  - Low
  - High Closing Price
  - Low Closing Price
  - Volume
- Portfolio Transactions - LOV
  - Tickers

Calls (Context)
- Call Id
- Call Notes
- Call Duration
- Num Calls
- Calls - Contact POV
  - Contact Id
  - Contact Name
  - Contact Phone
  - Contact Title
  - Contact Industry
  - Contact Company
  - Contact Ticker
  - Num Contacts

Equity Prices (Context)
- High
- Low
- High Closing Price
- Low Closing Price
- Average Closing Price
- Volume
- High Volume
- Low Volume
- Average Volume

Company (Common)
- Ticker
- Last Trade Date
- DOW 30
- Risk
- Buy Sell
- Industry ID
- Industry
- Company
- Num Companies
- Num Industries
- Company - Advanced
  - Ticker
    - DOW 30
    - Risk
    - Buy Sell

Dates (Common)
- Full Date
- Year Num
- Fis Year
- Qtr Num
- Fis Qtr
- Month Num
- Fis Period
- Month Name
- Day Name
- First Of Year
- End Of Year
- Days In Year
- Days Into Year
- Workdays In Year
- Workdays Into Year
- Fis First Of Year
- Fis End Of Year
- Days In Fis Year
- Days Into Fis Year
- Workdays In Fis Year
- Workdays Into Fis Year
- First Of Qtr
- End Of Qtr
- Days In Qtr
- Days Into Qtr
- Workdays In Qtr
- Workdays Into Qtr
- Fis First Of Qtr
- Fis End Of Qtr
- Days In Fis Qtr
- Days Into Fis Qtr
- Workdays In Fis Qtr
- Workdays Into Fis Qtr
- First Of Month
- Days In Month
- Days Into Month
- Workdays In Month
- Workdays Into Month
- First Of Week
- Days Into Week

Portfolio (Context)
- Manager
- Portfolio Transactions
  - Revenue Greater Than 2001 Average
  - Daily Price and Volume
  - Portfolio Transactions - LOV
- Equity Prices (Context)
- Calls (Context)
- Company (Common)
  - Company Ticker
  - Company - Advanced
- Dates (Common)
  - Date Range - Prompted
  - WTD - Prompted
  - MTD - Prompted
  - QTD - Prompted
  - YTD - Prompted
  - PYTD - Prompted

Objects in our Universe

Universe Objects

Universe objects identify data and the type of data that is available in a universe. They are created to allow report developers access the data that a universe points to (maps).

They not only access data, but describe how that data is to behave. There are three different types of objects that represent data behavior - Dimensions, Details, and Measures. There are also condition objects that allow for conditions to be placed in queries.

In the graphic, we can see that the objects are organized within folders. These folders are called Classes.

Therefore, universes are mappings of tables within databases. They do not contain data, but point to the locations of data. Universes are able to point to data through database connections - ODBC, Oracle Client, and others. We map the tables with joins and contexts. We map the fields with objects - Classes, Dimensions, Details, and Measures. We create conditions that allow report developers to focus on only data of interest.

We must create universes with all of these components, and at the same time make them easy for report developers to understand. I hope that through this book that I am able to teach you how to accomplish creating powerful and easy to understand universes.

Notes

Creating Queries

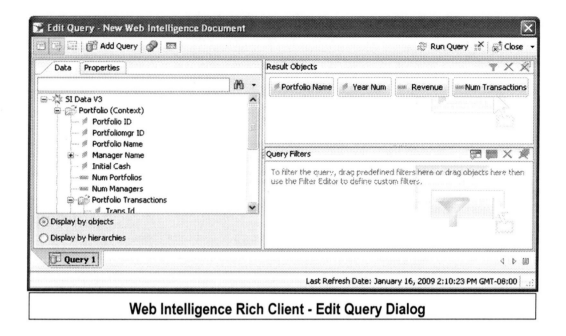

Web Intelligence Rich Client - Edit Query Dialog

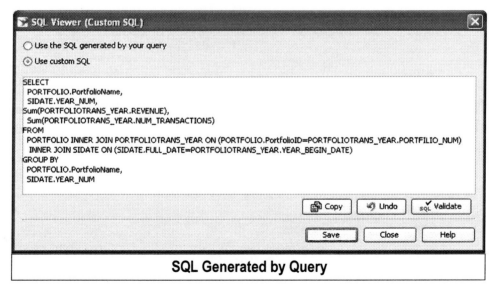

SQL Generated by Query

Portfolio Name	Year Num	Revenue	Num Transactions
Alternative Energy	2000	(89,221)	78
Alternative Energy	2001	303,886	96
Biotech	2000	(369,888)	91
Biotech	2001	449,314	93
DOW 30	2000	(4,385,413)	675
DOW 30	2001	5,736,866	816
Finance	2000	(507,101)	45
Finance	2001	574,563	75
Media	2000	(465,394)	62
Media	2001	386,854	58
Technology	2000	(1,116,767)	274
Technology	2001	1,059,497	317

Table of Results

Creating Queries

After the universe is created, then report developers can use the objects to create queries, and then format the results from the queries into useful reports. The advantage to the universe is that all of the complexities of the data relationships has been resolved in the universe design and consistently presented to the report developers through the query interface.

Report developers create queries by placing objects in the Result Objects section of a query dialog. Then, Business Objects will create SQL from the objects and their definitions, as shown in the graphic. After the SQL is created, the SQL is then sent to the database through the database connections, and when the query is executed, the data is sent back to the document. Then, the report developers format the data into useful information.

Notice that the report developers cannot see the table relationships. This means that the report developers have no idea of the complexities that have been resolved. This means that we must present the objects in a manner that makes it easy for them to select the correct objects for their reports. This is also something that I hope you learn while doing the examples throughout this course.

Notes

Chapter 1: Build a Basic Universe

In this chapter, we are going to build a one table universe with no condition objects. We will define our connection, insert a table, and then create objects from the fields in the table. We will be able to create queries with this universe in any application that uses Business Objects' Universes. In fact, this is how we test the universe to make sure that it is working.

Creating a one table universe will allow us to concentrate on universe behavior independent of any data complexities that may exist in a database. We will learn about object definition and behavior. We will also create a connection that allows Business Objects to communicate with the database. In addition, we will use Web Intelligence Rich Client to demonstrate and test our universe.

One interesting note on this chapter is how much analysis that we can actually perform on a single table.

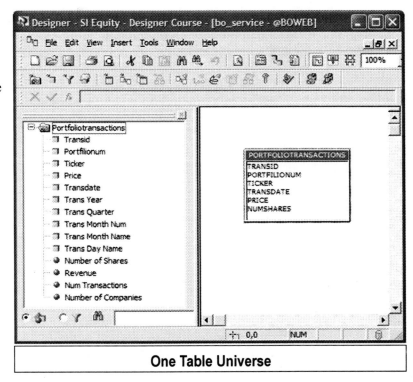

One Table Universe

Create a ODBC Data Source

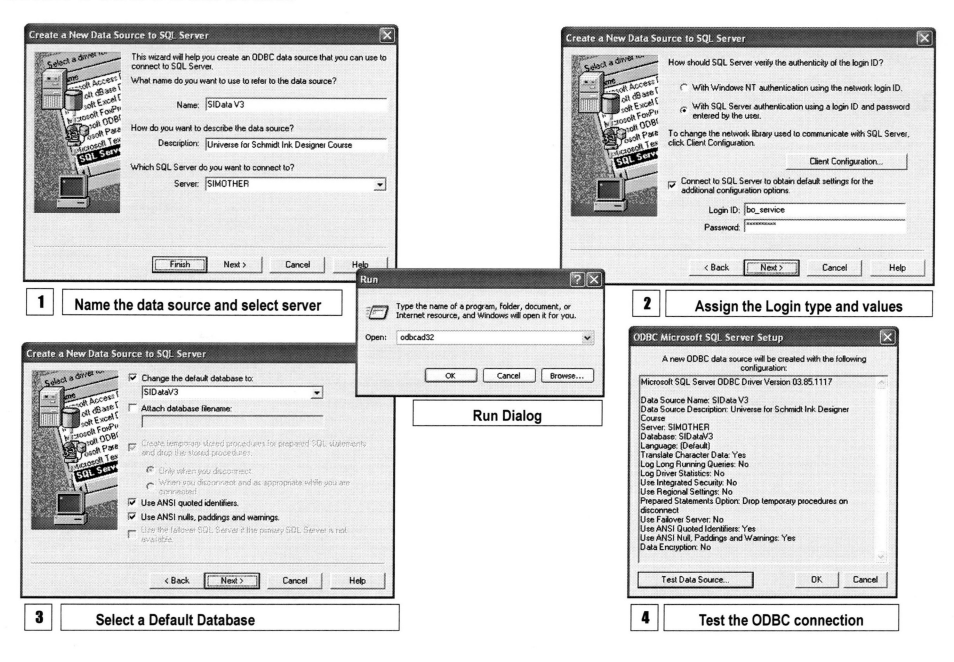

1 Name the data source and select server

2 Assign the Login type and values

Run Dialog

3 Select a Default Database

4 Test the ODBC connection

In the Beginning, There was Nothing...

Well, not exactly nothing. There was a database. In this database, there was data that we needed to supply our department with information. There were many discussions on how to get this data into our reports to form useful information, and Business Objects was the application selected to perform this task. That brings us to this page and the purpose of this book - How to get data from our database into well designed reports that supply our company with much needed information.

To get the data from the database and make it accessible to Business Objects, we can make a universe. We could retrieve the data using other methods, such as stored procedures, freehand SQL, MS Excel files, and so forth. However, this book is not about those topics, so we won't discuss them. In this class, we are going to create a universe on the SIDataV3 database to retrieve the data. The SIDataV3 data is on the CD accompanying this book.

To start our universe, or any universe, we need to know where the data is stored and what database server it is stored in. In this course, our data is stored in SQL Server or Oracle. Business Objects can retrieve data from many different data sources, including Apache Derby 10, HP Neoview, Hyperion Essbase, IBM DB2, Informix, MySQL, Netezza Server, NCR Teradata, Oracle, Salesforce.com, and of course SAP Business Warehouse.

If we are using SQL Server, then we will use an ODBC data source. If you are testing with Web Intelligence thin client, then you will need the ODBC data source to exist on both your local machine and on the Web Intelligence server. The copy on the server is needed, because the reports will use the universes stored on the server. With Web Intelligence Rich Client, only a local ODBC data source will be needed, as rich client can use a local universe. The steps that I used to create my ODBC data source are listed below.

---

1. Select Run from the Start menu located on the Windows Taskbar.
2. Enter 'odbcad32' into the *Open* edit field and click *OK*.
3. Click on the System DSN tab to activate the tab.
4. Click the *Add...* button to start the New Data Source Wizard.
5. Scroll down and Select SQL Server.
6. Click the *Finish* button
7. Enter the name of the Data Source, in my case it is SIData V3.
8. Select the Server Name from the *Server* drop list. If Server Name does not appear in the list, then you can usually just type it in.
9. Click *Next >*.
10. Select the type of authenticity for your login. I will use SQL Server.
11. Enter a *Login ID* and *Password* that has access to the database.
12. Click *Next>*.
13. Set the default database, in my case it is SIDataV3.
14. Click *Next >*, Click *Finish*.
15. Test the Data Source. If it is successful, then we are ready to create a universe.

Notes

Start and Login to Designer

Desktop Icon

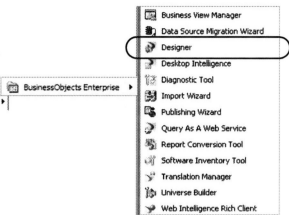

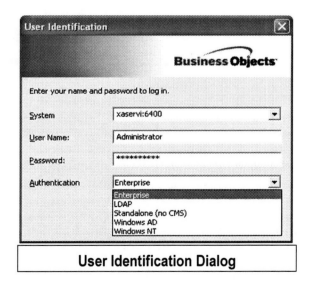

User Identification Dialog

Start and Login to Designer

Since Business Objects can be installed many different ways, you may need to start Designer differently. I start it by clicking on the Start menu and navigating to the Designer icon in the Business Objects Enterprise folder. I also start it by double-clicking on an icon on my desktop.

Once the application is started, the User Identification dialog will usually be displayed. Depending on how the security environment has been set up, you will have to enter various values. In my office I first enter the System. This is the Business Objects server that I want to use, for me the server is xaservi. The :6400 appended to the server name is the port where the log in information is sent. In many cases, there is no need for the 6400.

Next, enter a *User Name* and *Password*. This is the user name and password for the Business Objects system. Finally, I select Enterprise *Authentication*. Notice that there are several Authentication methods available. In this course, I am using Enterprise.

Notes

The Quick Design Wizard - Quick Universe Design?

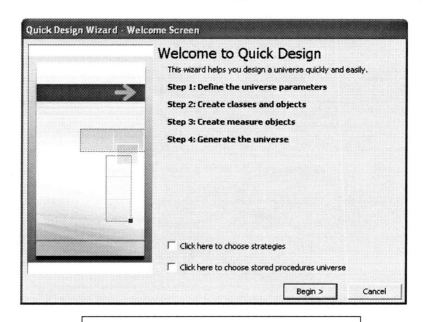

Quick Design Wizard

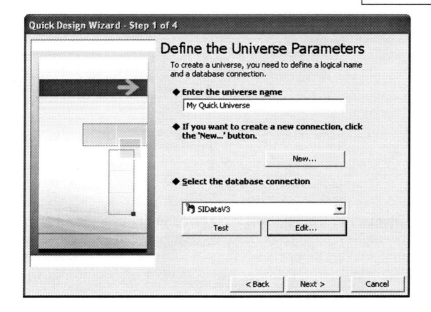

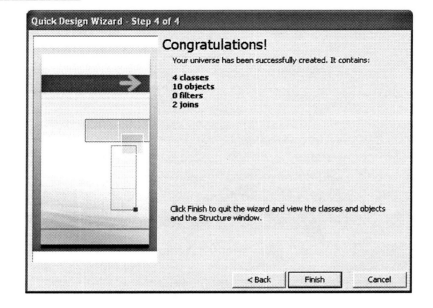

Quick Design Wizard

Wizards are called wizards, because they perform some kind of magic. If we could use magic in our jobs, then wizards and other types of magical people would be in high demand and, practice and education would help us little. Luckily, (not magically), practice and education does matter and many of us have little magic to help us with such matters. Therefore, I would like to suggest that we avoid this wizard, because you may spend more time trying to figure out why it did what it did, then actually doing what you think it did, which is designing your universe.

This is not to say that the Quick Design Wizard is of no value, and we may visit it later in this book. If anything, to show you how much you don't need it. Most universes take relatively little time to build. I know many people disagree with this and it is my experience that the closer you get to the data source, the more people like to argue. One of the most popular arguments is how many tables should be in a universe. I have heard some popular writers and consultants say there should be no more than 50 or so. I am not going to add to this argument, except to say that a universe should have as many tables as needed and no more. This may seem obvious, because if we don't include the needed tables, then we can't build our needed reports.

The most basic of universes should be able to be built within a day. In my experience, this is usually the case for me. I think that in recent years this is truer, since most data has been moved to data warehouses, where the data is organized for easy retrieval. Once in a while, I get a gig where the database is a complete mess and it takes me a couple of days just to figure out what is going on in there. So, I would say that the time it takes to build a universe is largely dependent on the data that it is to be built on. Clean organized data ensures a speedy development, where unorganized, confusing data almost ensures a lengthy development time (and many tricks).

Therefore, the word *Quick* in Quick Design Wizard is misleading. It may be quick - it may not. Much of the speediness depends on the database and not the method chosen to create the universe.

Notes

Universe Parameters - Definition

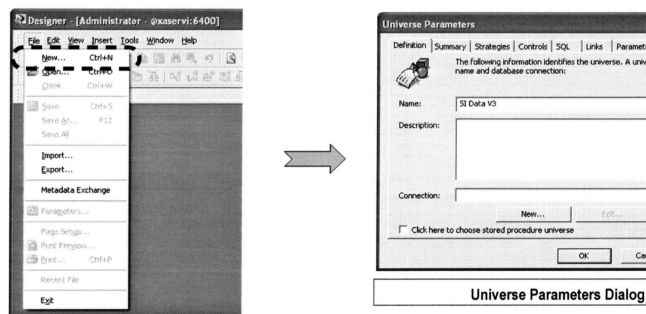

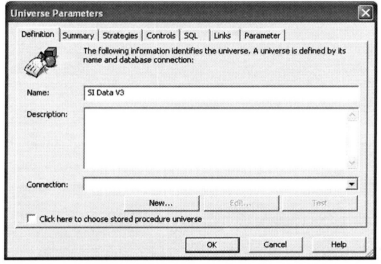

Universe Parameters Dialog

Universe Parameters - Definition

After closing the Quick Design Wizard, you are left with nothing, but an open application. This may seem scary and you may want to go and get the wizard back. However, I assure you that we can go at it alone. To get something again, we just need to select *File | New...* from the menu. This will open the Universe Parameters dialog.

All universes need at least two things to exist - a Name and a Business Objects Connection. The name identifies the universe in our reports and the connection allows us to use a database connection. The name is the easy part - just type it in. Remember that this is the name that users will see when they create a new document, so try to make it descriptive. However, don't make it too long, as it is only the name. You can enter a long description into the description field.

If you have just installed Business Objects, then you may have no connections. Business Objects' connections use database connections that we have defined to connect to our databases. In the case of SQL Server, this database connection is probably an ODBC data source, similar to the one that we created earlier in this course. The next slide discusses how to create a universe connection.

Note: The Universe Parameters dialog can be accessed after a universe has been created, by selecting *File | Parameters...* from the menu. You can also click the *Parameters* toolbar button, as shown in the graphic.

Notes

Define a New Connection

1 | Displayed After Clicking New...

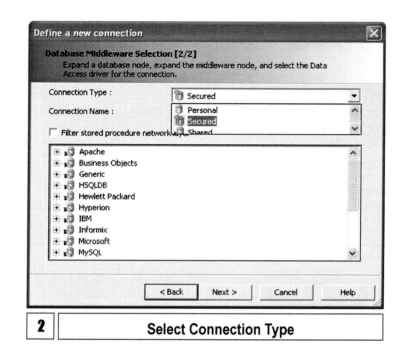

2 | Select Connection Type

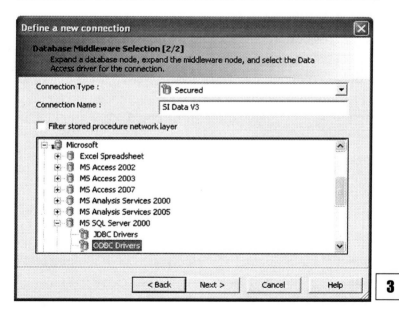

3 | Name the Connection and Select the Middleware

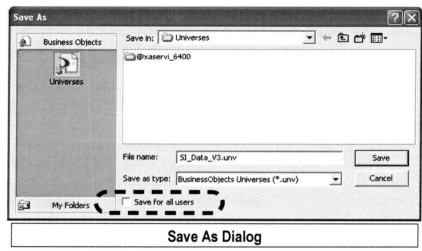

Save As Dialog

Connection Type and Middleware

When a system is brand new, there may not be any connections to a database from within Business Objects. There may be many ODBC or other types of connections that exist on a machine, but Business Objects cannot use these connections until a Business Objects connection is defined. To create a new connection from within Designer, click the *New...* button on the Definition tab, in the Universe Parameters dialog. This will display the Define a New Connection dialog.

To start the creation process click the *Next >* button. The first step is to select your *Connection Type*. There are three choices:

- Personal and Shared: These two types allow access to data from universes saved to your local machine. These universes can only work with thick client applications, such as Web Intelligence Rich Client or Desktop Intelligence, because these applications can open a local copy of a universe. Universes that use Personal or Shared connections cannot be exported to the CMS for other report developers to use. One advantage to these universe types is that you can *Save for All Users*, which removes all security from the universe. This allows you to email the universe to others outside of the system. (Note, you cannot save the universe until after the Connection Wizard is complete and the Universe Parameters dialog is dismissed. The Save As dialog is shown here, because it is important to note that unsecured universes can be emailed to others outside of the secured environment. This is usually done for support issues or archiving.)

- Secured: Secured universes can be used locally or exported to the CMS for all users with rights to the universe to use. Secured universes can only be used by people that have rights to the universe. Most universes created within a business environment are secured, because universes with Secured connections can be exported and have Business Objects security features. Universes must be secure, in order to link them to others.

We also need to give our connection a name. This name usually reflects the datasource that it is to talk to. For example, Finance Server - Development. If the server is MS SQL Server, then one connection can talk with any database on the server. Therefore, the name usually reflects the server name. I am naming ours SIData V3.

The next step is to select your middleware, as this will affect the rest of the steps. The middleware defines how Business Objects will communicate with the connection to your data source. As you can see, there are many different types of middleware available. These different types allow us to use Business Objects with many different types of data sources. In this class, we are going to select the ODBC Drivers for MS SQL Server 2000. Then, click the *Next >* button.

Notes

Define a New Connection (Continued)

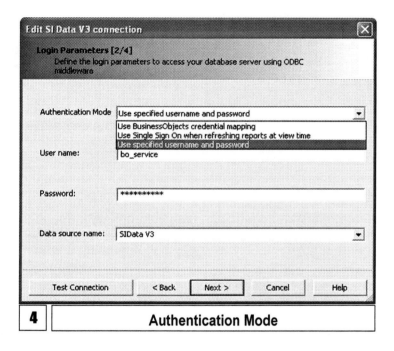

4   **Authentication Mode**

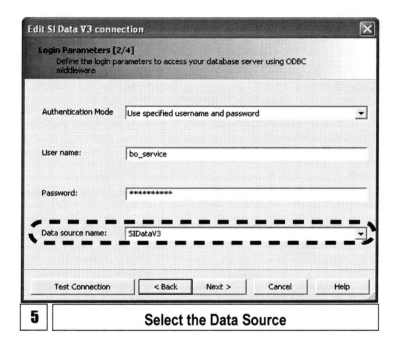

5   **Select the Data Source**

Authentication Mode

The next step is to select the Authentication Mode, and there are three to select from:

- Use Specified User Name and Password: Will use the user name and password on the dialog to log into the data source.

- Use Business Objects Credential Mapping: This option associates Business Objects users to database users via the dbuser and dbpass parameters that are set at the administrative level.

- Use Single Sign On When Refreshing Reports at View Time: This option uses the user name and password used to log into the Business Objects application to log into the database.

In this text, I am using the specified User Name and Password, so I need to enter a user name and password. These two parameters will be used to log into the database through the data source.

Next, I will select a data source. This will be the ODBC data source, SIData V3 that we created earlier. The *Data Source Name* drop list will be populated with only SQL Server ODBC data sources, because we selected Microsoft SQL Server ODBC as our middleware. If you do not see the data sources that you expected to see, then click the < *Back* button and make sure that you selected the proper middleware.

So there are two connections involved with a universe - There is the Business Objects connection that we are defining now and the data source connection that we defined earlier. The data source talks directly to the database and is usually available for any application to access. For example, you could use the SIData V3 data source to supply data to Microsoft Access. The Business Objects connection communicates with the data source to retrieve data from the database. Business Objects connections are only available to Business Objects' applications.

Notes

Define a New Connection (Oracle)

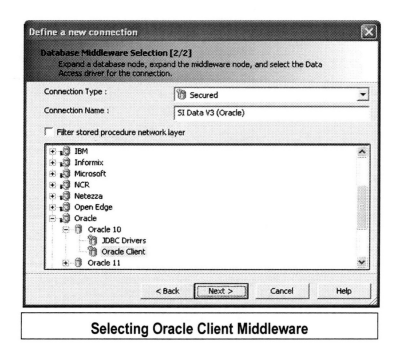

Selecting Oracle Client Middleware

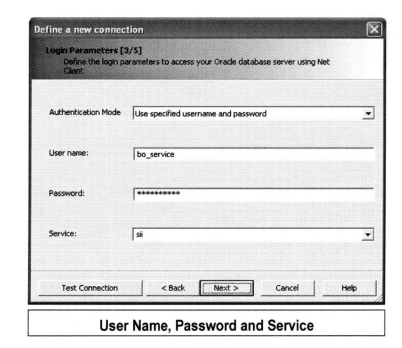

User Name, Password and Service

```
SII =
  (DESCRIPTION =
    (ADDRESS = (PROTOCOL = TCP)(HOST = xaservi)(PORT = 1521))
    (CONNECT_DATA =
      (SERVER = DEDICATED)
      (SERVICE_NAME = SII)
    )
  )
```

TNSNames.ora Entry for Service (SII)

Connection Type and Middleware (Oracle)

When using oracle middleware, we use Oracle Client for the version of Oracle where the data is stored.

The User Name must be associated with a schema to see the tables in the user's table space. For example, if you used SYS, then probably no tables will show up in the table browser when inserting tables. Also, there must be an entry in the TNSNames.ora file for the service. If there is no entry or the TNSNames file is not in the PATH environment variable, then you will get the following error: ORA-12154: TNS:could not resolve the connect identifier specified.

Note: If you still get the ORA-12154 error, then you can try adding these environment variables to your system,

- **ORACLE_HOME**: C:\oracle\product\10.2.0\client_1

- **OraClient10g_home1**: C:\oracle\product\10.2.0\client_1

Notes

Define a New Connection (Continued)

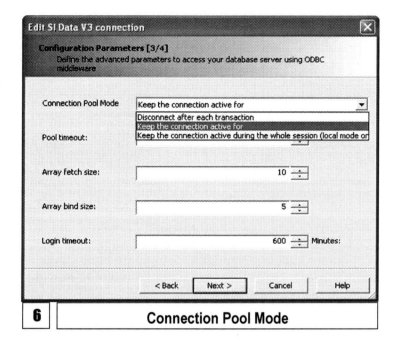

Edit SI Data V3 connection

Configuration Parameters [3/4]
Define the advanced parameters to access your database server using ODBC middleware

Connection Pool Mode	Keep the connection active for ▼
	Disconnect after each transaction
	Keep the connection active for
Pool timeout:	Keep the connection active during the whole session (local mode or
Array fetch size:	10
Array bind size:	5
Login timeout:	600 Minutes:

< Back | Next > | Cancel | Help

6 | **Connection Pool Mode**

Edit SI Data V3 connection

Configuration Parameters [3/4]
Define the advanced parameters to access your database server using ODBC middleware

Connection Pool Mode	Keep the connection active for ▼
Pool timeout:	10 Minutes:
Array fetch size:	10
Array bind size:	5
Login timeout:	600 Minutes:

< Back | Next > | Cancel | Help

7 | **Array Fetch Size**

Connection Parameters

The *Connection Pool Mode* defines how long the connection resource will be connected. The default is 10 minutes, which is defined by setting the mode to *Keep Connection Active For* and setting the *Pool Timeout* to 10 minutes. This means that the connection will stay connected for 10 minutes, which could be bad, if your query is to take more than 10 minutes. It is also important to note that this is a connection level parameter, so whatever you pick here will apply to every Business Objects resource using the connection. In addition, many resources, such as universes, have their own time limit, which means that the resource timeout must be less than or equal to the connection timeout. I have seen many examples where the setting on the universe level was increased beyond the Pool Timeout and the queries did not run as expected. I will discuss this again when we discuss the Universe parameter *Limit execution time*.

The other two options are:

- Disconnect after each transaction
  This means that the connection will terminate after a refresh. This will keep the minimum amount of users attached to the database. However, there will be some overhead with people refreshing many reports with the connection, since it must reconnect before each transaction.

- Keep the connection active during the whole session
  This is probably not good for those who never log out of their applications. It is also not good if there are more database connections than there are database licenses. Only works for local mode.

The next option *Array Fetch Size*, tells the connection how many rows to retrieve from the data source with each fetch. When a query is executed, the database caches the rows and waits for the connection to retrieve the rows. This option sets the number of rows retrieved in each fetch. The default is 10 rows, which seems a little low, since that is the same default that it was 15 years ago and systems have improved much since then. However, I am not sure if this number should be adjusted until after the universe has been created and tested. I am also not sure of any overall improvement that can be obtained by setting it higher.

The *Array bind size* is used when sending to the repository. It allocates memory to cache data before it is stored in the repository.

The *Login Timeout* is the number of seconds a connection will attempt to connect before it times out and displays an error message.

Notes

Define a New Connection (Continued)

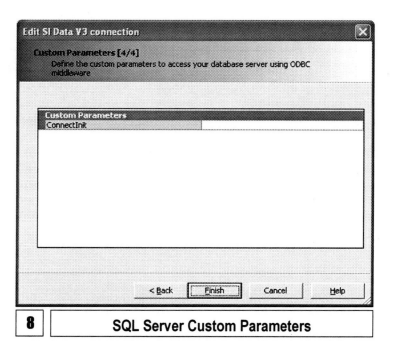

| 8 | SQL Server Custom Parameters |

Custom Parameters

This step allows custom parameters to be sent to the data source when connecting. I have heard of many uses for this dialog. For example, the connectinit parameter can be used to identify the document and the user id of the person refreshing the document. Then, some databases are able to track this information for auditing purposes. The user and document are identified through the use of @Variable functions, as in the following @VARIABLE('BOUSER'):@VARIBALE('DOCNAME'):. These variables can be passed using a procedure defined on the database. For example, if a procedure called set_bo_session was created on the database, and it expected the user and document name to be passed to it, then the following can be entered into the connectinit parameter,

    begin set_bo_session('@VARIABLE('BOUSER')', @VARIBALE('DOCNAME')); Commit; end;

There are also other parameters that can be used, such as END_SQL in Oracle, which will also allow you to pass values to the database.

To create the connection and return to the Universe Parameters dialog, click the *Finish* button. The connection will be used in this universe, and if it is secured, then will also be available for other universes. Many times, the universe designers do not create connections, as they are system resources. In these cases, the administrators create connections to the data warehouses and databases and make them available to designers who need them.

Notes

Universe Parameters

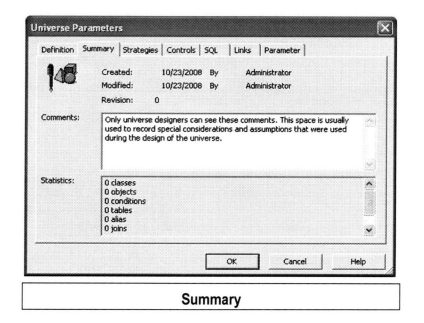

Summary

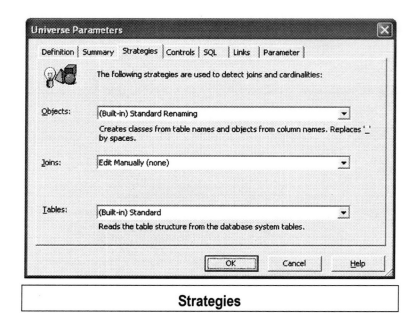

Strategies

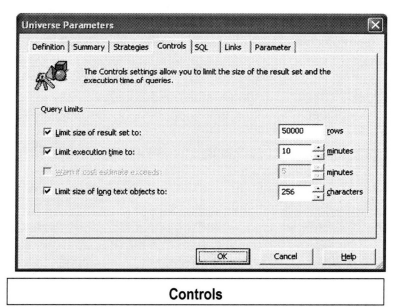

Controls

Defining Summary, Strategy and Controls

After defining a connection and assigning the universe a name, we should look at several other tabs of the Universe Parameters dialog.

The *Summary* tab contains the create and modify by information. It also contains a revision number that increments each time the universe is exported to the repository. The *Comments* allow universe designers to makes notes available to others that may also work on the universe. It is important to note any assumptions or irregularities, so that others designers will know how to maintain the universe. The *Statistics* section notes the number of universe objects that are in the universe. This number is rarely important, because each universe will require differing number of objects, and there really are no limits on these numbers.

The *Strategy* tab should rarely be used. It is for automatic creation of objects, joins and classes, which probably should never happen. It seems like the existing strategies are not perfect, and therefore much time could be spent auditing what the strategies actually do. If you want to use a custom external strategy, then you can create a STG file that contains the instructions for the strategies. To learn more about how to create the STG file, please refer to External strategies in Designer XI in the Universe Designer guide.

The *Controls* tab allows for limits to be placed on queries. The first option, *Limit size of result set to*, allows a limit to be placed on the number of rows returned by a query. Many companies set this to around 50,000. Remember that probably only 60 to 70 rows can fit on a page, therefore, in most cases, it is unusual to need more than 50,000 rows. The *Limit execution time to* option, limits the time a query can use to complete its operation. However, this number must be smaller or equal to the number used to define the connection time in the connection definition. The *Warn if cost estimate exceeds* option, will warn that a modified query may take longer than the threshold defined for this option. The *Limit size of long text objects to* option, allows for long text objects to be truncated to a specified number of characters. If a number other than 1000 is desired, then this option must be checked and a specific number entered into the field. In this example, I have entered 256.

Notes

Universe Parameters (SQL)

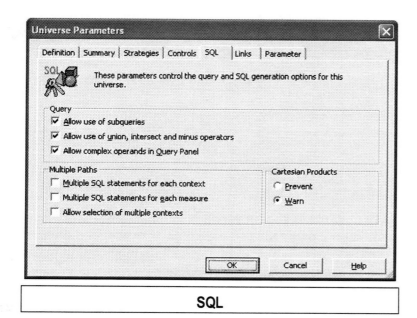

SQL

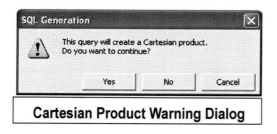

Cartesian Product Warning Dialog

Company	Industry
Business Objects S.A.	Airlines
Business Objects S.A.	Alternative Energy
Business Objects S.A.	Automotive
Business Objects S.A.	Biotechnology
Business Objects S.A.	Chemical
Business Objects S.A.	Consumer
Business Objects S.A.	Finance
Business Objects S.A.	Industrial
Business Objects S.A.	Media
Business Objects S.A.	Metals
Business Objects S.A.	Oil and Gas
Business Objects S.A.	Technology
Business Objects S.A.	Telecom

Select *
From Company, Industry

Cartesian product

Defining SQL Parameters

The *SQL* tab is very important, because it defines the behavior of the SQL generation in the report. SQL is the language that Business Objects uses to create instructions to retrieve data from a data source.

The *Query* section allows the designer to allow the use of subqueries, combination queries, and complex operands. It seems normal that in most cases report developers should be able to use subqueries and combination queries. These are two tools that allow for more complex and/or convenient queries to be used in a document. Complex operands are used in Desktop Intelligence, which uses these operands to create subqueries. I usually, leave all three of these options checked.

The *Cartesian Products* section specifies that if a Cartesian product exists between two tables, then the report refresher should either be prevented from refreshing the report, or warned that the product exists. Since, there is no Cartesian products are okay option, then your universes should not contain any Cartesian products. A Cartesian product is a relationship between two tables with no join between them. This causes every row in one table to be matched up to every row in the other table. In most cases, this makes little sense. In the example in the graphic, a Cartesian product would put every company in every industry. Some Cartesian products work very well. For example, one row tables with parameters, such as load date. Sometimes, we want to include load date on every row in another table. However, since there is no option that will allow this without a warning, then I recommend that you do not do this in a universe. In many cases, you can just create a view in the database that will do this join.

The *Multiple Paths* section applies to measures and contexts. This section is very important, because it affects the result sets of the queries. We cannot discuss these options here, but will in a later chapter. For now, clear all three options.

Notes

Universe Parameters - Links and Parameters

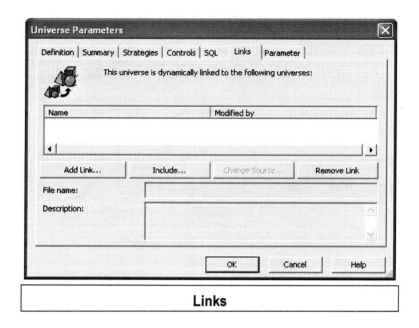

Links

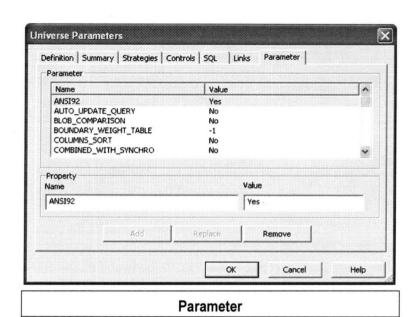

Parameter

Parameters in Dialog

ANSI92

AUTO_UPDATE_QUERY

BLOB_COMPARISON

BOUNDARY_WEIGHT_TABLE

COLUMNS_SORT

COMBINED_WITH_SYNCHRO

CORE_ORDER_PRIORITY

CORRECT_AGGREGATED_CONDITIONS_IF_DRILL

CUMULATIVE_OBJECT_WHERE

DECIMAL_COMMA

DISTINCT_VALUES

END_SQL

EVAL_WITHOUT_PARENTHESIS

FILTER_IN_FROM

FIRST_LOCAL_CLASS_PRIORITY

FORCE_SORTED_LOV

MAX_INLIST_VALUES

REPLACE_COMMA_BY_CONCAT

SHORTCUT_BEHAVIOR

THOROUGH_PARSE

UNICODE_STRINGS

Universe Parameters - Links and Parameters

The Links and Parameters tabs are used to make your universe design more efficient and to set SQL definitions.

The Links tab is used to link or include other universes into the current universe. This can make universe creation more efficient, because core universe components do not have to be redefined. We will cover this in more detail later in the course, so I will just touch on the topic here. Suppose that you have a Product table. There may or may not be other tables that are associated with this table. From this table and the associated tables, we will create objects and conditions.

Now, suppose that we have Inventory, Sales, and Marketing universes. Each of these universes will probably need the Products table and related objects. We can create the product structure in each of the other universes and this will work fine. However, as time goes by, we will begin to make alterations on the product structure in each of the universes. This will cause them to diverge and some of them may even become outdated. To avoid this situation, we can create a single Product universe, with all of the objects and conditions that make it perfect. Then, we can just link it into the other universes. Now, whenever a change is made to the Products universe, it will propagate throughout the other universes.

The Parameters tab allows you to set parameters for your middleware. For example the first one is ANSI92. If this is set to yes, then the SQL generated will be in ANSI92 format. We may want to set this option to yes in universes that have outer joins, since outer joins are less problematic for ANSI92. In this course, I am going to set this option to 'Yes'. The parameters displayed on this tab are the ones that are most common for most middleware. There is a *.prm file in the middleware directory of Business Objects that allows you to set more specific middleware parameters.

If there are no parameters listed on the Parameters tab, then click the *OK* button to dismiss the dialog. Then, select | *File* | *Parameters...* | from the menu to re-open the Universe Parameters dialog, and revisit the Parameters tab, which should now be populated with the parameters for the middleware in the connection.

After we have visited the Parameters tab of the Universe Parameters dialog, we are ready to click the *OK* button to begin the creation of our universe. We can always return to the dialog by clicking the *Universe Parameters* toolbar button or by selecting | *File* | *Parameters...* | from the menu.

Notes

The Designer Workspace

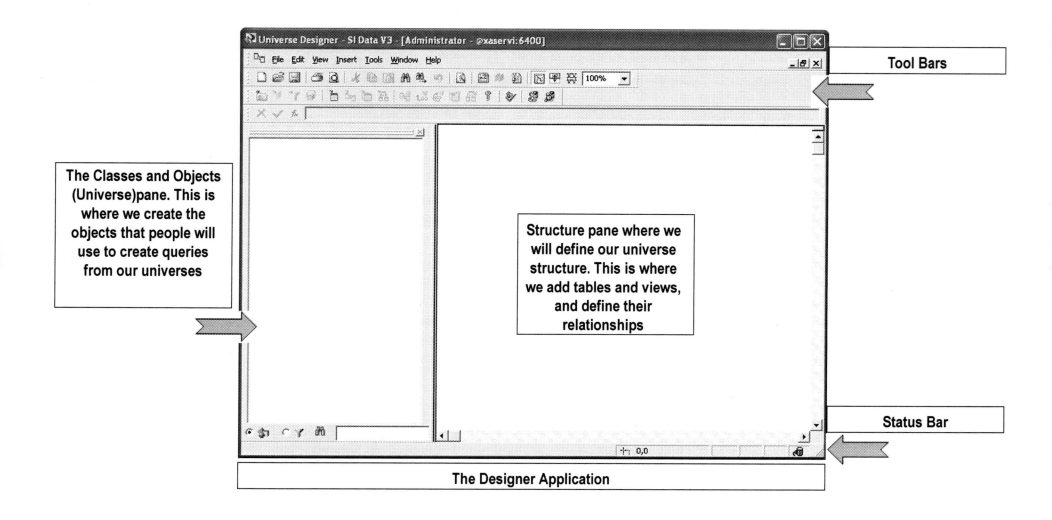

The Designer Workspace

After we set our new universe's parameters, we enter the Designer workspace. At first, it may be a little intimidating, because it is so empty. In time, you will see that this workspace is very convenient and friendly. It allows us to create the heart of most reports - the universe.

I am not going to describe each button and area here, as I will introduce them as we use them. I will tell you that we are going to create a universe by placing tables in the Structure pane, creating joins to define their relationships, and then creating objects and classes in the Universe section.

Notes

Table Browser

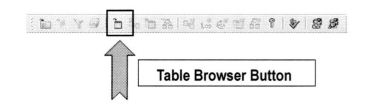

Table Browser Button

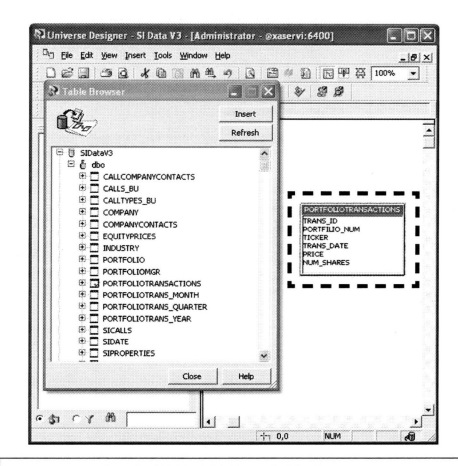

Our First Table SQL Server Table Browser

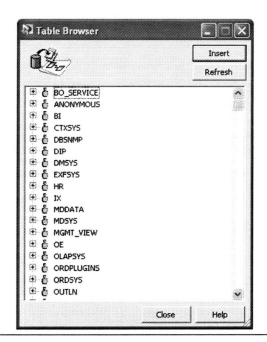

Oracle Table Browser

Let's Get Some Tables

We add tables and views to our workspace through the table browser. To open the browser, click the *Table Browser* button. You can also double-click on the white-space of the Structure pane. You can also right-click in the Structure pane to get a pop-up menu or select | *Insert* | *Tables* | from the menu.

In the Browser, the tables are organized by the databases on the server. (This is true for SQL Server, for Oracle and other databases, they may be arranged differently.) SQL Server is very convenient, because you can use tables and views from any of the databases on a server. To insert a table or view into the Structure pane, we can drag the table or view from the Table Browser or double-click the table or view in the browser.

In the screen shot above, we've inserted PORTFIOLIOTRANSACTIONS into the workspace.

Exercise: Insert a Table into the Workspace

1. Click the Table *Browser* button to display the Table Browser.
2. Locate the PORTFOLIOTRANSACTIONS table in the SIDataV3 database.
3. Drag the PORTFOLIOTRANSACTIONS table from the browser and drop it onto the Structure pane.
4. Close the Browser by clicking the *X* in the upper-right corner.

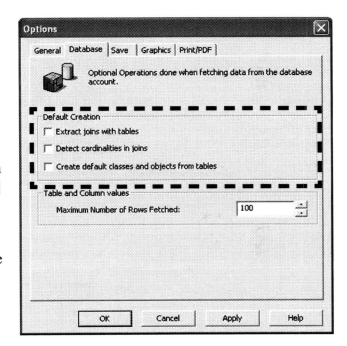

Adding a table to the structure pane should have cause no other objects to be created. If a class and objects were created in the Classes and Objects pane, then you have some Default Creation options set. In this class we won't use these options, so let's turn the options off. Select | *Tools* | *Options* | from the menu to display the Options dialog. Click on the Database tab and clear all checks in the option controls.

Delete any classes that may have been created - click on the class to select it, and then press the [Delete] key.

Notes

Viewing Table and Column Values

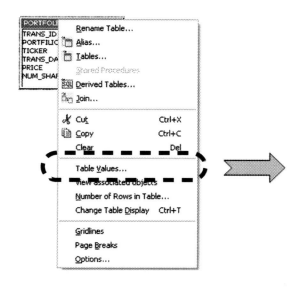

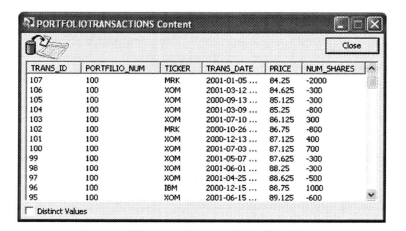

Table Values

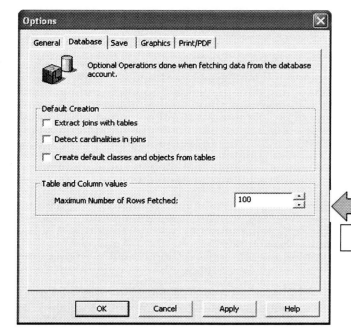

Maximum Number of Rows Fetched

Viewing Table and Column Values

Many times, especially in a new environment, you may need to check the values in a table. We may do this to make sure that the column values are in the form that we think they should be. For example, is the Customer number in a new format or an old one - D230067 vs 000067. We also view the data to find out what kind of values are stored or if a column has been populated.

To see a table's values, right-click on the table and select *Table Values...* from the pop-up menu. To view a single column, right-click on the column in the table and select *Column Values...* from the pop-up menu.

Sometimes, we only need to see a few rows and at other times, we may need to see hundreds of values. Sure, we could go to Query Analyzer and see the entire table, but sometimes, we don't have access to such database tools. To set the number of rows fetched when viewing values, we use the Database tab in the Options dialog.

Exercise: View the Values in a Table

1. Select | Tools | Options | from the menu.
2. Click on the Database tab to activate the tab.
3. Enter 200 in the *Maximum Number of Rows Fetched* control.
4. Click *OK* to accept the change and dismiss the Options dialog.
5. Right-click on the table in the Structure pane and select *Table Values...* from the pop-up menu.
6. After viewing the values, click the *X* in the upper-right corner to dismiss the dialog.
7. Right-click on a field in the table (Ticker, for example) and select *Column Values...* from the pop-up menu.
8. After viewing the values, click the *X* in the upper-right corner to dismiss the dialog.

Notes

Renaming Tables

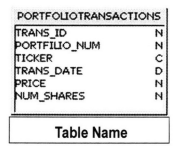

```
PORTFOLIOTRANSACTIONS
TRANS_ID          N
PORTFILIO_NUM     N
TICKER            C
TRANS_DATE        D
PRICE             N
NUM_SHARES        N
```

Table Name

```
SIDataV3.dbo.PORTFOLIOTRANSACTIONS
TRANS_ID          N
PORTFILIO_NUM     N
TICKER            C
TRANS_DATE        D
PRICE             N
NUM_SHARES        N
```

Fully Qualified Table Name

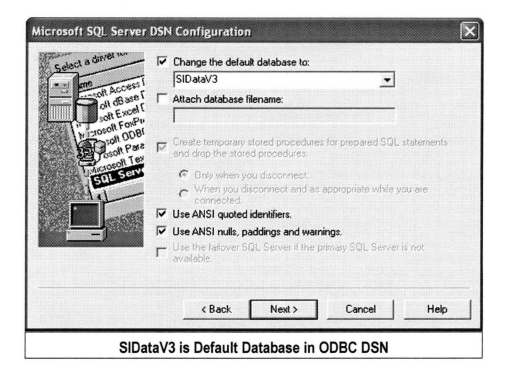

SIDataV3 is Default Database in ODBC DSN

Rename Table Dialog

Renaming Tables

We can rename tables in the structure, by selecting *Edit | Rename Table...* from the menu, while the table is selected in the structure. You can also right-click on table and select Rename *Table...* from the pop-up menu. In the graphic, there are two representations of PORTFOLIOTRANSACTIONS. One representation is just the table name, which will work fine if the default database in the ODBC connection is set to the database where the table resides, in this case SIDataV3.

The other representation is a fully qualified table name, which includes the database name and the owner name. You will have to fully qualify table names that are not identifiable with just the table name. For example, if the table does not reside in the default database of the ODBC connection, then it will have to be qualified with database name and owner name.

The table name must match the table name in the database, because Business Objects will build SQL with the table name. If the table name does not exist in the database, then the SQL will fail. Usually, we only rename tables if the name of the table in the database has changed.

Notes

Default Classes and Objects

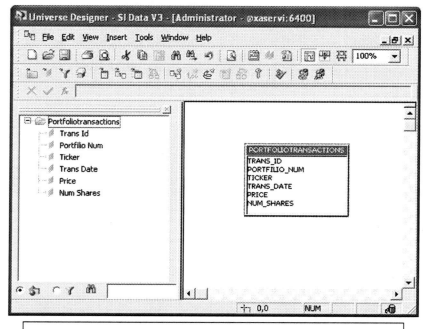

Classes and Objects Made From Table

Class Folder

Organizes objects in the Universe
Helps to organize Contexts in the Universe
No two Classes can share the same name

Dimension Object

Defines contexts in a report
Allows queries to be linked (merged) in a report
Not compatible with unlinked dimensions from other queries
Can be used to define filters in reports
Can be used to create Master-Detail (Section) reports
Can be used to define breaks in a table
Automatically aggregate to unique values in a table
Used to create hierarchies for drilling

Default Classes and Objects

The class in the above screen shot, was created by simply dragging the table from the Structure pane and dropping it into the Classes and Objects (Universe) pane. This created a class with the same name as the table, which is usually not the best name for a class. It also created dimension objects from each of the fields that are in the table.

Class folders are used to organize the objects in a universe. They usually contain objects that represent certain aspects of a business. For example, Products, Employees, Regions, Dates, Orders, Invoices, and so forth. A single folder can, and usually does, contain objects created from multiple tables. Class folders can even contain subclass folders to better organize folders that have many objects. For example, an Invoice class may have the following subclasses: Invoice Date, Ship to Address, Mail to Address, and so forth. I have heard many rules of thumb about creating classes, but I have found that you need what you need. Whatever makes it easiest for people to find the objects that they need to create reports. One important note is that no two Class folders can share the same name.

Dimension objects define the data framework of a report. These frameworks are called Report Contexts. They are called contexts, because all calculations and groupings take place in some context. For example, in the table below, the context is Region, Department, and Year. The Sales values

Region	Department	Year	Sales
West	Hardware	2005	$500,000
West	Hardware	2006	$400,000
East	Software	2005	$300,000
East	Software	2006	$200,000

sum to the rows created by these contexts. One other important note about dimensions is that they aggregate to unique values. For example, the document that contains the above report may have thousands of rows. However, it can be said for sure, that there are only four unique combinations of values for the three dimensions, as shown in the table.

Exercise: Drag the Table to the Classes and Objects Pane

Notes

Table Options

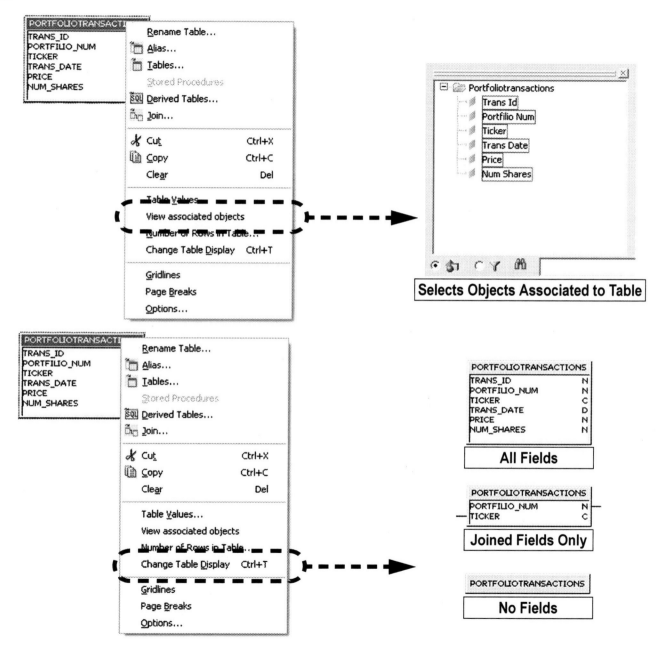

Table Options

We have already used the Table Values menu command to view the rows in a table. There are also three more menu items that are related to a selected table. These are View Associated Objects, Number of Rows in Table, and Change Table Display.

Quite often, we have to find all of the objects that are associated with a table. To find all of the associated objects, we right-click on the table, and then select *View Associated Objects* from the pop-up menu.

Knowing the number of rows in a table is also often of interest. To view the number of rows, right-click on the table and select *Number of Rows in Table...* from the pop-up menu. This action will display the row count just beneath the table in the structure. You can hide the number of rows by selecting *Tools | Options...* from the menu, and then unchecking the *Show Row Count* option on the Graphics tab.

Each table has three viewing states - Expanded, Joined Fields Only, and No Fields. To change the view state, right-click on the table and select *Change Table Display* from the pop-up menu. Double-clicking on the table header will also change the display state. By default, the expanded table displays eight columns (fields). To display more or less fields, just click on the bottom edge of the table and adjust the size of the table. To change the default number of columns, select *Tools | Options...* from the menu, and then change the number in the *Default Number of Columns* option on the Graphics tab.

Notes

Dimension Properties

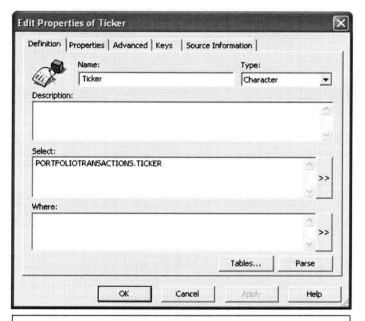

Definition tab of Edit Properties Dialog

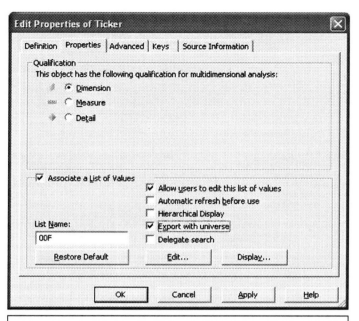

Properties tab of Edit Properties Dialog

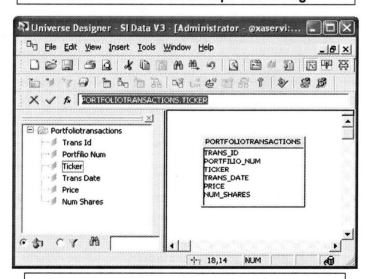

Edit Formula in Formula Bar

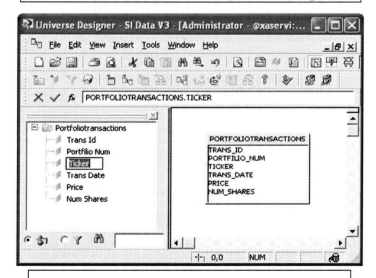

Edit Object Name in Place

Dimension Properties

We created the dimensions in our universe by dragging the PORTFOLIOTRANSACTIONS table into the Classes and Objects (Universe) section of the Designer. This works well in most cases, but sometimes, we need to change existing dimensions or create new ones. We can change or create objects through the Edit Properties dialog.

The Definition tab of the Edit Properties dialog has five fields:

1. Name: This is the name that people see when they use the universe to create queries. It is also the default column header in most applications.
2. Type: This is the data type of the field. It can be Number, Character, Date, or Long text. It is important to select the correct type, because it is part of the behavior definition of the object. In addition, improperly typed objects are not displayed properly in Web Intelligence.
3. Description: This field lets you describe the object to people using it. It is a good idea to describe most of your fields to help eliminate confusion.
4. Select: This field is where the object's data comes from. It can be as simple as a field in a table. It can also be a complicated case statement.
5. Where: This field allows for a where condition to be placed on the object. It is important for objects that must be accompanied with a constraint. (Conditions in an object's Where section will appear in the Where clause of a SQL statement. This means that it will apply to the entire query and not just the object where it is defined. This could limit data in an unexpected way, so care should be taken when defining conditions in an object's Where section.)

The Properties tab has two sections:

1. Qualification: This is where the object is actually defined has a Dimension object. Notice that there are two other object types that we will discuss later.
2. Associate a List of Values: This section allows you to assign a list of values to an object. By default, all dimension objects have a list of values.

Sometimes, we just need to quickly change the name of an object. We can do this by clicking on an object in the Classes and Objects section and then just letting the cursor rest on the object. The object will then go into edit mode and you can alter the name by editing the current name.

There are also times that we want to quickly change the formula of an object, without going into the Edit Properties dialog. We can do this by clicking on the object in the Classes and Objects section and then modifying the formula in the Formula toolbar. For the change to be permanent, you must press the [Enter] key or click the *Validate Object* check button on the toolbar.

Notes

Editing Object Names

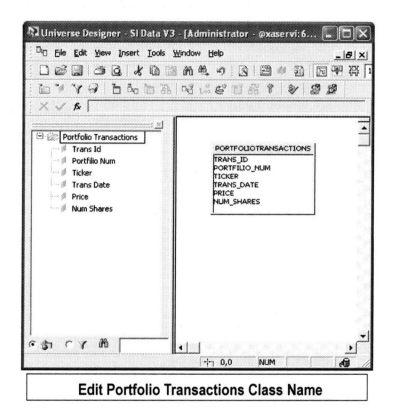

Edit Portfolio Transactions Class Name

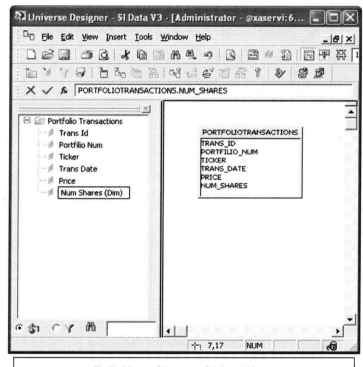

Edit Num Shares Object Name

Edit Object Names

When we dragged the Portfolio Transactions table to the Universe window, a default class and objects were created. The names of these objects were derived from the names of the database objects: Table Name to Class Name, and Field Names to Object Names. In most cases, these default names are not appropriate and we should change them in the universe window. We can do this by simply clicking on an object and waiting for the edit mode field. When the edit mode field appears, we simply type a new name in for the object.

In most cases, we can simply rename any object in the universe at any time, as this should not cause existing reports to not find the objects. The reason for this is that Business Objects identifies objects by both their name and internal ID, and we cannot change the internal ID, unless we delete the object and recreate it.

Exercise: Modify Some Dimensions

1. Save the Universe
   - Select | *File* | *Save* | from the menu.
   - Name the file: SI Data V3 Designer Course.unv
   - Click the *Save* button
2. Change the Name of Num Shares
   - Click on the Num Shares object in the Classes and Objects section.
   - Let the cursor rest until the edit field is displayed.
   - Type Num Shares (Dim) into the edit field.
   - Press [Enter].

3. Change the Name of the Portfoliotransactions class
   - Click on the Portfoliotransactions class in the Classes and Objects section.
   - Let the cursor rest until the edit field is displayed.
   - Type Portfolio Transactions into the edit field.
   - Press [Enter].
4. Save the Universe.

Notes

List of Values

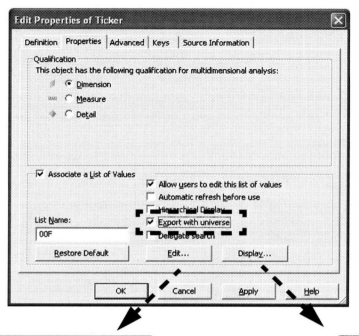

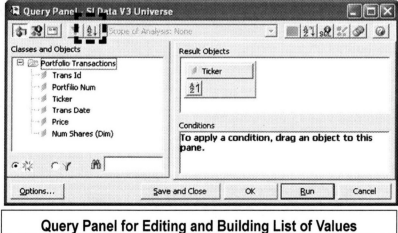

Query Panel for Editing and Building List of Values

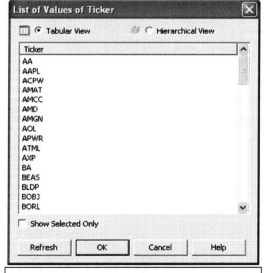

List of Values Dialog

List of Values

Most of the time the default list of values is sufficient and we need not do anything. However, there are certain attributes and behaviors that we must consider. To display the List of Values for an object, click the *Display...* button on the Properties tab of the Edit Properties dialog. This will display the same list that a person will see in Desktop Intelligence. In WEB Intelligence it is presented differently, but the list is still the same. Probably one of the most import aspects of the list is how the values are sorted. To sort the list, a person can click on the header in the list, in this case Ticker, and the list will sort. However, it would probably be better if we sorted the list for them. Notice that there is also a *Refresh* button on the dialog. This allows the list to be refreshed with the most current values.

To edit the List of Values, we need to edit the query that creates it. To edit the query, click on the *Edit...* button, in the Edit Properties dialog. This will display a Query Panel that is very similar to the one used in Desktop Intelligence. To sort the values in the list, click on the object to select it and then click the *A-Z* toolbar button. This will place a sort icon on the object, as shown in the graphic. Notice that we can also place conditions on the object. This may help us to eliminate any junk data that may be present in our database. After editing the query, you can click either *Save and Close*, *OK*, or *Run*. All three buttons will save the query.

It is important to note that an edited list of values is only available on the machine that it was edited on. This means that it will be available to Desktop Intelligence, Web Intelligence Rich Client, and other applications that run locally. However, Web Intelligence thin client and other machines using local applications will not be able to use the custom list of values. To make the custom List of Values available to others, it must be *Exported with Universe*. This option is highlighted in the screenshot.

Also notice the List Name of the object, which is also the internal identifier of the object.

Exercise: Modify Ticker List of Values

1. Modify the Ticker list of values.
   - Double-click on the ticker object, in the Classes and Objects section, to display the Edit Properties dialog.
   - Click on the Properties tab to activate the tab.
   - Click on the *Edit...* button to display the Query Panel.
   - Click on the Ticker object in the Result Objects section.
   - Click the *A-Z Sort* button to place the sort icon on the object.
   - Click the *Run* button to run and commit the change.
2. Click on the *Display...* button to make sure that the list is indeed sorted properly.
3. Click *Ok* to exit all dialogs.
4. Save the Universe.

Notes

Exporting a Universe

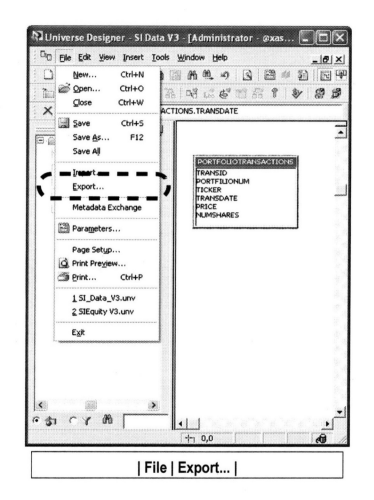

| File | Export... |

Export Universe Dialog

Exporting a Universe

Whenever you have made progress on a universe, you should export it. Exporting it saves the universe to a repository database. It is more secure in the repository, because the repository is usually managed by the IT department of a company, which means that the repository is probably backed-up often and safeguarded against unusual use. We can retrieve it and replace the file on our local computer by selecting | *File* | *Import...* | from the menu.

When we export a universe, we must decide where it goes and who will be able to use it. Universes are stored in a universe domain. In your company, there may be one universe domain or many. Sometimes there is a production domain and a development domain. Other times they are categorized in other ways. In this class, we will use the */webi universes* domain. Since Business Objects can be set-up in a variety of ways, you will probably have to select which domain on your system is best for you.

The domain places a level of security on a universe, because the domain itself has security. This means that only privileged people can see certain domains. However, in most case all users have access to a certain domain. This in of itself is probably not that secure. This is why there are user groups that you can assign to your universe. The user groups are usually divided up into departments, because each department employee will usually have similar rights and needs. In this class, I am going to export to Everybody.

We are exporting the universe, because if you are using WEB Intelligence to test your universe, then the universe will have to be exported. If you are using Desktop Intelligence, then you will not have to export the universe in order to use it. However, it is a good idea to export it, because this will always preserve your latest copy.

Exercise: Export the universe

1. Save the Universe, by selecting | *File* | *Save* | from the menu.
   Saving the universe will save a copy to your local machine. This is your copy and you may modify it without changing the corporate copy in the repository. However, when you export it again, then it will replace the copy in the repository.
2. Select | *File* | *Export* | from the menu.
3. Select a Domain to export to.
4. Select a Group that will have rights to use the Universe.
5. Click the *OK* button.

Notes

Dimension Object Behavior

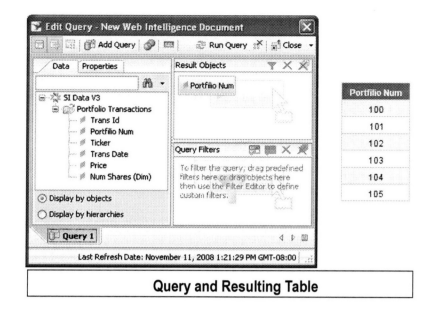

Query and Resulting Table

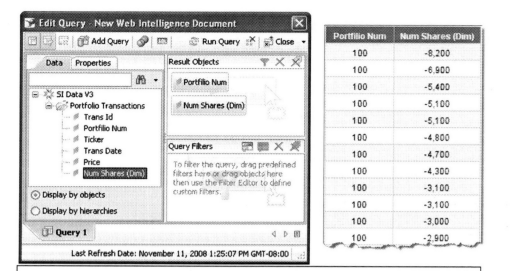

Query with Portfolio Num and Num Shares (Dim)

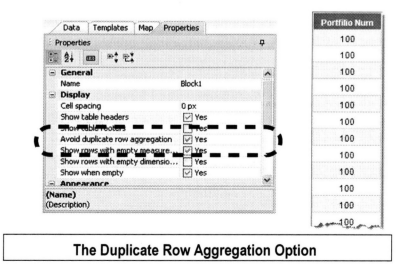

The Duplicate Row Aggregation Option

Dimension Object Behavior

Let's have a look at how the Dimension objects in our universe will behave in a reporting environment. In this example, I am using Web Intelligence Rich Client.

The first step is to create a query with the Portfolio Num object and then click *Run Query*. Web Intelligence creates a table that displays each portfolio number one time. Therefore, there are six rows, each with a unique portfolio number. This is what Web Intelligence is displaying, but it is not what the query returned. Actually, the query returned 2680 rows of portfolio numbers. However, since most of these rows are duplicates (we only have six portfolio numbers in the database), Web Intelligence just shows the six unique portfolio numbers. This is called Duplicate Row Aggregation, and the way Dimension objects do this, is to just display unique values.

In Web Intelligence, the Duplicate Row Aggregation can be turned off by selecting the *Avoid Duplicate Row Aggregation* option in the Properties section, while the table is selected, as shown in the bottom graphic. By the way, if only dimension objects are selected for a query, the report developer should select distinct values, as this would cause only the six unique values to be returned.

Next, I add the Num Shares (Dim) object to the query. When people add number of shares to a query, they usually expect to see the number of shares for each portfolio number in the query. However, when we run the query, we no longer see just the six unique portfolio values, as shown in the graphic, in the upper-right section. What we are seeing is the unique combinations of portfolio number and number of shares. This is not all of the shares, just the unique shares involved in any trade. Therefore, if we were to total the Num Shares (Dim) column, the answer would not be what we expect. It would not be the total number of shares - it would be the total of unique number of shares. For example, if we traded 100 shares 10 times, the report would only show 100, not 10 * 100, which is 1000. If we were to select the *Avoid Duplicate Row Aggregation* option, and sum the values, then the totals would be as we expect.

This means that the Num Shares (Dim) object probably should not be a dimension, as it did not total the way we expected it to. What we wanted to see, was simply each portfolio number and the total number of shares for each portfolio. We also expected the query to only return 6 rows, and not the 2680 that it did return. By the way, it returned 446 times more rows than we needed!

Notes

Measure Object Definition

To turn Numshares into a measure, add the Sum function to the Select

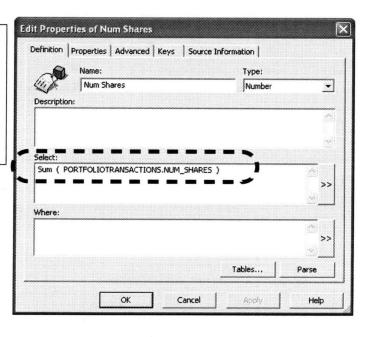

The Sum function usually sets the object Qualification to Measure on the Properties tab.

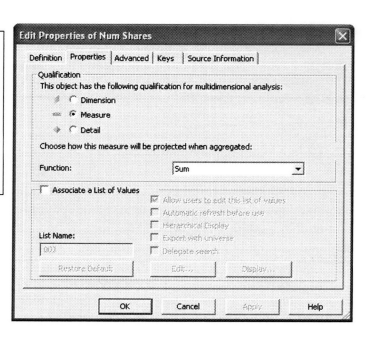

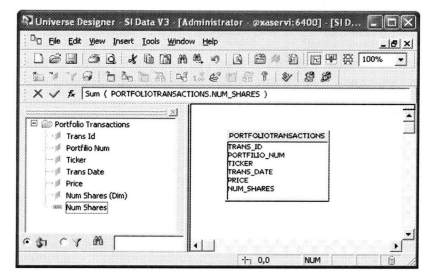

Measure Object

Conforms to contexts in a report
If defined with aggregate function, causes a Group by
Does not have to be linked to other queries to be compatible

Measure Object Definition

Earlier, we learned that dimension objects define the contexts in reports. One of the biggest reasons for contexts in a report, is for calculations to conform to the contexts. For example, suppose that you had the following data in a database (table on the left):

Product	Quantity
Hard Drives	200
Hard Drives	200

Product	Quantity
Hard Drives	400

When a query is created to return Product and Quantity, then you probably want to return only the product and the total quantity for each product, as in the table on the right. This would be the most efficient way for the data to be returned. This is how Business Objects works when Dimension and properly defined measures are combined in a query. If you understand SQL, then I will note the SQL generated by Business Objects

Select Product, *Sum*(Quantity)
From Sales
Group by Product

The sum function in the object definition causes the SQL to have the Group By statement, that causes the Quantity to aggregate to each unique combination of dimension values. So what does the Sum function on the Properties tab do? This tells the Business Objects application (Desktop or WEB Intelligence) how to handle the data if it is placed in a context other than the default created by the query. For example, when a dimension column is deleted from a table, then the context of the table will change, and any measures in the table will conform to the new context.

Exercise: Create the Number of Shares Measure

1. Copy the Num Shares (Dim) object
- Click on Num Shares (Dm) to select it.
- Select | Edit | Copy | from the menu.
- Select | Edit | Paste | from the menu.
2. Double-click on the copy of Num Shares (Dim)
3. This will display the Properties dialog for the object.
4. Change the name to Num Shares
5. Change the Select to:
   Sum(PORTFOLIOTRANSACTIONS.Numshares)
6. Check the Properties tab to make sure it is qualified as a Measure.
7. Click OK to create Num Shares measure.

Notes

Create the Revenue Measure

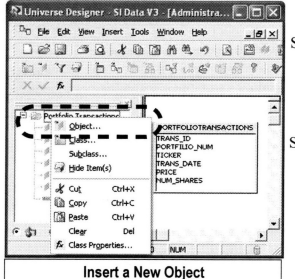

Insert a New Object

Sum(@Select(Portfolio Transactions\Price) * @Select(Portfolio Transactions\Num Shares (Dim))) * (-1)

Revenue Definition Using Existing Objects

Sum(PORTFOLIOTRANSACTIONS.PRICE * PORTFOLIOTRANSACTIONS.NUM_SHARES) * (-1)

Revenue Definition Using Fields from Table

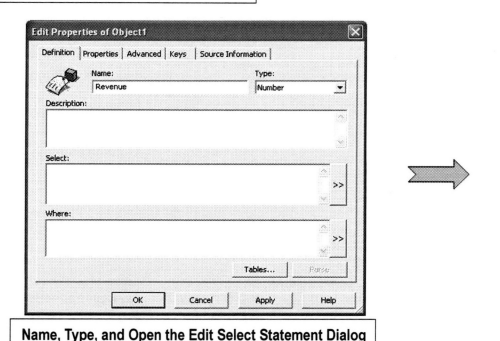

Name, Type, and Open the Edit Select Statement Dialog

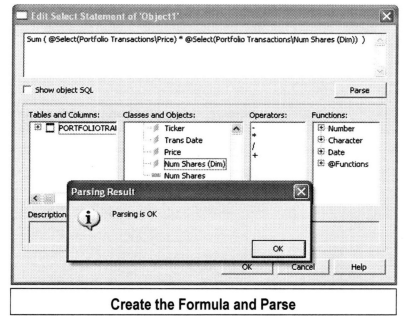

Create the Formula and Parse

Creating a Measure

In the previous example, we added the sum function to an existing dimension to turn it into a measure. This works in a lot of cases, but sometimes, we need to start from scratch. In this example, we want to create an object for Revenue. Revenue is the sum of Price * Num Shares.

To create the new object, click the *Insert Object* button on the Editing toolbar. This action will display the Edit Properties dialog for a new object (probably Object 1). We will start by entering a name and a type for our new object. Next, we will click the >> button, to the right of the *Select* edit field, to display the Edit Select Statement dialog. In this dialog, we can create formulas for our objects using database fields, already defined objects, operators, and functions that are native to the database.

In this example, the formula is: Sum (@Select(Portfolio Transactions\Price) * @Select(Portfolio Transactions\Num Shares (Dim))) * (-1). The *@Select* function allows us to use existing objects in the universe. The @Select function is convenient, because if the definition of Price or Num Shares (Dim) changes, then the change will be reflected in the Revenue formula. We cannot use the Num Shares measure, because it contains an aggregate function, and in SQL, we cannot Sum an aggregate function.

After we create the formula, it is a good idea to click the *Parse* button. The parse function checks the SQL syntax of the formula and will return if the database accepts the formula or finds it in error. If the parse returns, "The expression type is not compatible with the object type", then the formula probably does parse, but it is typed wrong. Click the OK button(s) to return to the Edit Select Statement dialog and set the type as a number. Desktop Intelligence will work with improperly Typed objects, but Web Intelligence will not display the values correctly.

We multiply the formula by -1, because Revenue flows in the opposite direction of shares. When we buy something, we gain a product, but money leaves our account. When we sell something, Money goes into our account, but product leaves our inventory. This is common in many databases.

Exercise: Create the Revenue Object

1. Select | Insert | Object | from the menu.
2. Enter Revenue into the *Name* field & Enter Number in the *Type* list.
3. Click on the >> button on the right of the Select control.
4. Type *Sum(* into the Edit field.
5. Double-click on the Price object in the Classes and Objects section.
6. Type a space, an *, and a space.
7. Double-click Num Shares(Dim) in the Classes and Objects section.
8. Type:) * (-1), to finish the formula.
9. Click the Parse button to make sure that it parses.
10. Click the *OK* button, to exit the Edit Select dialog.

Notes

No Group By Measure

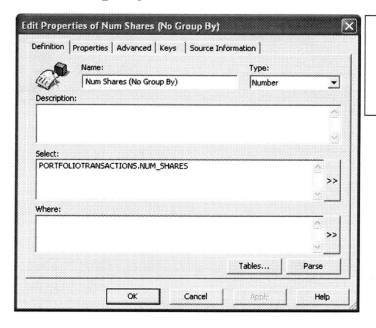

No Group By
Measures have
no aggregate
function in the
Select formula

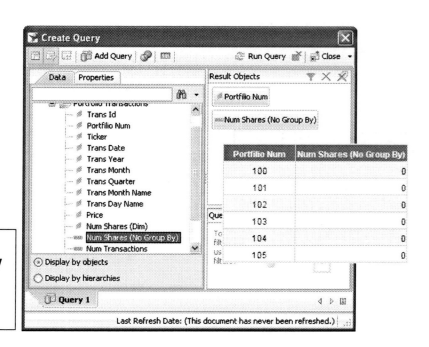

A table created
with a No Group By
Measure appears
the same as any
other table

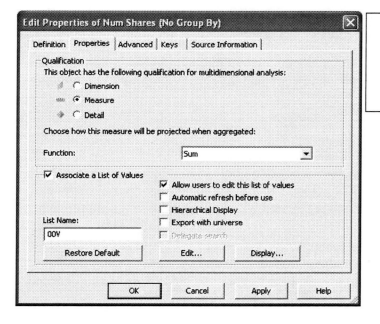

No Group By
Measures can
have a Function
selected on the
Properties tab

If there is no
Group By, then the
query will return
non-aggregated
data to a document

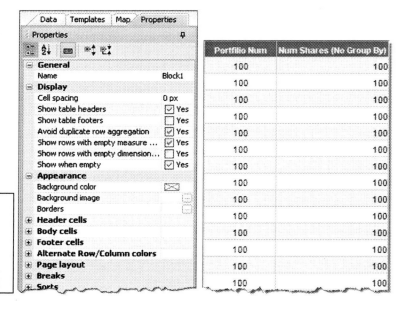

No Group By Measure

To create the Revenue measure, we use the Sum function in the Select formula: Sum(Price * NumShares) * (-1). We also selected the Sum function in the *Function* drop list, on the *Properties* tab. The Sum function in the *Select* statement (formula) causes the SQL to add the Group By clause to the SQL statement, which causes the Revenue to total to the context created by any dimensions in the query. In our example, it was Portfolio Num.

The Sum function in the *Function* list, on the *Properties* tab tells Business Objects to summarize on the report. In other words, sum to the context in which the measure is placed. If a Group By measure is placed with a dimension in a query, then the query will return only the summarized data. In the case of Revenue, this meant that only unique Portfolio Num's would be returned and the total Revenue for each Portfolio Num will accompany the Portfolio ID's.

In the case of our No Group By Num Shares measure, the query will not summarize the data set. This means that it will return every transaction from the transaction table. However, the reporter will summarize the data, as shown in the upper-right graphic. It will summarize on the report, because of the Sum function selected in the *Functions* drop list, on the Properties tab, of the *Edit Properties* dialog. To see the complete data set with no summarization, select the edge of the table on the report, and then check the *Avoid Duplicate Row Aggregation* option in the *Display* section of the Table Properties, as shown in the lower-right graphic.

Most of the time, these No Group By measures are a mistake, because the Designer simply forgot to add the aggregate function to the Select formula. These mistakes are very costly, because even though the report looks correct, it returned more rows than needed to display the correct information. For example, in our universe, when the correctly defined measure is combined with Portfolio ID, in the Result Objects section of a query, the query will return only 6 rows. When the No Group By measure is combined with Portfolio ID, the query will return 2680 rows! These extra rows will make reports cumbersome and difficult to work with.

Notes

Objects in SQL

Num Shares (Dim)

```
SELECT
  PORTFOLIOTRANSACTIONS.NUM_SHARES
FROM
  PORTFOLIOTRANSACTIONS
```

Num Shares (No Group By)

```
SELECT
  PORTFOLIOTRANSACTIONS.NUM_SHARES
FROM
  PORTFOLIOTRANSACTIONS
```

Num Shares

```
SELECT
  PORTFOLIOTRANSACTIONS.TICKER,
  Sum(PORTFOLIOTRANSACTIONS.NUM_SHARES)
FROM
  PORTFOLIOTRANSACTIONS
GROUP BY
  PORTFOLIOTRANSACTIONS.TICKER
```

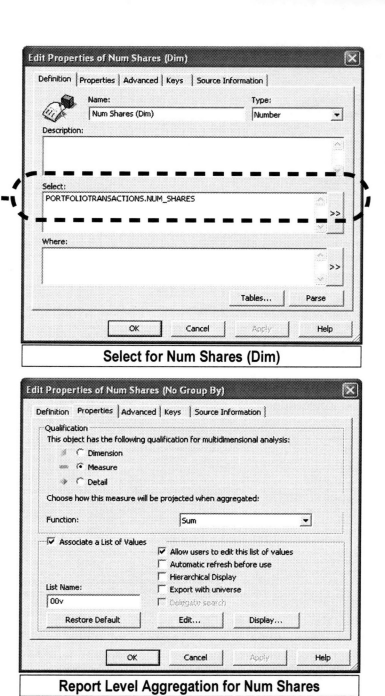

Select for Num Shares (Dim)

Report Level Aggregation for Num Shares

Objects in SQL

Business Objects uses the contents of the *Select* field in the Edit Properties dialog to create the Select clause in the SQL generated for a report. Notice that Num Shares (Dim) and Num Shares (No Group By) create identical SQL statements, even though they behave differently on a report. Business Objects universes must define two behaviors for objects. The first is SQL generation and the other is how to behave in a report. Since the Select field for both the Dim and No Group By versions is identical, they create identical SQL. However, on a report they will behave differently, because the Dim version will add to the context definition of a table, and the No Group By will simply conform to any contexts by summing. So, both of these objects will return identical data sets to a report (document).

The Num Shares object is a true measure, because it will summarize in the SQL before the data is returned to a document. It is able to do this, because the *Select* field in the Edit Properties dialog includes the sum function. This aggregate causes Business Objects to create a summary SQL statement using a Group By for all non-aggregating objects. This is why we included Ticker in the example, so the Group By clause will be formed in the SQL statement. Both Num Shares and Num Shares (No Group By) will aggregate on a report, if the default context is changed. We know this, because we set the report level aggregation to Sum on the Properties tab of the Edit Properties dialog.

Notice that the table in the From clause of the SQL is part of the *Select* field definition in the Edit Properties dialog. Business Objects gets the table(s) in the from clause from the object definition in the Edit Properties dialog. If the objects come from several tables, then Business Objects will include all of the tables necessary to relate the objects.

Notes

NULL or Contsant Objects

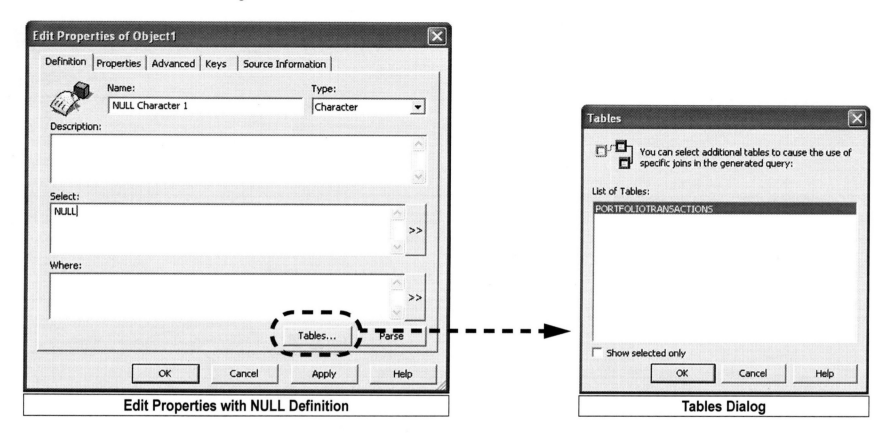

Edit Properties with NULL Definition

Tables Dialog

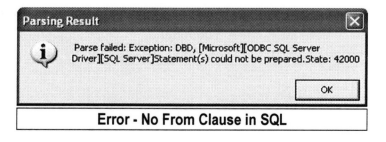

Error - No From Clause in SQL

```
SELECT
    NULL
FROM
    PORTFOLIOTRANSACTIONS
```

Tables Property Adds Table to SQL

NULL or Constant Objects

We often want to add constant or NULL objects to our universe. We often do this for union queries. The constants label the data from one query in the union. For example,

> Select "First Data Set", x, y, z
> Union
> Select "Second Data Set", a, b, c

The NULL is usually a placeholder for a column in one of the sets, because all queries involved in the union, must have the same number and types of columns.

> Select "First Data Set", x, y, z
> Union
> Select "Second Data Set", a, NULL, c

If you create a constant or NULL object, then the objects will not parse with the *Parse* button, because there will be no From clause in the SQL. However, when the object is included with other objects that do have Where clauses, then the SQL will correctly generate. Therefore, even though the objects do not individually parse, they will function properly in an SQL statement with other objects.

Sometimes, companies will not allow a universe to be exported, if there are any errors, even errors such as this that make sense and are no problem. If this is the case, the *Tables* button can be used to relate the object to a table. The Tables button will include selected tables in the query, and also all SQL related tables. This is really not a good solution, because if the table is not required for the SQL, then it will introduce extra joins into the statement. Many designers use this button to force joins in SQL statements.

Notice that my NULL in the graphic is typed as a character. This is needed, because Business Objects types all objects, and you will need Character, Numeric, and Date NULLS, if reporters are planning on creating unions with these types of columns. Many times I will create four of each type of NULL objects and include them in a NULLs class. I will not use the Tables button to associate them to a table, as this may cause errors in the SQL. The objects will not individually parse, but when combined with other objects, they will perform properly.

Notes

Counting Measures

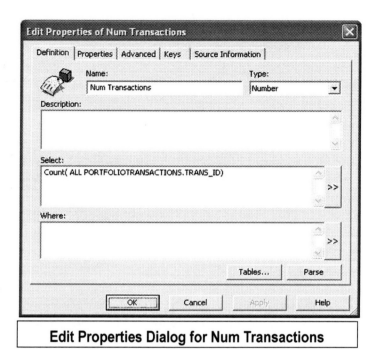

Edit Properties Dialog for Num Transactions

Edit Properties Dialog for Number of Companies

Count(ALL PORTFOLIOTRANSACTIONS.TRANSID)

> The ALL
> Keyword causes
> the Count to
> return the count
> of all Non-Null
> Values

Count(DISTINCT @Select(Portfolio Transactions\Ticker))

> The Distinct
> keyword causes
> the Count to
> count only
> unique
> Non-Null values

Counting Measures

We have already calculated Num Shares and Revenue. Now, we will create two more measures that count the number of transactions and the number of distinct companies in a query. We create count measure objects by using the database's local Count function and keywords.

First, we will create the Num Transactions measure. We can do this by copying the Trans Id object and opening the copy by double-clicking on it. Next, we simply modify the formula to: Count(ALL PORTFOLIOTRANSACTIONS.TRANS_ID). Notice the ALL keyword in the formula, this keyword will cause the formula to count all id's, even if they are duplicated. This is the default in many databases, but it is good to explicitly put the keyword in the formula. Also, notice that we are using the database field, and not the Trans Id dimension object. The reason for this is that Trans Id is a primary key in the PORTFOLIOTRANSACTIONS table, and probably will not change throughout development. Another reason for using the field directly is that many project managers will want the primary key objects deleted from the classes.

In the Num Companies formula: Count(DISTINCT @Select(Portfolio Transactions\Ticker)), we are using the Ticker Dimension object, because the object does not represent a primary key and can change definition of the object that we are counting. Also, notice that we are using the DISTINCT keyword. This will cause the formula to only count unique values of Ticker and ignore any duplicates. This should be the case with most counting measures.

Exercise: Create the Num Transactions and the Number of Companies Measure Objects

1. Copy the Trans Id object and paste it near the end of the object list.
2. Enter Num Transactions into the Name field.
3. Make sure that Number is selected in the Type drop list.
4. Click on the >> button on the right of the Select control.
5. Type: Count(ALL , into the edit field..
6. Locate the TRANSID field in the Tables and Columns section.
7. Double-click on the TRANSID field, to place it into the formula.
8. Make sure that there is a space between ALL and TRANSID.
9. Type:), to complete the formula.
10. Click the *OK* button, to return to the Edit Properties dialog.
11. Parse the formula.

12. Select | Insert | Object | from the menu.
13. Enter Num Companies into the Name field.
14. Make sure that Number is selected in the Type drop list.
15. Click on the >> button on the right of the Select control.
16. Type: Count(DISTINCT , into the edit field..
17. Double-click Ticker in the Classes and Objects section.
18. Type:), to complete the formula.
19. Click the *OK* button, to return to the Edit Properties dialog.
20. Parse the formula.

Notes

Automatic Time Hierarchy

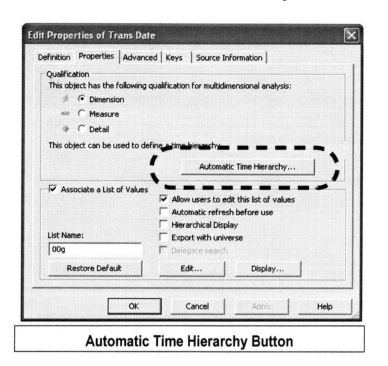

Automatic Time Hierarchy Button

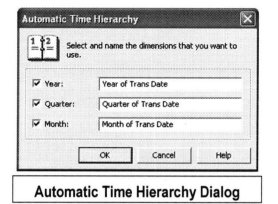

Automatic Time Hierarchy Dialog

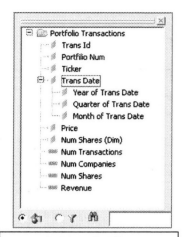

Automatic Time Hierarchy Objects

Formulas for Automatic Time Hierarchy Objects (SQL Server)

Year: {fn year(PORTFOLIOTRANSACTIONS.TRANSDATE)}
Quarter: datepart(qq,PORTFOLIOTRANSACTIONS.TRANSDATE)
Month: {fn month(PORTFOLIOTRANSACTIONS.TRANSDATE)}

Formulas for Automatic Time Hierarchy Objects (Oracle)

Year: TO_NUMBER(TO_CHAR(PORTFOLIOTRANSACTIONS.TRANS_DATE,'SYYYY'))
Quarter: TO_NUMBER(TO_CHAR(PORTFOLIOTRANSACTIONS.TRANS_DATE,'Q'))
Month: TO_NUMBER(TO_CHAR(PORTFOLIOTRANSACTIONS.TRANS_DATE,'MM'))

Automatic Time Hierarchy

Many times there is just a date in a table. However, we often need to retrieve data that is summarized by Year, Quarter, and/or Month. Therefore, we often need to create derived date summary objects from the date field of a table. Business Objects gives us an automated method of creating these derived time objects, which is known as the Automatic Time Hierarchy.

To access the Automatic Time Hierarchy double-click on any date object in the Classes and Objects pane. This action will display the Edit Properties dialog for the date object, in our case Transdate. Once the dialog is displayed, click on the Properties tab. On the Properties tab, there is a button called *Automatic Time Hierarchy*. Click this button to display the Automatic Time Hierarchy dialog. This dialog allows you to choose Year, Quarter, and/or Month. After the option has been checked, you can also edit the name of the derived object. Then, just click the OK button to create the objects, as shown in the screenshot.

Each database probably will use different functions to create the objects. The default functions for SQL Server and Oracle are shown above. Business Objects knows to use these functions, because they are defined in the sqlsvr.prm file. This file has many such functions and parameters defined for SQL Server. Many companies modify this file and many do not - it just depends on how their system is set up.

Notice that when the hierarchy is created, they become sub-objects of the date they were derived from. This is convenient from an organizational point of view, but what if you want other derivatives of the date, such as Month Name or Day Name? If this is the case, then it may just be better to explicitly create the objects without the Automatic Time Hierarchy.

Exercise: Automatic Time Hierarchy

1. Double-click on the Trans Date object, to access the Edit Properties dialog for the object.
2. Click on the Properties tab to activate the tab.
3. Click the *Automatic Time Hierarchy* button to display the Automatic Time Hierarchy dialog.
4. Check all three options
5. Click *OK* to create the derived time objects.
6. Click OK to exit the Edit Properties dialog.

Notes

Explicitly Creating the Time Hierarchy

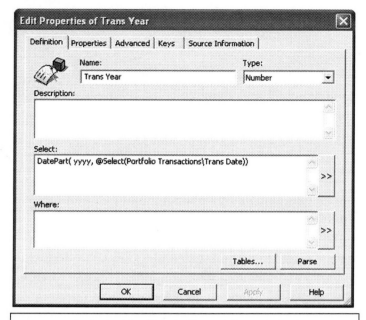

DatePart to Create Trans Year Object

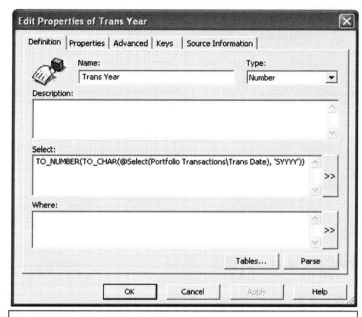

DateName to Create Month Name Object

SQL Server Formulas

Object	Formula	Type
Trans Year	DatePart(yyyy, @Select(Portfolio Transactions\Trans Date))	Number
Trans Quarter	DatePart(q, @Select(Portfolio Transactions\Trans Date))	Number
Trans Month	DatePart(m, @Select(Portfolio Transactions\Trans Date))	Number
Trans Month Name	DateName(mm, @Select(Portfolio Transactions\Trans Date))	Character
Trans Day Name	DateName(dw, @Select(Portfolio Transactions\Trans Date))	Character

Oracle Formulas

Object	Formula	Type
Trans Year	TO_NUMBER(TO_CHAR(@Select(Portfolio Transactions\Trans Date), 'SYYYY'))	Number
Trans Quarter	TO_NUMBER(TO_CHAR(@Select(Portfolio Transactions\Trans Date), 'Q'))	Number
Trans Month Num	TO_NUMBER(TO_CHAR(@Select(Portfolio Transactions\Trans Date), 'MM'))	Number
Trans Month Name	TO_CHAR(@Select(Portfolio Transactions\Trans Date),'Month')	Character
Trans Day Name	TO_CHAR(@Select(Portfolio Transactions\Trans Date),'DAY')	Character

Using SQL Date Functions

In the previous example, we used the default functions defined in the sqlsvr.prm file, by using the Automatic Time Hierarchy button. This method works okay, unless you want to modify the objects, then you will have to modify the sqlsvr.prm file and recreate the objects. It also doesn't work well if you want other types of objects, such as Day Name. To overcome these limitations, most people just explicitly use the native database date functions.

The Automatic Time Hierarchy button also causes the date derivatives to be hidden within the Date object, from which they are derived. This is okay, but it makes it difficult for some report developers to locate the objects, because the developers must click on the plus (+) in front of the object to display the derivatives. This is another reason to use the native database functions and explicitly create each derivative object.

Notice that in the formulas, we are using the object definition for date (**@Select (Portfolio Transactions\Trans Date)**), and not the field directly from the database table. This is important when creating such objects, because we may need them to point to a different date in the future.

I have worked at many companies throughout the years, and in my younger days, one of the most difficult tasks in modifying existing universes was learning how they created their date derivatives. It seems like almost every company uses different methods and functions. Later in this book, I will present a method that will work in universes created with any database. Until then, we will use these native formulas and functions.

A good place to find MS SQL Server Date functions is at the following URL,

http://msdn.microsoft.com/library/default.asp?url=/library/en-us/tsqlref/ts_fa-fz_2c1f.asp

I have been using the following site for Oracle formatting strings with the TO_CHAR function,

http://www.techonthenet.com/oracle/functions/to_char.php

Exercise: Create the five date objects listed on the graphic page.

Notes

Using a Subclass to Hold Date Objects

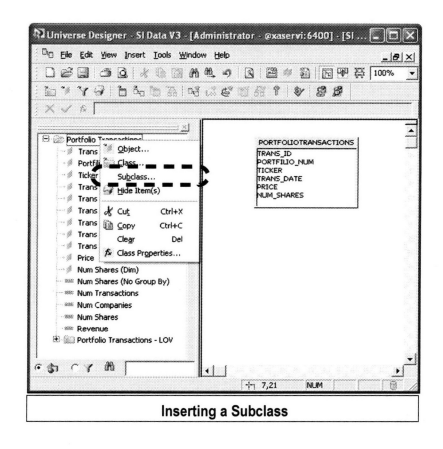

Inserting a Subclass

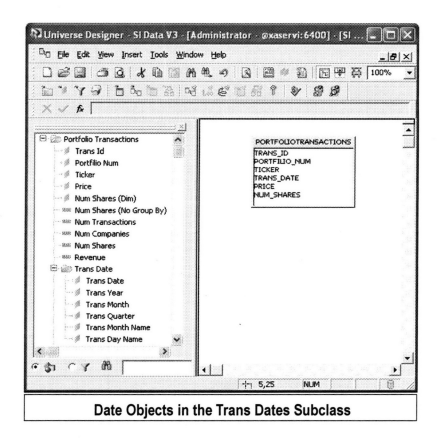

Date Objects in the Trans Dates Subclass

Using a Subclass to Hold Date Objects

Earlier, we created a date hierarchy using the Automatic Time Hierarchy button on the Properties tab, in the Edit Object dialog. This created three date hierarchy objects - Year, Quarter, and Month. These date hierarchy objects were sub-objects to the Trans Date object The Trans Date object was preceded by a plus (+) sign to let people know that there were date hierarchy objects associated with it. The problem with the plus(+) sign in front of an object is that many people do not realize that an object can have sub-objects. Therefore, many people will not realize that there are date derivative objects, such as year, quarter, and month.

Another method of organizing Date Derivative objects is to create a subclass within a class that has a lot of date derivatives. In this case, we can create a subclass named Trans Dates and move all of our date derivative objects into this subclass. Most people realize that a plus in front of a class (folder) means that there are objects or other classes stored within the folder. This will make your date objects well organized and easy to locate.

Exercise: Create the Trans Date Subclass and Move the Date Objects into the Subclass.

1. Right-click on the Portfolio Transactions folder and select *Subclass...* from the pop-up menu.
2. Name the new class - Trans Dates.
3. Select the Date objects in the Portfolio Transactions class and move them to the new Trans Dates subclass.

Notes

Preformatting Object Output

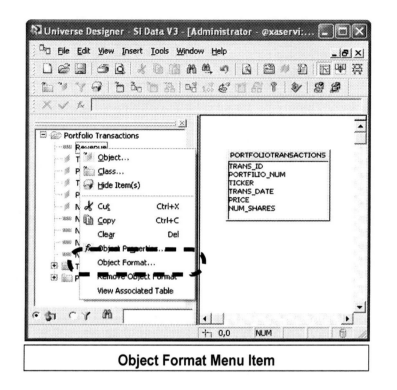

Object Format Menu Item

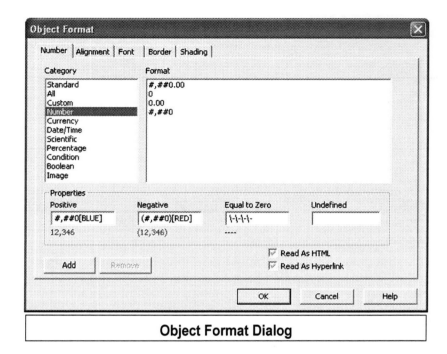

Object Format Dialog

Trans Date	Mmm dd, YYYY	Sep 03, 2006
Trans Quarter	0	3
Trans Month	0	11
Number of Shares	0	230
Revenue	#,##0[BLUE], (#,##0)[RED], \-\-\-\-	2,300, (2,300), ----
Num Transactions	#,##0, (#,##0), 0, 0	5
Number of Companies	#,##0, (#,##0), 0, 0	10

Defining Object Report Format

Business Objects assigns a default format to all objects. For character objects there is no real need for formatting, but for numbers and dates, we may want to override the default format. For example the default for number is #,##0.##. This means that your years will look like 2,006. This format is very distracting and many people viewing the report may not even know that this is a year. Therefore, it would be a good idea to preformat it to 0, as shown in the graphic.

Notice that for numbers there are four format fields: Positive, Negative, Equal to Zero, and Undefined. This allows you to format each state of a number. For example, you may format Revenue to #,##0[Blue], (#,##0)[RED], \-\-\-\-.

The value [RED] in the square brackets assigns a color to the format. Other colors could be Yellow, Blue, Green, Cyan, and Magenta. This is not a complete list, it is just the colors that I have used.

Exercise: Override the Default Formats

1. Right-click on any of the objects listed on the graphics page.
2. Select Object Format from the pop-up menu.
3. Click on the Number tab to activate the tab.
4. Select the Category for the format (Date for Trans Date - Number for the rest)
5. Enter the format shown in the graphic (or you can use formats that you normally use)

Notes

Checking the Universe Integrity

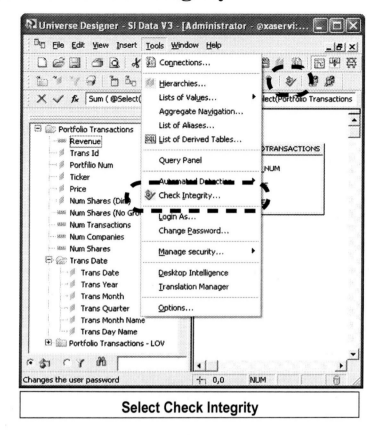

Select Check Integrity

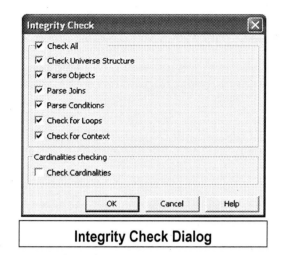

Integrity Check Dialog

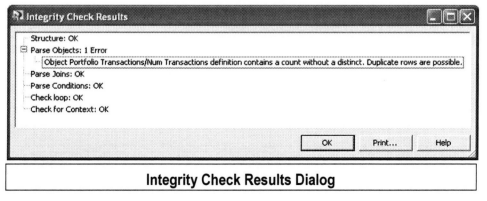

Integrity Check Results Dialog

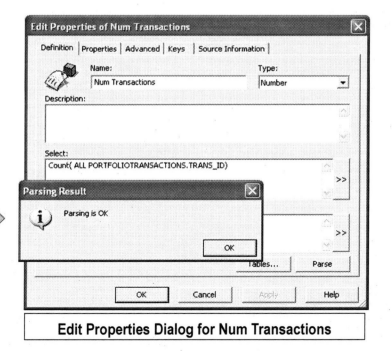

Edit Properties Dialog for Num Transactions

Checking the Universe Integrity

It is a good idea to check the integrity of the universe, especially before you export it and other employees start using it. Currently, all we have is one table and some objects, so the integrity check will parse the objects and make sure that the data connection is working.

The integrity check will make sure that the database is able to use all of the definitions in your universe design. It will parse every object with its algorithm, which may be different from the Parse button located within the Object Properties dialog.. For example, the Num Transactions objects parses in the Properties dialog, but the integrity check still complains that it may count the same object more than once (Duplicate rows are possible), because we did not use the Distinct keyword. If we double-click on the error in the Integrity Check Results dialog, the Object Properties dialog for the Num Transactions object will appear. In this dialog, we can change the ALL keyword to the DISTINCT keyword.

The Integrity Check dialog allows you to choose which aspects of the universe that you want to check. It doesn't hurt to leave them all checked, as this may cause you to find out something that you've overlooked. However, the Check Cardinalities option is sometimes very expensive, because it could take a very long time to complete. We will talk more about cardinalities later in this course.

The integrity check displays the results in the Integrity Check Results dialog. If all is okay for a selected group, then the group will be followed by the affirmation OK. If there are errors for a group, then the group will be followed by the error count. If the group is expanded, then the individual errors for the group can be viewed. To go to the error, double-click on the error message and the properties dialog will be displayed for the object with the error, as shown in the graphic.

Exercise: Check Universe Integrity

1. Select | *Tools* | *Check Integrity* | from the menu.
2. Select all of the options and click *OK*.
3. View the Integrity Check Results and notice the warning on our Num Transactions object.
4. Double-click on the error to display the Edit Properties dialog for Num Transactions.
5. Click the Parse button to make sure the object parses.
6. Change the ALL keyword to DISTINCT.
7. Exit all dialog boxes.

Notes

Our Universe, So Far...

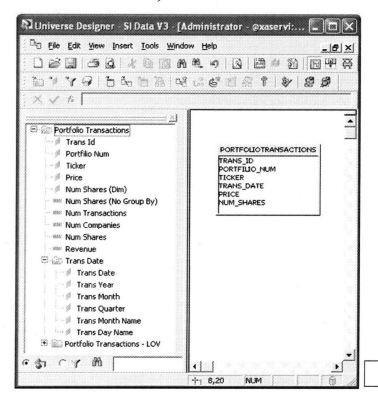

Our Universe

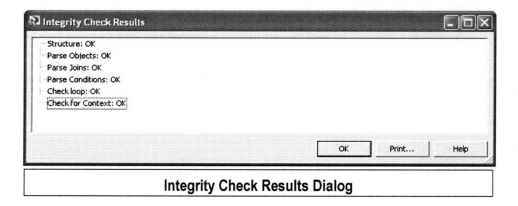

Integrity Check Results Dialog

Object	Qualification	Formula
Trans Year	Dimension	DatePart(yyyy, @Select(Portfolio Transactions\Trans Date))
Trans Quarter	Dimension	DatePart(q, @Select(PPortfolio Transactions\Trans Date))
Trans Month Num	Dimension	DatePart(m, @Select(Portfolio Transactions\Trans Date))
Trans Month Name	Dimension	DateName(mm, @Select(Portfolio Transactions\Trans Date))
Trans Day Name	Dimension	DateName(dw, @Select(Portfolio Transactions\Trans Date))
Num Shares (Dim)	Dimension	PORTFOLIOTRANSACTIONS.Numshares
Num Shares (NGB)	Measure	PORTFOLIOTRANSACTIONS.Numshares
Num Transactions	Measure	Count(DISTINCT PORTFOLIOTRANSACTIONS.TRANSID)
Num Companies	Measure	Count(Distinct @Select(Portfoliotransactions\Ticker))
Revenue	Measure	Sum(@Select(Portfolio Transactions\Price) * @Select(Portfolio Transactions\Num Shares (Dim))) * (-1)
Num Shares	Measure	Sum(PORTFOLIOTRANSACTIONS.Numshares)

* NGB = No Group By

What We Have Learned So Far

We created a one table universe. We did this by inserting a table into the Structure pane and then dragging it into the Classes and Objects pane (Universe Section). Dragging it into the Classes and Objects pane created a default class with the same name as the table. Each field in the table also created a dimension object.

We learned that dimension objects create contexts on a report. They also perform duplicate row aggregation, which means that each row in a report table only displays unique combinations of dimension objects. Since the rows roll-up, it is difficult to get a correct sum of any dimension numerical values. Therefore, we created measures. Measures aggregate using an aggregate function, such as Sum, Max, Min, Average, Count, and so forth. The measures will aggregate to the contexts that are defined by the dimensions in the query. We also learned that measures with aggregate functions will cause a Group By statement to be added to the SQL. This Group By statement can greatly reduce the number of rows returned to a document, because only unique combinations of the dimensions are returned with the measures aggregating the numeric fields.

We learned that we can use the @Select function to insert already created objects into the definition of other objects. This allows us to create many derivatives of a single object. For example, we can create Year, Quarter, Month, and Day from a single date object. Then, later if we need to change the source for the date object (Invoice to Order date), then all of the derived objects will also update. We learned how to use the SQL Server and Oracle date functions to create time hierarchies using DatePart and DateName for SQL Server, and to_number and to_char for Oracle.

We also used the *Parse* button to check our objects. The *Parse* button sends the object definition to the server and if it is correct, then it will display *Parsing is OK* in the Parsing Results dialog. If there is an error, then it will display the error message in the Parsing Results dialog.

In addition, we discovered that we can preformat objects before they are used in a report. This is especially important for Year objects, Count objects, Percentage objects, Numerical ID objects, and others.

Lastly, we used the Integrity Check dialog to check our universe. The Integrity check will check all aspects of a universe, and then display the results in the Integrity Results dialog. If there is an error in the dialog, then we can double-click on it to go to the definition of the object in error.

Notes

Testing the Universe

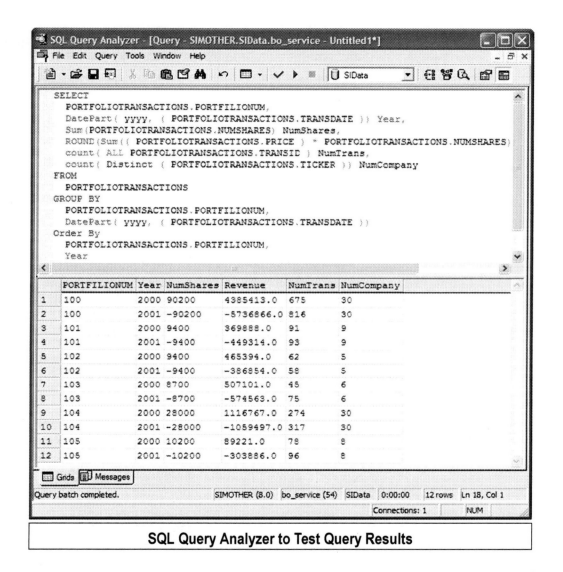

SQL Query Analyzer to Test Query Results

Rich Client Query Panel

Portfolio Num	Trans Year	Num Shares	Revenue	Num Transactions	Num Companies
100	2000	90,200	(4,385,413)	675	30
100	2001	-90,200	5,736,866	816	30
101	2000	9,400	(369,888)	91	9
101	2001	-9,400	449,314	93	9
102	2000	9,400	(465,394)	62	5
102	2001	-9,400	386,854	58	5
103	2000	8,700	(507,101)	45	6
103	2001	-8,700	574,563	75	6

Table Created in Rich Client

Testing the Universe

It is very important to test the universe to see if it functions and it returns the expected results. There are many ways to check a universe. One way is to explore the data through Query Analyzer. This will help you to know what the results of different combinations of objects should be. Then, create the queries in Desktop Intelligence or WEB Intelligence and compare the results. They should match identically.

Another way to test is to have several accepted *Gold Standard* reports. Then create queries with the universe that should yield the same results. Again, the results should match.

Many times the later of the two methods is the best way to test, since you know they are correct. Sometimes, people create SQL in the Analyzer that yields erroneous results. Then they spend hours, or even days, trying to get the universe to match the results of the query. It has been my experience that if you have created the universe using proper design rules, then it will almost always return the proper results. This is why I like to use the accepted gold standard reports.

The gold standard reports will only match, if the data has not changed. For example, sometimes people build a data warehouse. During the process of building the warehouse, they may *massage* the data to make it more correct. For example, combine duplicate customers or realign regions. If the gold standard reports are built using the transactional data before it is warehoused, then the universe results may not match exactly. I have seen people spend weeks trying to reconcile data from two different sources. I guess it's got to be done, but it seems like a waste of good talent. People should know ahead of time of any changes that were made to the data that will cause it to diverge from the gold standard reports. Then, they can create queries that isolate the data portion that should match. This will save large amounts of time and break the testing into smaller, targeted pieces.

Notes

Chapter 2: Conditions in Our Universe

In this chapter, we are going to learn how to create conditions in our universe. Conditions that are defined at the universe level make our universes more friendly and complete. People appreciate having a variety of conditions to use in their queries.

While universe-defined conditions are convenient for people to use in their queries, it is also important to note that some universe-defined conditions cannot be created on the query side and must be defined in the universe.

In this chapter, we will learn to create a variety of conditions, including prompted conditions that prompt for user input when a query is refreshed and subquery conditions that allow us to use a summary condition that is separate from the main query.

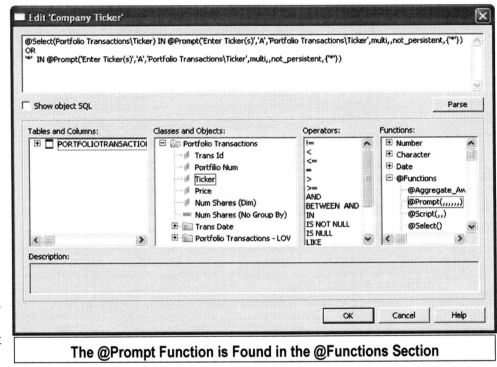

The @Prompt Function is Found in the @Functions Section

This chapter is called Conditions in our Universe. However, it is important to note that these conditions are also known as Query Filters in WEB Intelligence. We will continue to call them conditions throughout this book.

Conditions Defined

Opps, forgot to place conditions on a query!

Portfilionum	Transdate	Number of Shares	Revenue	Num Transactions	Number of Companies
100	Jul 13, 2000	3000	164,138	30	30
100	Jul 14, 2000	2600	131,375	5	5
100	Jul 17, 2000	3100	124,538	5	5
100	Jul 18, 2000	2300	142,875	4	4
100	Jul 19, 2000	1200	59,475	3	3
100	Jul 20, 2000	2000	158,025	3	3
100	Jul 21, 2000	1700	105,038	6	6
100	Jul 24, 2000	2700	144,963	5	5
100	Jul 25, 2000	3200	162,825	7	7
100	Jul 26, 2000	3800	228,950	6	6
100	Jul 27, 2000	1600	80,175	5	5
100	Jul 28, 2000	2500	161,563	5	5
100	Jul 31, 2000	3000	108,000	5	5
100	Aug 01, 2000	2600	117,850	5	5
100	Aug 02, 2000	2500	184,575	7	7
100	Aug 03, 2000	1300	41,175	4	4
100	Aug 04, 2000	2600	147,813	6	6
100	Aug 07, 2000	1200	60,488	3	3
100	Aug 08, 2000	400	(4,863)	3	3
100	Aug 09, 2000	-1000	(62,525)	9	9
100	Aug 10, 2000	500	10,288	4	4
100	Aug 11, 2000	1700	75,588	4	4
100	Aug 14, 2000	2600	126,225	6	6
100	Aug 15, 2000	2800	144,550	8	8
100	Aug 16, 2000	2300	169,200	5	5
100	Aug 17, 2000	-600	(27,075)	3	3
100	Aug 18, 2000	2200	95,600	7	7
100	Aug 21, 2000	-500	(43,300)	6	6
100	Aug 22, 2000	3200	145,063	4	4
100	Aug 23, 2000	1800	120,313	8	8
100	Aug 24, 2000	0	11,150	3	3
100	Aug 25, 2000	300	12,300	1	1
100	Aug 28, 2000	600	32,838	3	3
100	Aug 29, 2000	-1100	(77,863)	5	5
100	Aug 30, 2000	-1700	(110,075)	4	4
100	Aug 31, 2000	-300	(28,800)	4	4

Reports with No Conditions are Overwheming

Conditions - Bring Back the Data that You Want

Conditions are very important to any universe, because they allow people to isolate data of interest. Reports with no conditions are usually quite overwhelming and, sometimes, even incorrect. We use conditions to limit data. We can also use them to make reports correct. For example, some conditions inhibit multiple counts due to erroneous relationships in the universe.

Many times, conditions can be created in a document and don't really need to be created in a universe. Other times, the conditions are too complicated for the reporting tool and must be created in a universe.

I have worked in companies that have very little conditions (only the complicated ones) in their universes and I have worked in others that have every conceivable condition. I am not sure which is better, but I'll bet that it is somewhere in between the two extremes.

Conditions can be hard-coded, which means that they need no input from the person refreshing the report. They can also be parameterized, which means that they will need user input when the query is refreshed. Most universes have both cases, and they should.

In this chapter, we are going to explore the different types of condition objects that we can create. In addition, we will continue to discuss conditions throughout the course, because we will need to create additional conditions as we add more tables and objects to our universe.

Notes

Creating Conditions

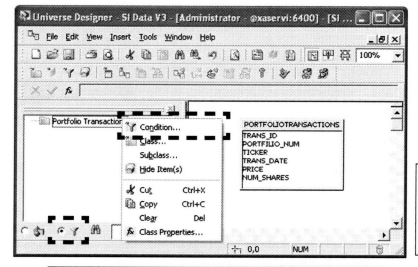

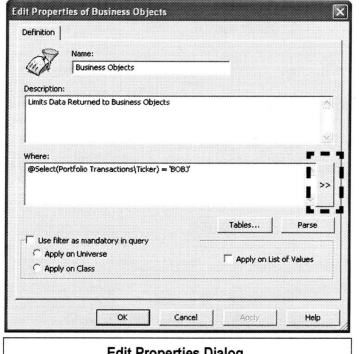

Edit Properties Dialog

To access the Conditions pane in the Designer, click on the Yellow Filter Funnel located beneath the Classes and Objects (Universe) pane.

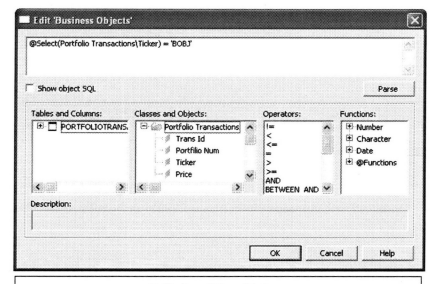

Edit Condition Dialog

Creating Conditions

Conditions are accessed in the Conditions list of the Universe workspace. To access the Conditions list, click the Yellow Filter Funnel located beneath the Classes and Objects (Universe) window. All condition objects in the universe are located in this pane.

To insert a Condition object, you can right-click and select *Condition...* from the pop-up menu. You can also use the Editing toolbar or the | *Insert* | *Condition...* | menu item. All of these actions will display the Edit Properties dialog where you can create a new condition object or modify an existing one.

The Edit Properties dialog has three fields: Name, Description, and Where. There is no *Select* field, as there was in the Edit Properties dialog for result objects. To create the condition, we simply enter the condition logic in the *Where* field of the dialog. Many times, it is more convenient to click the >> button to display the Edit dialog. With this dialog, we can access fields from tables, result objects, operators, and local database functions.

Since it is better (easier to maintain) to use results objects (as opposed to columns in tables), we usually use the objects in the Classes and Objects section of the dialog. When we double-click on an object, it will appear in the formula field. It will be enclosed within the @Select statement, which simply inserts the SQL from the Select field of the Edit Properties dialog for the object into the Where condition that we are working on. Notice that the object is referred to as Class/object within the @Select statement. This is why we cannot have two classes with the same name, because it will confuse the @Select function.

Most conditions are defined by an object, operator, and an operand. In the case in the graphic, the object is Ticker, the operator is Equal to, and the operand is the constant: 'BOBJ'. Over the next few slides we will create various condition objects for our universe.

Exercise: Create a Simple Condition Object

1. Click on the Yellow Condition Funnel, located beneath the Classes and Objects section of the Designer.
2. Right-Click on the class name and select *Condition...*
3. Enter Business Objects into the Name field.
4. Enter Limits data returned to Business Objects, into the Description field.
5. Click on the >> button to display the Edit dialog.
6. Locate and double-click Ticker in the Classes and Objects section.
7. Double-click on the equal sign in the operators section.
8. Type 'BOBJ'
9. Click the Parse button to check the condition.
10. Click the OK's to exit all dialogs and create the object.

Notes

Creating Prompted Conditions

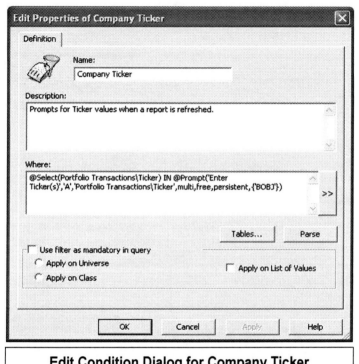

Edit Condition Dialog for Company Ticker

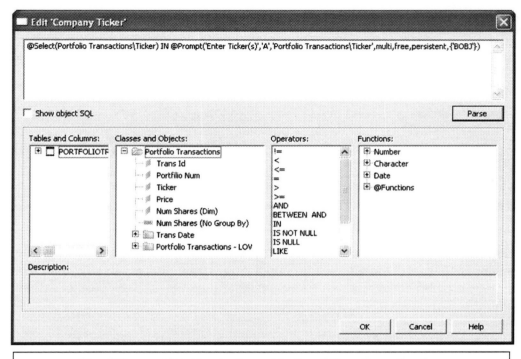

The @Prompt Funtion is Found in the @Functions Section

@Select(Portfolio Transactions\Ticker) IN @Prompt('Enter Ticker(s)','A','Portfolio Transactions\Ticker',multi,free,persistent,{'BOBJ'})

The @Prompt
Allows User
Input at
Refresh
Time

Prompted Conditions

The BOBJ condition that we created works well for conditions on objects with only a few values. For example, Yes - No, On - Off, Active - Not Active, and so forth. However, this technique is not practical for objects that can have many conditions placed on them. For example, there are thousands of ticker values and we cannot make a condition object for each value. In these cases, it is best to prompt for the ticker value(s) when the report is refreshed. We create prompted conditions with the @Prompt function.

The @Prompt function is very versatile and allows for different configurations through the use of the following seven arguments:

1. **Message:** This is the label that prompts for input. It is also used to identify the prompted input to various functions that can be used to access the inputted value. For example, the UserResponse function that allows the prompt value to be accessed for formulas within a report.
2. **Type:** This is 'A' for Alpha, 'N' for Number, or 'D' for Date. Acronym - 'AND'.
3. **List of Values:** Optional argument that supplies a list of values from which to select the value(s) for the prompt. This list can be provided by an object or a hard-coded list. The syntax to use an object is 'Class\Object' ('Portfolio Transactions\Ticker'). To provide a hard-coded list use {'value1','value2',..., 'value(n)'} ({'BOBJ','IBM','SAP'}).
4. **Mono|Multi:** Mono allows for only one value to be selected. Used with the following operators: =, >, >=, <, <=, LIKE, and so forth. Multi allows for multiple values to be selected and is used with the IN or NOT IN operators. Mono is the default.
5. **Free|Constrained|Primary_Key:** Free allows for values to be freely typed into the prompt field. Constrained limits the values entered to values selected from the list. Therefore, a list must be provided if the Constrained option is used. Primary key also constrains the selected values to values from the list. However, Primary Key will allow the index awareness of an object to be taken advantage of. Free is the default.
6. **Persistent|Not_Persistent:** Persistent will remember the last value(s) used to satisfy the prompt. Persistent will override any default values assigned to the prompt. Not Persistent will not remember any previous values selected. Not Persistent will allow default values to be selected when the prompt dialog is displayed. Persistent is the default.
7. **Default Value:** Allows for default values to be assigned to a prompt. The default values are assigned with the following syntax: {'value1','value2',...,value(n)'} ({'BOBJ','IBM'}.

The first five arguments are the original five arguments and only the first two are required. Desktop Intelligence only recognizes these first five arguments. The minimum syntax is @Prompt('Label', 'A',,,)

Notes

Prompted Condition Examples

@Select(Portfolio Transactions\Ticker) = @Prompt('Enter Ticker(s)','A',,,,)

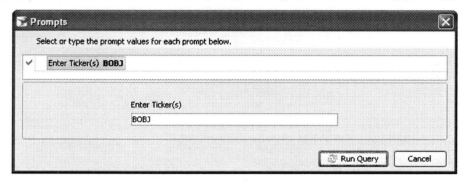

@Select(Portfolio Transactions\Ticker) IN @Prompt('Enter Ticker(s)', 'A', 'Portfolio Transactions\Ticker', multi,,)

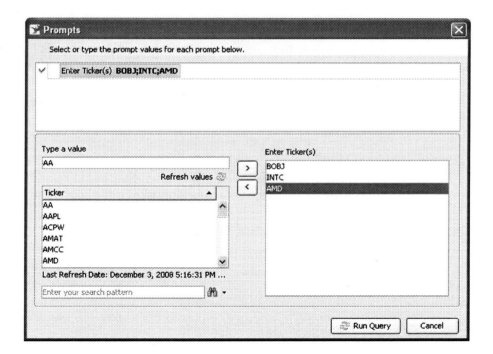

Prompted Condition Examples

To prompt for a single value, with no list of values, ability to type in value, persistent value, and no default value:
    @Select(Portfolio Transactions\Ticker) = @Prompt('Enter Ticker(s)','A',,,)

To prompt for multiple values, with no list of values, ability to type in value(s), persistent value(s), and no default value(s):
    @Select(Portfolio Transactions\Ticker) IN @Prompt('Enter Ticker(s)','A',,multi,)

To prompt for multiple values, with list of values, ability to type in value(s), persistent value(s), and no default value(s):
    @Select(Portfolio Transactions\Ticker) IN @Prompt('Enter Ticker(s)','A','Portfolio Transactions\Ticker',multi,)

To prompt for multiple values, with list of values, ability to type in value(s), persistent value(s), and default value(s):
    @Select(Portfolio Transactions\Ticker) IN @Prompt('Enter Ticker(s)','A','Portfolio Transactions\Ticker',multi,,,{'BOBJ','IBM'})

To prompt for multiple values, with list of values, constrained to the list of values, non persistent value(s), and no default value(s):
    @Select(Portfolio Transactions\Ticker) IN @Prompt('Enter Ticker(s)','A','Portfolio Transactions\Ticker',multi,constrained,not_persistent,)

To prompt for multiple values, with hard-coded list of values, ability to type in value(s), non persistent value(s), and no default value(s):
    @Select(Portfolio Transactions\Ticker) IN @Prompt('Enter Ticker(s)','A',{'BOBJ','INTC','AMD'},multi,,not_persistent,)

Exercise: Create a Prompted Condition (Bottom Condition in the Graphic)

1. Click on the Yellow Condition Funnel located beneath the Classes and Objects window.
2. Delete the Business Objects condition.
3. Click the *Condition...* toolbar button.
4. Enter *Company Ticker* into the Name field.
5. Click the >> button to launch the Editor.
6. Double-click the Ticker dimension object to add it to the formula.
7. Double-click the IN operator.
8. Expand the @Function folder in the Functions section.
9. Double-click the @Prompt function.
10. Type *'Enter Ticker(s)'* for the first argument.
11. Right-arrow past the comma and enter *'A'*.
12. Right arrow past the next coma and type ', double-click on the Ticker dimension object, and type another '.
13. Right arrow past the comma and type *multi*.
14. Right arrow past the next comma, and then delete the final two commas.
15. Click Parse, if it parses, then click the OK buttons to accept it.

Notes

Create All or Selected Conditions

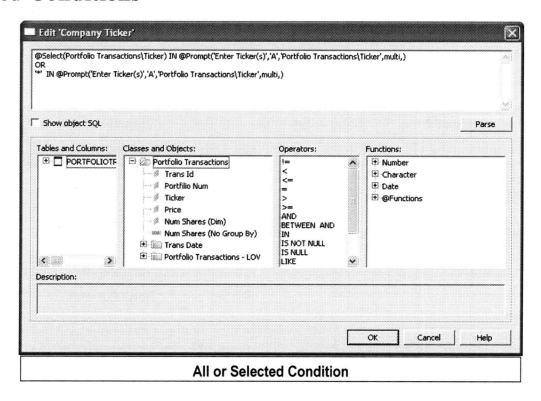

All or Selected Condition

@Select(Portfolio Transactions\Ticker) IN @Prompt('Enter Ticker(s)', 'A', 'Portfolio Transactions\Ticker', multi,)
Or
'*' IN @Prompt('Enter Ticker(s)', 'A', 'Portfolio Transactions\Ticker', multi,)

```
Select
 COMPANY.TICKER
FROM
 COMPANY
WHERE
 ( (COMPANY.TICKER) IN ('*')
OR
'*' IN ('*') )
```

```
Select
 COMPANY.TICKER
FROM
 COMPANY
WHERE
 ( (COMPANY.TICKER) IN ('AA','AAPL','AMAT')
OR
'*' IN ('AA','AAPL','AMAT') )
```

Create All or Selected Conditions

There are limits to how many values that can be selected from a list of values. The limits vary from database to database, and even within different versions. However, Business Objects only allows you to select 99 values from the list. This limit can be overridden by modifying the sqlsvr.prm file and entering the following in the [RDBMS] section: MAX_INLIST_VALUES. It is probably is not very efficient to select all values in a list of values either. So, to overcome this limitation, we can use the following statement:

@Select(Portfolio Transactions\Ticker) IN @Prompt('Enter Ticker(s)', 'A', 'Portfolio Transactions\Ticker', multi,)
Or
'*' IN @Prompt('Enter Ticker(s)', 'A', 'Portfolio Transactions\Ticker', multi,)

The first clause of the statement (the part before the Or), is exactly like the original. It simply allows people to select values from a list in the Prompt dialog. The second clause looks for the value '*'. If an '*' is entered into the prompt dialog, then this second clause is true and all rows will be returned. This is much more efficient than selecting all values in the list.

I have worked at companies that create a dimension object to hold the asterisk. This object could be called *For All Constant* and the Select field would contain '*'. This object will not parse, because it is not associated with any table. However, it will work just fine when it is part of a query. The statement would then change to:

@Select(Portfoliotransactions\Ticker) IN @Prompt('Enter Ticker(s)', 'A', 'Portfolio Transactions\Ticker', multi,)
Or
@Select(*For All Constant*) IN @Prompt('Enter Ticker(s)', 'A', 'Portfolio Transactions\Ticker', multi,)

Exercise: Create All or Selected Condition

1. Double-click on the Company Ticker condition to display the Edit Properties dialog for the object.
2. Modify the existing Where formula to the formula shown in the graphic.
3. Click Parse to make sure the object's syntax is correct.
4. Click *OK* to exit the Edit Properties dialog.

Notes

Working with All or Selected Conditions

@Select(Portfolio Transactions\Ticker) IN @Prompt('Enter Ticker(s)','A','Portfolio Transactions\Ticker',multi,,not_persistent,{'*'})
OR
'* IN @Prompt('Enter Ticker(s)','A','Portfolio Transactions\Ticker',multi,,not_persistent,{'*'})

Set Asterisk as the Default Value for the Prompt

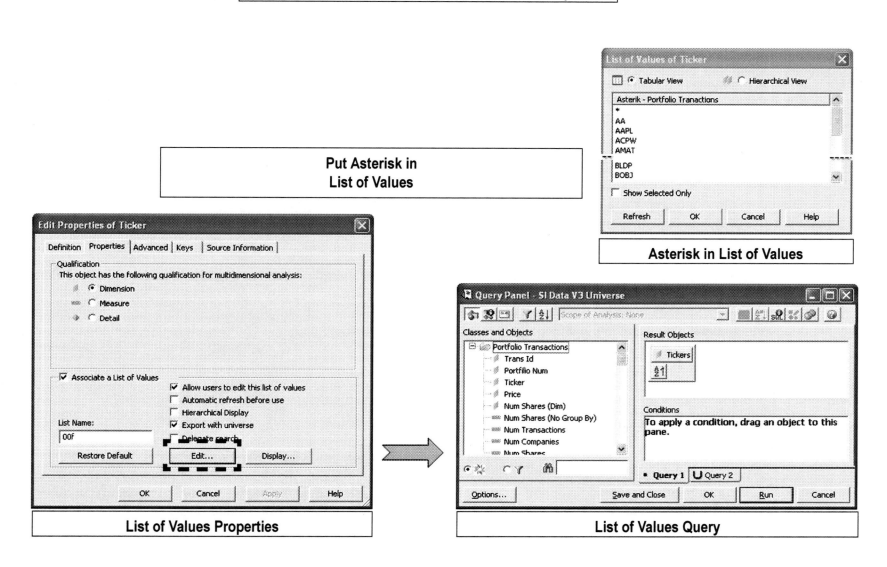

**Put Asterisk in
List of Values**

Asterisk in List of Values

List of Values Properties

List of Values Query

Working with All or Selected Conditions

Now that we allow people to enter an asterisk to retrieve all of the list items, we now need to make it easier for them to work with. One way to do this is to make the asterisk the default value.

@Select(Portfolio Transactions\Ticker) IN @Prompt('Enter Ticker(s)','A','Portfolio Transactions\Ticker',multi,,not_persistent,{'*'})

OR

'*' IN @Prompt('Enter Ticker(s)','A','Portfolio Transactions\Ticker',multi,,not_persistent,{'*'})

Notice the two new arguments in the @Prompt. The first one - not_persistent, allows for the default value to be displayed when a document is refreshed more than once. The last argument is the default value enclosed in {}.

Another trick is to add the asterisk to a list of values for an object. Then, the asterisk will be one of the choices in the list. Even though this is an advanced topic, I wanted to put it here to keep it in context. We will discuss the Tables... button (used in the exercise (3d)) later in the book.

Exercise: Place '' in List of Values (Optional Exercise, Slightly Advanced)*

1. Right-click on the Portfolio Transactions folder and select Subclass.
2. Name the new subclass - Portfolio Transactions - LOV.
3. Create an Asterisk object for Portfolio Transactions
   - Right-click on the new folder and select *Object...*
   - Name the Object : *Tickers.*
   - In the Select field, enter '*'.
   - Click the Tables button and select PORTFOLIOTRANSACTIONS
   - Click OK, OK to create the *Asterisk - Portfolio Transactions* object.
4. Edit the Ticker objects list of values to contain the Asterisk object
   - Double-click on the Ticker object.
   - Click on the Properties tab to activate it.
   - Click the Edit... button in the List of Values section.
   - Click the Combine Queries button in the Query Panel.

- Click on the Query 1 tab to activate it.
- Click on the Ticker object in the Results Objects section, and press the [Delete] key to delete it.
- Locate the Asterisk - Portfolio Transactions object int the Classes and Objects section and double-click it to place it in the Result Objects section of the Query Panel.
- Click the A-Z sort button on the left side of the dialog to sort the object values.
- Click Run to exit the Query Panel.
- Click Display to see the List of Values, and then click Ok to exit.
- Select Export with Universe to make the list available to others.
- Click OK to exit.

Notes

Using a Subquery Condition

Revenue Greater Than 2001 Average Edit Dialog

@Select(Portfolio Transactions\Price) * @Select(Portfolio Transactions\Num Shares (Dim)) * (-1) >
  (Select Avg(@Select(Portfolio Transactions\Price) * @Select(Portfolio Transactions\Num Shares Dm)) * (-1))
  From PORTFOLIOTRANSACTIONS
  Where @Select(Portfolio Trnactions\Trans Year) = 2001)

Using a Subquery Condition

When a standard condition, such as Revenue Greater than 200,000, is applied to a query, it will work on the resolution of the Dimensions in the Result objects section. This resolution is known as the context, so we can say that the condition will apply to the context created by the dimensions. This means that if Trans Year and Revenue are selected in the Result objects window, then the condition Revenue Greater than 200,000 will return years where revenue is greater than 200,000. If the same condition is used in a query with Trans Year, Trans Month, and Revenue, then the query will return months where revenue is greater than 200,000.

Sometimes, we need this condition to be independent of the objects in the Results Objects section of the query, such as in the case Revenue Greater than the Average Revenue. To create a condition that is independent of the Result Objects, we can use a subquery. The subquery works, because it will return a value that is independent of the outer query.

Exercise: Create a Subquery Condition

1. Click the Yellow Condition funnel to enter into the Conditions section of the universe.
2. Right-Click on the class name and select | *Condition...* | from the pop-up menu.
3. Name the Condition: Revenue Greater Than 2001 Average.
4. Describe the object as: Returns Where Transaction Revenue Greater Than 2001 Average.
5. Enter the formula displayed in the graphic.
6. Parse the object to ensure the proper syntax.

Note: You can test this condition by running a query with Trans Id and Revenue. Then, place a filter to limit the data to 2001 and average the Revenue values. The average will be 5,849. Then, make a new query with Trans Id and Revenue. This time, use the *Revenue Greater than 2001 Average* condition. Sort the Revenues on the report from lowest to highest, and you will see that the lowest revenue on the report is 5,850, which is 1 dollar larger than the 2001 average. If you wanted to make the 2001 a variable, then you could replace it with an @Prompt, such as:

@Select(Portfolio Transactions\Price)*@Select(Portfolio Transactions\Num Shares (Dim))*(-1) >
    (Select Avg(@Select(Portfolio Transactions\Price)*@Select(Portfolio Transactions\Num Shares (Dim))*(-1))
    From PORTFOLIOTRANSACTIONS
    Where @Select(Portfolio Transactions\Trans Year) = *@Prompt('Enter Year for Average', 'N',,,))*

Notes

Date Conditions (SQL Server)

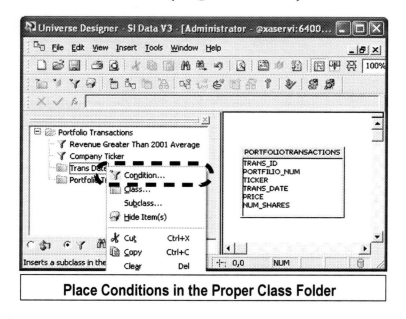

Place Conditions in the Proper Class Folder

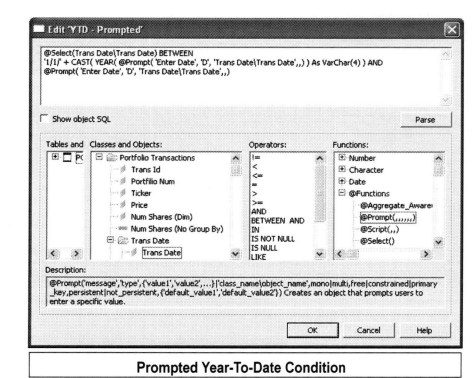

Prompted Year-To-Date Condition

Year-To-Date

@Select(Trans Date\Trans Date) BETWEEN
'1/1/' + CAST(YEAR(@Prompt('Enter Date', 'D', 'Trans Date\Trans Date',,)) As VarChar(4)) AND
@Prompt('Enter Date', 'D', 'Trans Date\Trans Date',,)

Month-To-Date

@Select(Trans Date\Trans Date) BETWEEN
STR(MONTH(@Prompt('Enter Date', 'D', 'Trans Date\Trans Date',,))) + '/ 01/' +
STR(YEAR(@Prompt('Enter Date', 'D', 'Trans Date\Trans Date',,))) AND
@Prompt('Enter Date', 'D', 'Trans Date\Trans Date',,)

Date Range

@Select(Trans Date\Trans Date) BETWEEN
@Prompt('Enter Begin Date', 'D', 'Trans Date\Trans Date',,) AND
@Prompt('Enter End Date', 'D', 'Trans Date\Trans Date',,)

Date Conditions (SQL Server)

Dates are implemented in many different fashions in today's data warehouses. Sometimes conditions are fast and easy to create. In these cases, the data warehouse usually has a date table with every conceivable attribute of a date. However, there are times that there is only a date to work with, as in our one-table universe. In these cases, we need to perform some kind of date logic to get the date ranges that we are interested in. Most of the time, if the database is indexed efficiently and there are not millions of rows, this type of date manipulation is efficient enough.

We have three examples in the graphic - YTD - Prompted, MTD - Prompted, and Date Range. Of the three, the Date Range condition will be the most efficient, because it will utilize the indexes in the most efficient manner. The other two may not work as well for your situation. However, we got to do, what we got to do, to get the job done. If a date is all we have to work with, then so be it - let's create the date conditions.

You can see that with SQL Server and a little imagination that we can build date conditions that can do almost anything that we need them to. The available functions are Year, Month, Day, GetDate, DateAdd, DatePart and DateDiff. We may also need some other support functions, such as Cast or STR to force types.

Notice that in the prompt functions that I did not populate the last two arguments. This is because the Mono/Multi argument defaults to Mono and the Free/Constrained argument defaults to Free. Free is a good option for dates, because most people don't like searching a list for a date.

Exercise: Create the Three Date Conditions Shown in the Graphic

1. Select the Condition option, located under the Universe section.
2. YTD Condition
    * Right-Click on the Trans Date class and select *Condition...*
    * Enter YTD - Prompted into the *Name* field.
    * Click on the >> button to display the Edit dialog.
    * Create the Year-to-Date condition formula shown in the graphic.
    * Click the Parse button to check the syntax.
    * Close the dialogs by clicking OK.
3. MTD Condition
    * Right-Click on the Trans Date class and select *Condition...*
    * Enter MTD - Prompted into the *Name* field.
    * Click on the >> button to display the Edit dialog.
    * Create the Month-to-Date condition formula shown in the graphic.
    * Click the Parse button to check the syntax.
    * Close the dialogs by clicking OK.
4. Date Range Condition
    * Right-Click on the Trans Date class and select *Condition...*
    * Enter Date Range - Prompted into the *Name* field.
    * Click on the >> button to display the Edit dialog.
    * Create the Date Range condition formula shown in the graphic.
    * Click the Parse button to check the syntax.
    * Close the dialogs by clicking OK.

Notes

Date Conditions (Oracle)

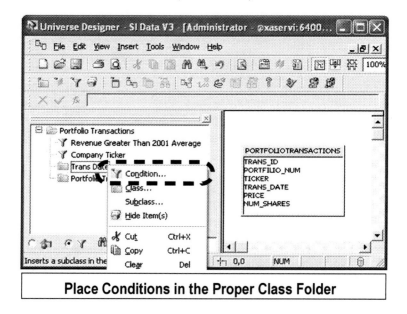

Place Conditions in the Proper Class Folder

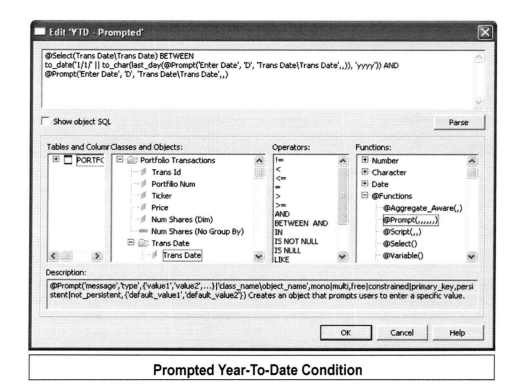

Prompted Year-To-Date Condition

Year-To-Date

@Select(Trans Date\Trans Date) BETWEEN
  to_date('1/1/' || to_char(last_day(@Prompt('Enter Date', 'D', 'Trans Date\Trans Date',,)), 'yyyy')) AND
    @Prompt('Enter Date', 'D', 'Trans Date\Trans Date',,)

Month-To-Date

@Select(Trans Date\Trans Date) BETWEEN
  add_months(last_day(@Prompt('Enter Date', 'D', 'Portfolio Transactions\Trans Date',,)),-1)+1 AND
    @Prompt('Enter Date', 'D', 'Portfolio Transactions\Trans Date',,)

Date Range

@Select(Trans Date\Trans Date) BETWEEN
  @Prompt('Enter Begin Date', 'D', 'Trans Date\Trans Date',,) AND
    @Prompt('Enter End Date', 'D', 'Trans Date\Trans Date',,)

Date Conditions (Oracle)

Dates are implemented in many different fashions in today's data warehouses. Sometimes conditions are fast and easy to create. In these cases, the data warehouse usually has a date table with every conceivable attribute of a date. However, there are times that there is only a date to work with, as in our one-table universe. In these cases, we need to perform some kind of date logic to get the date ranges that we are interested in. Most of the time, if the database is indexed efficiently and there are not millions of rows, this type of date manipulation is efficient enough.

We have three examples in the graphic - YTD - Prompted, MTD - Prompted, and Date Range. Of the three, the Date Range condition will be the most efficient, because it will utilize the indexes in the most efficient manner. The other two may not work as well for your situation. However, we got to do, what we got to do, to get the job done. If a date is all we have to work with, then so be it - let's create the date conditions.

You can see that with Oracle and a little imagination that we can build date conditions that can do almost anything that we need them to. The available functions are Year, Month, Day, sysdate, add_months, last_day, to_char, to_date, and so forth.

Notice that in the prompt functions that I did not populate the last two arguments. This is because the Mono/Multi argument defaults to Mono and the Free/Constrained argument defaults to Free. Free is a good option for dates, because most people don't like searching a list for a date.

Exercise: Create the Three Date Conditions Shown in the Graphic

1. Click on the Yellow Condition Funnel, located beneath the Classes and Objects section of the Designer.
2. YTD Condition
   - Right-Click on the Trans Date class and select *Condition...*
   - Enter YTD - Prompted into the *Name* field.
   - Click on the >> button to display the Edit dialog.
   - Create the Year-to-Date condition formula shown in the graphic.
   - Click the Parse button to check the syntax.
   - Close the dialogs by clicking OK.
3. MTD Condition
   - Right-Click on the Trans Date class and select *Condition...*
   - Enter MTD - Prompted into the *Name* field.
   - Click on the >> button to display the Edit dialog.
   - Create the Month-to-Date condition formula shown in the graphic.
   - Click the Parse button to check the syntax.
   - Close the dialogs by clicking OK.
4. Date Range Condition
   - Right-Click on the Trans Date class and select *Condition...*
   - Enter Date Range - Prompted into the *Name* field.
   - Click on the >> button to display the Edit dialog.
   - Create the Date Range condition formula shown in the graphic.
   - Click the Parse button to check the syntax.
   - Close the dialogs by clicking OK.

Notes

Mandatory Conditions (Filters)

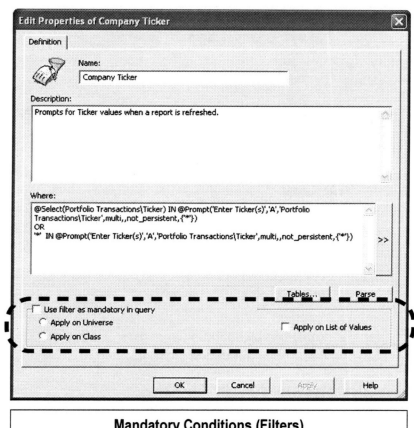

Mandatory Conditions (Filters)

Mandatory Conditions (Filters)

Many conditions represent Business Rules within a company. For example, only select active customers. If all of the reports made in a company only contain active customers, then every report would have to contain the Active Customer condition. In a large company with thousands of report developers, it is a big thing to ask every report developer to remember to place the Active Customer condition on every report that they create, as many will forget to place the condition. Since some reports will have the condition and others will not, the reports will diverge and people will become confused, as they are presented with two different sets of numbers - those that have the condition and those that don't.

For this reason, Business Objects has included the Mandatory Filter section on the Edit Properties dialog for conditions. This section allows you to select two different options - Apply on Universe and Apply on Class. Apply on Universe will place the condition on every query created with the universe. Apply on Class will apply the condition to all queries created using any object from the class where the condition resides, including subclasses of the class. If the condition is placed in a subclass, then it will apply to the subclass and all subclasses of the condition's class. However, it will not apply to the parent of the subclass.

The Apply on List of Values checkbox will also place the condition on any list of values in the conditions scope. With the Apply on Universe option selected, the Apply on List of Values checkbox will apply the condition to all list of values in the universe.

> **Note on Filters and Conditions:** In Business Objects' earlier years, there was only the full client version. In this version there were only Conditions to be placed on queries. Then, later the Web Intelligence version was created. The Web Intelligence designers decided that Query Filter was a better descriptor than Condition, so they referred to conditions as query filters. This has cause confusion with Universe Designers, because the Designer application refers to conditions as both conditions and filters.

Notes

Chapter Summary

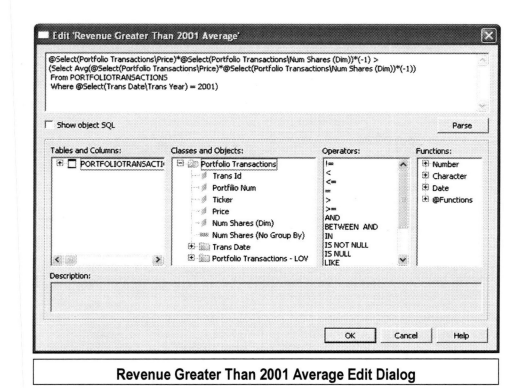

Revenue Greater Than 2001 Average Edit Dialog

Chapter Summary

In this chapter, we learned the importance of condition objects. We also learned how to create simple and complex conditions. Many universes have too many or not enough condition objects. I guess finding the right balance for your company will take some discovery. I also think that it is better to err on the side of having too many conditions than not enough.

It is also important to know how people may use or interoperate your conditions. For example, in this chapter, we created a subquery condition. The subquery of this condition will return the average trade revenue in the year 2001. Then, the complete condition will compare the revenue on each row of the database to this average revenue. If it is larger, then it will return the row. If people do not understand this behavior, then they may assume that it does something else.

Having standardized conditions allows all reports to use the same condition logic. This logic is usually based on business rules in the company. Therefore, they are very effective at keeping reports consistent throughout the company.

Notes

Chapter 3: Inserting Tables and Joins

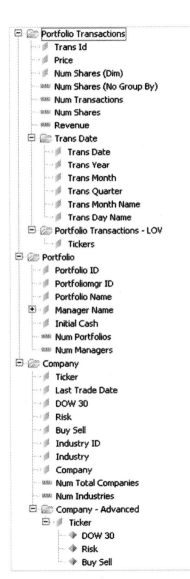

In this chapter, we are going to expand our one-table universe into a professional level universe. We are going to insert more tables and work with joins to relate the tables. We are going to implement a properties table solution that will allow us to use all of the properties in a table with no special business logic on the query side. We are also going to create and organize the objects that we derive from the fields of the tables.

We are going to discover four different methods to fix the chasm trap created by the SIProperties table. One of these methods will include using a derived table. We will also use a derived table to create a Last Trade Date summary table.

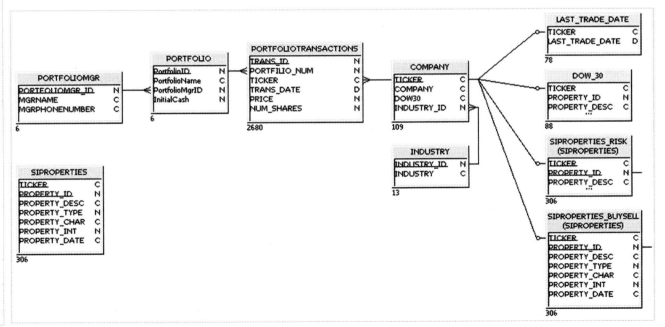

Table Types - Fact and Dimesion

Fact Table (Transactions)

PORTFOLIOTRANSACTIONS

TRANS_ID
PORTFILIO_NUM
TICKER
TRANS_DATE
PRICE
NUM_SHARES

PORTFIOLIOTRANSACTIONS

Dimension Tables (Look up)

PORTFOLIO

PortfolioID
PortfolioName
PortfolioMgrID
InitialCash

PORTFOLIO

PORTFOLIOMGR

PORTFOLIOMGR_ID
MGRNAME
MGRPHONENUMBER

PORTFOLIOMGR

COMPANY

TICKER
COMPANY
DOW30
INDUSTRY_ID

COMPANY

INDUSTRY

INDUSTRY_ID
INDUSTRY

INDUSTRY

Multi-Dimension (Look-Up)

SIPROPERTIES

TICKER
PROPERTY_ID
PROPERTY_DESC
PROPERTY_TYPE
PROPERTY_CHAR
PROPERTY_INT
PROPERTY_DATE

SIPROPERTIES

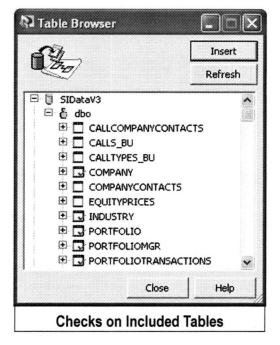

Checks on Included Tables

Table Types - Fact and Dimension

Almost all databases have two types of tables - Fact and Dimension. I know that this is a great area of discussion (defining fact tables) and I hear many arguments about if a table is a fact table, a slowly changing dimension table, or a dimension table. To me, these arguments are a waste of time, because sooner or later, we have to start using them in our universe. Regardless of what type of table it is, it has to work in the universe. This is why I say that there basically two types of tables - Fact and Dimension. These tables also can go by different names - a fact can be called a transactions table and a dimension can be called a look-up table.

We need to know which type of table each of the the tables in our universe is. We need to know this, because tables must logically cooperate. Meaning that one table cannot make another return erroneous results by multiplying the measure columns.

Fact tables usually contain some sort of transactional data, such as invoices, orders, experiments, inventory, payroll, trades, and so forth. They also contain measure type data, such as quantity, volume, amount, revenue, and so forth. The data that is not a measure is usually an ID or some sort of identifier, such as invoice number, date, employee id, and so on. Fact tables are also usually one of the largest tables in the database, at least by number of rows. For example, a shipping company can have a very large shipments fact table or a bank can have a very large transactions table.

The table PORTFOLIOTRANSACTIONS in our universe is a fact table. This is the table that we have based our simple universe on. It has transactional key data - TRANSID, PORTFOLIONUM, TICKER and TRANSDATE. These four key type data form the context for the measures in the table, which means that we can calculate number of shares for any combination of the four key fields.

Dimension tables usually have data that is more static and have unique keys defined by one or more key fields. The important phrase here is that each row in the table can be identified by a unique, non-repeating key. For example, in the COMPANY table, TICKER is the unique key. Each company in the table is identified by a unique ticker value. In the PORTFOLIO table, each portfolio is identified by a unique PortfolioID. The SIPROPERTIES dimension table has rows that are identified by a unique combination of keys - TICKER and PROPERTYID.

Exercise: Insert all of the tables shown in the graphic

1. Select | *Insert* | *Tables* | from the menu.
2. Locate each of the tables in the Table Browser and double-click on them.
3. Click the *Close* button to dismiss the browser.

Notes

Simple Joins

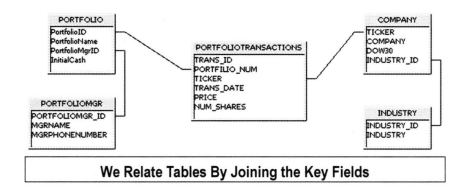

We Relate Tables By Joining the Key Fields

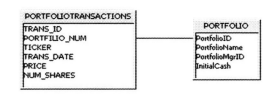

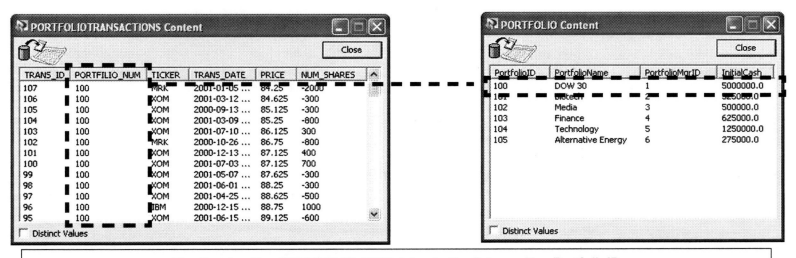

The Foreign Key PORTFOLIO_NUM Joins to the Primary Key PortfolioID

Simple Joins

Probably the most prevalent join in most universes is just a simple join. A simple join is where we just click on a primary key in one table and drag it over to the matching key in another table. All we need to do is identify the key fields in the tables.

Joins allow us to access data in a table through a key field. For example, the PORTFOLIOTRANSACTIONS table has a portfolio identifier. This identifier is PORTFOLIO_NUM. Many companies may be happy referring to a portfolio by its number. For example, portfolio 100 for the DOW 30 portfolio. However, we may also need to know the manager of the portfolio and how to contact the manager. The PORTFOLIO table has this information.

Once the foreign key in a table is identified, it is time to locate the table that the key accesses. Sometimes this is easy, for example, the employee id probably joins to the employee table. Other times it is more difficult, especially if you are using a generic database that ships with some application. In these databases, many of the fields and tables have completely unidentifiable names. In these cases, you will probably have to contact the application company and ask them for a relational diagram. I am surprised at how many application companies will not provide the diagram. I am even more surprised at the number of companies that purchase an application without first demanding the diagram.

Now that we know the keys in the two tables, we simply join the two tables, by dragging one key on top of the other. Make sure that the table is not selected before trying to drag the key from the table, because if the table is already selected, then you will simply drag the table and not the key.

Now that the tables are joined, they can be used as one single logical table. This means that we do not have to worry about this relationship again, unless the join is too restrictive and eliminates valid data. Now, instead of PORTFOLIO_NUM, we can refer to a portfolio by its name. We also now have the portfolio manager id and the initial cash for each portfolio.

Exercise: Join the tables shown in the graphic

1. Click on PORTFOLIO_NUM in PORTFOLIOTRANSACTIONS and drag it to PortfolioID in the PORTFOLIO table.
2. Click on PortfolioMgrID in the PORTFOLIO table and drag it to PORTFOLIOMGR_ID in the PORTFOLIOMGR table.
3. Click on TICKER in PORTFOLIOTRANSACTIONS and drag it to TICKER in the COMPANY table.

Notes

Edit Join Dialog

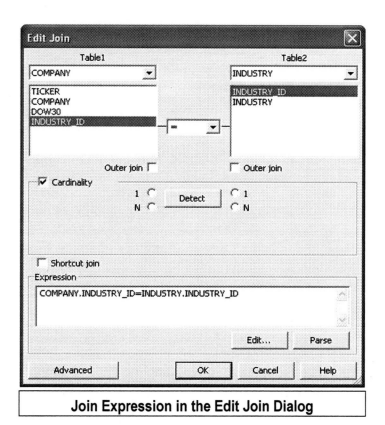

Join Expression in the Edit Join Dialog

Edit Join Dialog

The Edit Join dialog allows us to create a join by selecting fields in two tables. The top part has two drop lists that allow the selection of tables in the workspace. The lists below the tables contain the fields of the table selected in the drop list above it. To create a join, select the key field in each list.

Notice that the join expression is displayed in the *Expression* field. In this case, it says COMPANY.INDUSTRY_ID=INDUSTRY_.INDUSTRY_ID. This expression can be modified, and it often is. We will have an example of modifying this expression later in this chapter.

Sometimes, tables have to be joined on more than one field. In these cases, simply select the sets of keys in the field lists. For example, suppose that there were two tables Table_1 and Table_2. Then, the expression should be:

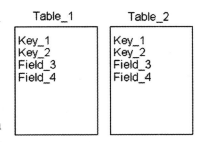

    Table_1.Key_1=Table_2.Key_1 AND Table_1.Key_2=Table_2.Key_2.

To do this with the Edit Join Dialog, select Table_1 and Table_2 in the drop lists. If you selected the tables in the workspace before launching the dialog, then the tables will already be selected in the lists. Then, select Key_1 in both lists, by clicking on them. Next, hold down the [CTRL] key, and select Key_2 in both lists. Now, the join expression will be similar to the one displayed above.

Notice the following check boxes: Outer Join, Cardinality, and Shortcut Join. The Edit Join dialog allows us to set these options. We will talk more about these check boxes later. For right now, we just want to consider the join between two tables.

Exercise: Use the Edit Join Dialog to Create the Company-Industry Join

1. Click on the COMPANY table to select it.
2. Hold down the [CTRL] key and click on the INDUSTRY table to select it.
3. Select *Insert | Join...* from the menu.
   - Select the field INDUSTRY_ID in both lists of the dialog.
   - The Join Expression: COMPANY.INDUSTRY_ID=INDUSTRY.INDUSTRY_ID

Notes

View Options

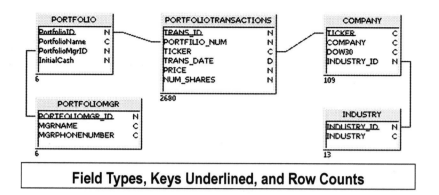

Field Types, Keys Underlined, and Row Counts

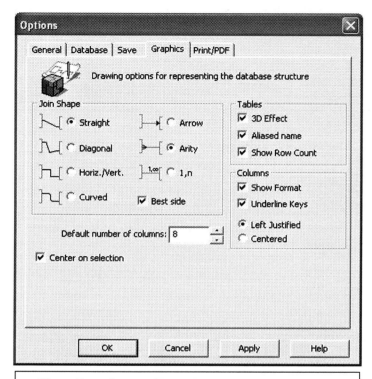

Show Row Count, Show Format, Underline Keys

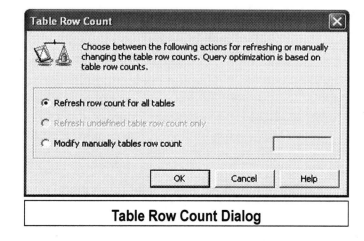

Table Row Count Dialog

View Options

In order to join two fields, the fields must be of the same type - Number to Number, Character to Character, and Date to Date. Earlier, we joined the tables without checking the data types of the fields. Now, it is time to make sure that we did the right thing. We can do this by asking Business Objects to display the field types in the tables. To do this, we select | *Tools* | *Options...* | from the menu. We then click on the Graphics tab, to activate it. In the Columns section, select *Show Format*.

It is also helpful to observe that the joins are made on indexed fields, because if the joins are on indexed fields, then we can expect better query times. To see if the keys are indexed, select the *Underline Keys* option. Then, select *View* | *Refresh Structure*, from the menu, to update the tables. This will only underline the keys if they are indexed in the database.

It is also a good idea to know how many rows are in each table. If there are only a few (10's of thousands), then queries and other operations will be relatively quick. If they are very large (10's of millions), then we need to be more careful, because operations on very large tables may take a relatively long time. Also, if the tables are rather large, then we should build more efficient conditions. To see the row counts of the tables, check the *Show Row Count* option in the Tables section. This will not cause the counts to be displayed, until you select | *View* | *Number of Rows in Table...* | from the menu. The Table Row Count dialog will be displayed - click *Yes* to refresh the counts for all tables.

Notice that there are also other view options on the Graphics tab. You can set these options to your preference. I usually don't change them, as it may cause some unexpected behavior. Plus, it may make your universe look different from others, and thus make it more difficult for other designers to work on it.

Exercise: Show Field Types, Underline Keys, and Show Row Counts

1. Select | *Tools* | *Options* | from the menu.
2. Check the *Show Row Count* option in the Tables section.
3. Check the *Show Format* and *Underline the Keys* options in the Columns section.
4. Click OK to accept the changes and dismiss the dialog.
5. Select | *View* | *Number of Rows in Table...* | from the menu, to display the row counts in the Structure pane.

Notes

Create Classes and Objects

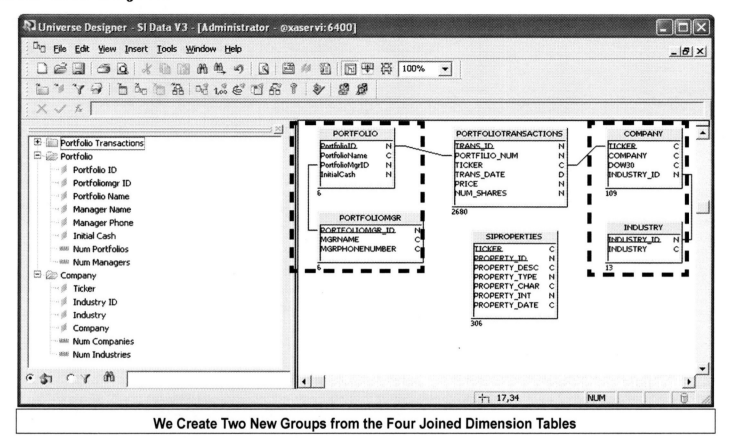

We Create Two New Groups from the Four Joined Dimension Tables

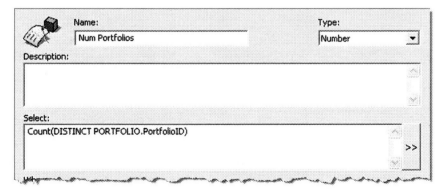

Name: Num Portfolios
Type: Number

Description:

Select:
Count(DISTINCT PORTFOLIO.PortfolioID)

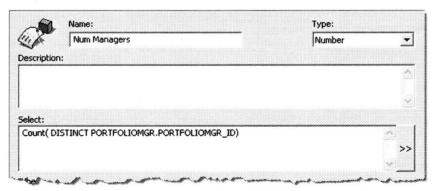

Name: Num Managers
Type: Number

Description:

Select:
Count(DISTINCT PORTFOLIOMGR.PORTFOLIOMGR_ID)

Create Classes and Objects

Earlier, we joined four dimension (look-up) tables to our table structure. We now need to create classes and objects for our newly added tables. Our first observation should be that the two Portfolio dimension tables can be grouped into one logical class. We will call this class Portfolio. We should also observe that the two company dimension tables could also be represented by one class, we will call this class Company.

To create the Company class, we just drag the COMPANY table over to the Classes and Objects section. This is how I work the objects in the new class. It won't always work like this, but in most cases, this is what I do. I delete any foreign keys and unwanted fields. In the case of Company, I delete INDUSTRY_ID (foreign key) and DOW30 (don't need it). Then, I create a copy of the primary key and drag the copy to the bottom of the class. I then create a count on the key, by double-clicking on it and changing the formula to Count(DISTINCT COMPANY.TICKER). I then change the count object's name to Num Companies. Then, I drag the wanted fields from INDUSTRY to the Company class, which are INDUSTRY_ID and INDUSTRY. I copy the Industry ID object to the bottom of the class and do a Count Distinct on it. Then, I modify any of the dimension names that need to be modified. In this case, I just capitalize the ID portion of the primary keys.

If I follow this procedure for all of my Dimension classes, then I should end up with only dimension objects and counts of the primary keys from the tables. I really do not want measures that sum, because this can, and probably will, cause fan-traps. I can have count distinct , min, max, or similar functions, because these usually are independent of any fan-traps that may exist in the data structure. We will discuss fan-traps in greater detail later.

Exercise: Create Classes and Objects from the Dimension tables

1. Make sure that the Portfolio Transactions class is not opened.
2. Drag the PORTFOLIO table to the Classes and Objects section.
3. Copy the Portfolioid object to the bottom of the class.
   - Double-click on the copy and change the name to Num Portfolios. Change the formula to:
   Count(DISTINCT PORTFOLIO.PortfolioID). Click OK.
4. Delete the Portfoliomgrid object (Foreign Key).
5. Name the objects as shown in the graphic.
6. Drag the fields from PORTFOLIMGR to the Portfolio class.
7. Copy the Portfoliomgr Id object to the bottom of the class

- Double-click on the copy and change the name to Num Managers. Change the formula to:
Count(DISTINCT PORTFOLIOMGR.PORTFOLIOMGR_ID). Click OK.
8. Rename the objects as shown in the graphic.

Notes

Organize and Create New Objects

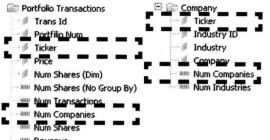

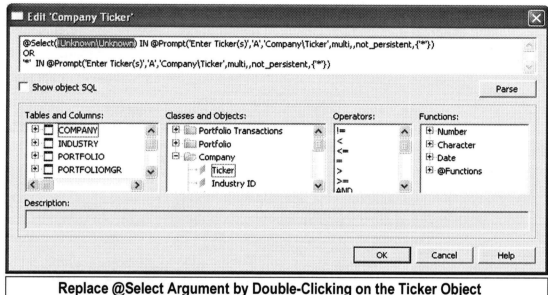

Replace @Select Argument by Double-Clicking on the Ticker Object

Broken

@Select(*!Unknown\!Unknown*) IN @Prompt('Enter Ticker(s)','A','***Portfolio Transactions\Ticker***',multi,,not_persistent,{'*'})
OR '*' IN @Prompt('Enter Ticker(s)','A','***Portfolio Transactions\Ticker***',multi,,not_persistent,{'*'})

Fixed

@Select(*Company\Ticker*) IN @Prompt('Enter Ticker(s)','A','*Company\Ticker*',multi,,not_persistent,{'*'})
OR '*' IN @Prompt('Enter Ticker(s)','A','*Company\Ticker*',multi,,not_persistent,{'*'})

Organize and Create New Objects

We have Ticker in both the Portfolio Transactions and Company class. Since Ticker is a foreign key in the Portfolio Transactions class, we will delete it. This will break the Company Ticker condition in two ways, the @Select no longer points to an existing object and the list of values argument in the prompt now points to an object that does not exist. To fix the prompt, simply point the @Select and the List of Values to the Company\Ticker object. After we fix the Company Ticker condition, we should move it to the Company class, because it now points to the COMPANY table.

We also want to delete Portfolio Num, because it is a foreign key. We don't need foreign keys, because they are joined to the primary keys in other tables. If they are not joined, then you may need to keep it. Remember, when I say that we should delete foreign keys that this is my design strategy. One could argue to keep them, and their argument may be valid. I don't like to keep them, because they may render misleading results.

We also have Num Companies in each class. I want to delete the Num Companies from the Portfolio Transactions class, but before we do, we should have a discussion, which we will have on the next page.

Exercise: Organize the Objects

1. Make sure that the Portfolio class is not opened.
2. Drag the Company table to the Classes and Objects section.
3. Copy the Ticker object to the bottom of the class.
   - Double-click on the copy and change the name to Num Companies. Change the formula to:
   Count(DISTINCT COMPANY.TICKER). Click OK.
4. Delete the Industry Id object (Foreign key).
5. Delete the DOW30 object. (Not Needed)
6. Drag the fields from INDUSTRY to the Company class.
7. Copy the Industry Id object to the bottom of the class
   - Double-click on the copy and change the name to Num Industries. Change the formula to:
   Count(DISTINCT INDUSTRY.INDUSTRY_ID). Click OK.
8. Rename Industry Id to Industry ID.
9. Delete Portfolio Num Portfolio Transactions (Foreign key).

10. Delete Ticker from Portfolio Transactions.
11. Click the Condition option and double-click on the Company Ticker condition. Notice that the formula has changed and won't parse.
12. Click the >> button to enter into the Condition Editor.
13. Highlight the *!Unknown\!Unknown* argument in the @Select and then Double-click the Ticker object in the Company class.
14. Highlight the List of Values argument in the @Prompts and then Double-click the Ticker object in the Company class. (If the @Select is added to the List of Values argument, then the @Select must be removed.
15. Fix the Num Companies object in the Portfolio Transactions class, by replacing the @Select(!Unknown\Unknown) with the Ticker field from the table:
   Count(DISTINCT PORTFOLIOTRANSACTIONS.TICKER)

Notes

Counting Foreign Keys

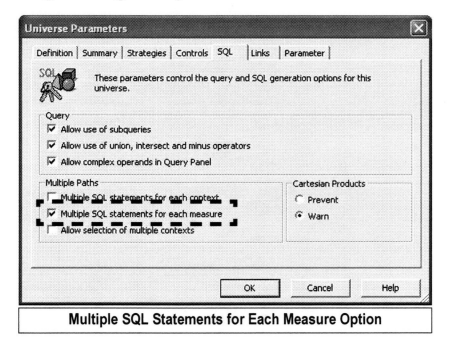

Multiple SQL Statements for Each Measure Option

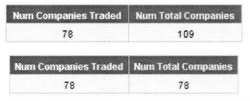

Num Companies Traded	Num Total Companies
78	109

Num Companies Traded	Num Total Companies
78	78

Counts on Foreign Keys can Yield Differing Results

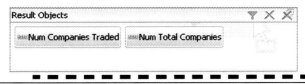

A Query with Two Measures Can Make Two Synchronized Queries

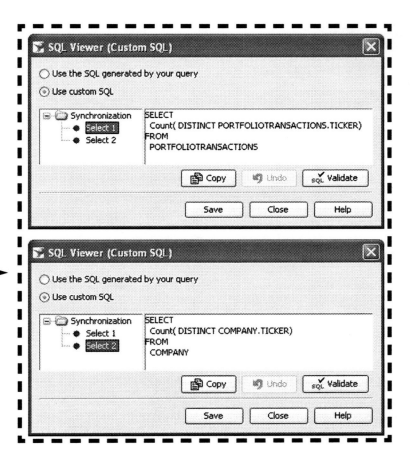

Counting Foreign Keys

Many people will count both the primary keys and foreign keys. In our example, this would be Num Companies. They will call the count of the Primary key, Num Companies Traded, and they will call the count of the Foreign key, Num Total Companies. This seems to make since, because Num Companies Traded will count the companies in the Transactions table, and Num Total Companies will count the companies in the Company dimension table. In order for this to work, the *Multiple SQL statements for each measure* option must be selected on the SQL tab in the Universe Parameters dialog. It is able to do this, because it queries each table independently of the other, as shown in the graphic. However, if I add a dimension from each class (Portfolio Transactions and Company), then the join between the tables will be forced and Num Companies Traded will equal Num Total Companies. For example, if I add Ticker from both Portfolio Transactions and Company to the query, then both measures will return 78, which is the number of distinct companies in the PORTFOLIOTRANSACTIONS table.

This means that if I include dimensions in my query, then Num Companies Traded can equal Num Total Companies, which is very confusing to most developers. So, I simply only count Primary keys to avoid this confusion, I also do not check the *Multiple SQL statements for each measure* option, because if I select objects from both tables, then I want the join between two tables to be activated.

Notice that this is a subjective argument, as I believe that this is the correct way to count keys 90% of the time. The *Multiple SQL statements for each measure* option is placed in the Parameters dialog, so this option can be toggled on and off. Some may believe that it is best to keep it checked. I am not arguing that this position is incorrect. I simply believe that this option is misleading and tends to confuse report developers.

Exercise: Delete the Num Companies Object from the Portfolio Transactions Class

---

Notes

Detail Objects

Manager Phone Can Be a Detail Object

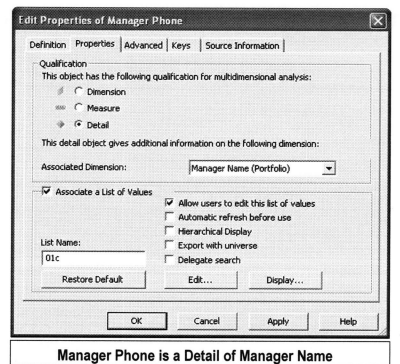

Manager Phone is a Detail of Manager Name

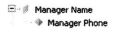

Manager Phone the Dimension
* Assumes that there will be more than one phone number per manager.
* Assumes that reports will be created, where the information will be grouped by phone number.

Manager Name
  Manager Phone

Manager Phone the Detail
* Assumes that each manager has only one phone number.
* It will not be used to Link (Merge) data providers in a document.
* Will not be as restrictive as a dimension object and can go into any structure that its parent Demension is in.

Detail Objects

So far, we have learned about Dimension and Measure objects. Now, we will have a look at the Detail object. The detail object has data that is similar to dimensions, but the data is somehow related to a dimension. We know that Dimensions uniquely identify aspects of our business or company. They are usually proper nouns, but don't have to be. Proper noun examples are Customer, Product, State, Region, Employees, and so forth. Dimensions can also be verbs, such as Buy/Sell, Shipped/Not Shipped, Ordered/Not Ordered, and so forth. In any case, we usually group information on a report by dimensions. Details don't have such power, because they do not usually uniquely represent anything. They are usually a single attribute of a dimension. For example, employee id uniquely identifies an employee, where employee name may or may not uniquely identify an employee. In this case Employee id is the dimension and employee name is the detail.

When data providers in a document are linked (merged), they are linked on the dimensions in the data providers. All linked dimensions are allowed in a table in the report, since they are linked and dimensions define the contexts within the table. Now, let's place an unlinked dimension in the table. We are allowed to place unlinked dimensions from one of the data providers. These new unlinked dimensions, along with the linked dimensions will define the new context of the table. Therefore, unlink dimensions from any other data provider will not be allowed in the table and are labeled as incompatible. They are incompatible, because the unlinked dimensions can have many values for each dimension defined context in the table, and thus may cause the rows to multiply.

However, details from the other data providers will be allowed in the table, if their parent dimension is in the table, because they are assumed to have only one value for each of the parent dimension's values. The details are allowed in, because if the parent dimension is in the table, then the detail will not alter the context. They will not alter the context, because they only have one value for each of their parent's values, and therefore will never increase the number of rows in the table.

By the way, we could have made Manager Name and Manager Phone details of Portfoliomgr ID, and many people will do this. This is correct, because each Portfoliomgr ID has only one name and one phone number. However, in cases where we want the Manager Name to be a dimension, we can just make Manager Phone a detail of Manager Name. Either way could be correct, and I have seen companies use both scenarios successfully.

One last note: The qualification Detail or Dimension does not affect the SQL in any way. The database does not recognize the qualification of an object. Qualifications are just tools to help Business Objects create accurate reports with the data sets contained within a document.

Exercise: Create a Detail Object

1. Double-click on the Manager Phone dimension object in the Portfolio class.
2. Activate the Properties tab, by clicking on the tab.
3. Select the Detail qualification.
4. Select Manager Name (Portfolio) in the *Associated Dimension* drop list.
5. Click *OK*.

Join Cardinalities

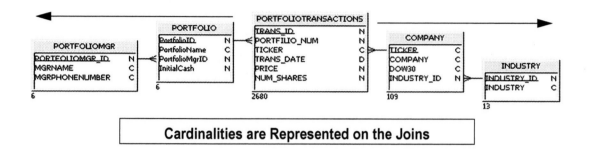

Cardinalities are Represented on the Joins

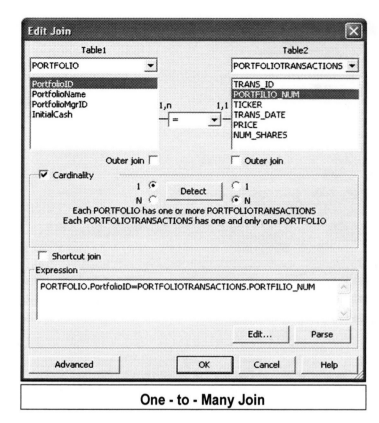

One - to - Many Join

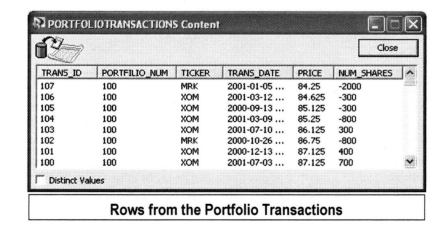

Rows from the Portfolio Transactions

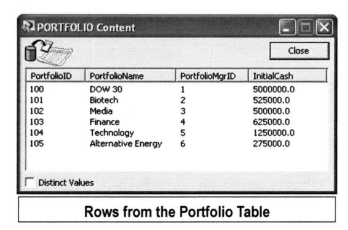

Rows from the Portfolio Table

Join Cardinalities

Join cardinalities help us to understand the relationships between two tables. Earlier, we said that all dimension tables should have a unique key (or set of keys) that uniquely identify each row of data in the table. Fact tables do not need this rule and can have redundant data rows. For example, the Portfolio ID can show up many times in the Portfolio Transactions table, because it is a foreign key. It will show up in the Portfolio Transactions table each time the Portfolio makes a transaction. However, a Portfolio ID value can only show up once in the Portfolio table, because it is a primary key. The Portfolio ID in the Portfolio table uniquely identifies each portfolio in the table. Since the value can show up many times in one table and only once in the other table, the join has a cardinality of *Many-to-One* join.

It is important to note that every table in a relational diagram multiplies the rows of any table that is joined to it. For example, the Industry table has 13 rows. When it is joined to Company, Company will expand the number of rows to 109. It does this, because the Company table has 109 rows and each company belongs to an industry. Most of the time, this multiplication is of no matter, because the table being multiplied has no summing quantitative measure field. For example, there are no summing measures in the Industry table. The Portfolio Transactions table **does have** summing measures - Revenue and Num Shares, and it is being multiplied by the other tables in the diagram. However, this is not a problem, because the other tables are multiplying the Portfolio Transactions table by one. We know this, because the opposite side of every cardinality is one. Therefore, any simple query made with this universe will not return more than the number of rows in the Portfolio Transactions table, which is 2680. If you think of the cardinalities as arrows, then all arrows should shoot away from the fact table, as shown in the graphic. If any arrows shoot back, then the many side will multiply the rows in the fact table. This will cause the summing measure to sum duplicate values, which will cause any sums to be larger than they actually are.

We set the cardinality of a join in the Edit Join dialog. To access the dialog, you can double-click on a join. You can also highlight the join and select *Edit | Properties...* from the menu. We set the cardinality in the Cardinality section of the dialog, which can be done manually or automatically. To manually set the cardinality, just select the *1* or the *N* option under the respective tables. This does require some knowledge of the tables and the data that they contain, because you must make sure that the join is valid and that it is not a many-to-many join. The Detect button will automatically detect the cardinality between two tables. However, it is not always correct and it may take some time to complete. Therefore, I do not recommend the use of this button.

Notes

Cardinality Argument

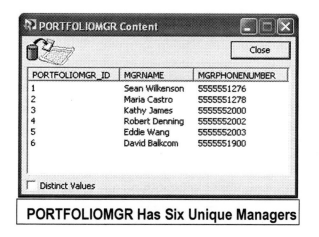

PORTFOLIOMGR_ID	MGRNAME	MGRPHONENUMBER
1	Sean Wilkenson	5555551276
2	Maria Castro	5555551278
3	Kathy James	5555552000
4	Robert Denning	5555552002
5	Eddie Wang	5555552003
6	David Balkcom	5555551900

PORTFOLIOMGR Has Six Unique Managers

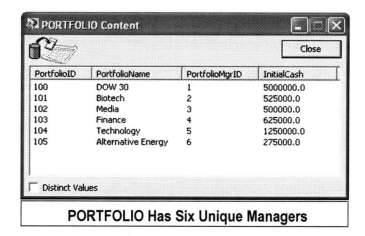

PortfolioID	PortfolioName	PortfolioMgrID	InitialCash
100	DOW 30	1	5000000.0
101	Biotech	2	525000.0
102	Media	3	500000.0
103	Finance	4	625000.0
104	Technology	5	1250000.0
105	Alternative Energy	6	275000.0

PORTFOLIO Has Six Unique Managers

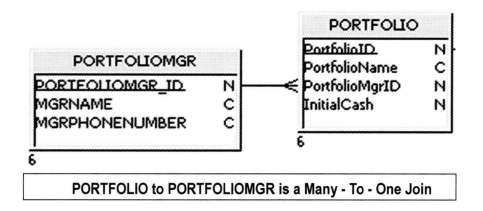

PORTFOLIO to PORTFOLIOMGR is a Many - To - One Join

Cardinality Argument

Earlier, we said that if a column has no repeating value and all values are unique, then that is the one side of a Many - To - One join. But, what if both sides of the join meet this criterion? For example, look at Portfolio and PortfolioMgr. They both have a unique list of Manager Id's that is identical to the other. Many believe that this should be a One - To - One join. However, this is not a One - To - One join.

It is not One - To - One, because the keys to not constrict the data to this assumption. In the PortfolioMgr table, the PortfolioMgr_Id is the primary key and its values cannot be repeated. In the Portfolio table, the PortfolioMgrId is a foreign key and there are no duplicate restrictions, which mean that the values can repeat, and will if one manager manages two different portfolios. Therefore, this is a Many - To - One join, Portfolio to PortfolioMgr.

By the way, if the keys are set and the Underline Keys option on the Graphics tab of the Tools dialog is set, then the detect button will usually detect this join as a Many - To - One, as we have argued. However, if the keys are not defined and the Detect button is used, then Business Objects will consider the cardinality to be One - To - One, which is probably not correct.

Exercise: Set the Cardinalities in Our Universe

1. Double-click on the join between PORTFOLIOMGR and PORTFOLIO.
   Set the cardinality to 1 on the PORTFOLIOMGR side and N on the PORTFOLIO side.
2. Double-click on the join between PORTFOLIO and PORTFOLIOTRANSACTIONS.
   Set the cardinality to 1 on the PORTFOLIO side and N on the PORTFOLIOTRANSACTIONS side.
3. Double-click on the join between PORTFOLIOTRANSACTIONS and COMPANY.
   Set the cardinality to N on the PORTFOLIOTRANSACTIONS side and 1 on the COMPANY side.
4. Double-click on the join between COMPANY and INDUSTRY.
   Set the cardinality to N on the COMPANY side and 1 on the INDUSTRY side

Notes

Dealing with Chasm Traps

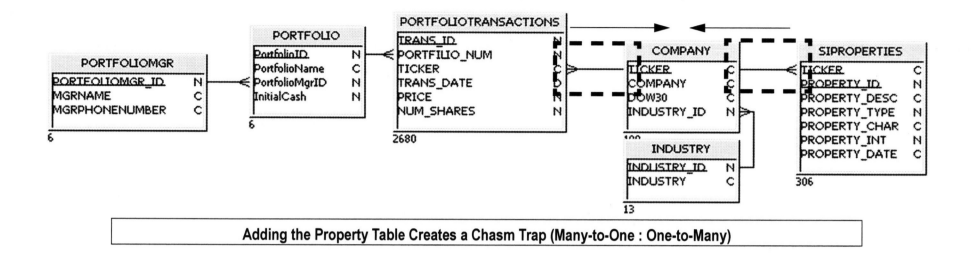

Adding the Property Table Creates a Chasm Trap (Many-to-One : One-to-Many)

Ticker	Property Id	Property Desc	Property Type	Property Char	Property Int	Property Date
AA	1	DOW30	1	Y	0	
AA	2	RISKLEVEL	2		1	
AA	3	BUYSELL	2		1	
AAPL	2	RISKLEVEL	2		2	
AAPL	3	BUYSELL	2		1	
ACPW	1	DOW30	1	N	0	
ACPW	2	RISKLEVEL	2		3	
ACPW	3	BUYSELL	2		0	
AMAT	2	RISKLEVEL	2		2	
AMAT	3	BUYSELL	2		1	

Some Rows from the Property Table

Dealing with Chasm Traps

Property tables usually have more than one key per row - a unique combination of keys to identify a row. This is true of many dimension tables, however, all the keys in a property table may not join to the table using the property table as a look-up. This creates a problem, because the relationship is no longer many-to-one : many-to-one. It is now many-to-one : one-to-many. This relationship is known as a chasm trap. Notice that in the diagram, the cardinality arrow is shooting back towards the PORTFOLIO TRANSACTIONS fact table and its summing measures. This means that the Properties table will multiply the rows in the PORTFOLIOTRANSACTIONS table, and thus cause the measures to return values that are larger than the actual values.

Since there are multiple matching keys in SIPROPERTIES for the key values in PORTFOLIOTRANSACTIONS, when the keys are joined there will be a multiplying effect. This multiplying effect happens when each property that has a matching key is assigned to a single Portfolio Transactions row. This will cause the measure in the Portfolio Transactions table to be multiplied by the number of duplicate keys, in this case the number of properties for each ticker.

By the way, simply changing the cardinality in the Edit Join dialog will not fix the chasm trap. The SQL generated by the universe is completely independent of any cardinality set in the universe. The cardinalities are set to help us observe data relationship problems, such as chasm traps. The setting of the cardinality has no effect on SQL generation.

Exercise: Join SIProperties to Company

Notes

Chasm Trap Example

Queries that Don't Include SIProperties Aren't Affected

Ticker	Revenue
AA	172,813
AAPL	(24,927)
ACPW	19,648
AMAT	12,667

Queries that Include SIProperties Objects Will Multiply Revenue

Ticker	Property Id	Property Desc	Property Char	Property Int	Revenue
AA	1	DOW30	Y	0	172,813
	2	RISKLEVEL		1	172,813
	3	BUYSELL		1	172,813
AA				Sum:	518,438

Ticker	Property Id	Property Desc	Property Char	Property Int	Revenue
AAPL	2	RISKLEVEL		2	(24,927)
	3	BUYSELL		1	(24,927)
AAPL				Sum:	(49,854)

Ticker	Property Id	Property Desc	Property Char	Property Int	Revenue
ACPW	1	DOW30	N	0	19,648
	2	RISKLEVEL		3	19,648
	3	BUYSELL		0	19,648
ACPW				Sum:	58,943

Ticker	Property Id	Property Desc	Property Char	Property Int	Revenue
AMAT	2	RISKLEVEL		2	12,667
	3	BUYSELL		1	12,667
AMAT				Sum:	25,335

Chasm Trap Example

In the graphic, we create a query with Ticker and Revenue. These objects come from the COMPANY and PORTFOLIOTRANSACTIONS tables. This query will only involve the join between these two tables, and therefore, no chasm trap exists in the query. So, the revenue in the table for this query is correct. If we look at the revenue for AA (Alcoa), the revenue is 172,813. We will use this value as a reference throughout our development. If we ever get an amount different from this, then we need to reexamine our universe for errors. Let's also look at AMAT (Applied Materials), whose revenue is 12,667.

The second query in the graphic includes items from the SIProperties table. This causes the chasm trap to become active, since SIProperties must be joined to COMPANY. Notice that this causes multiple rows to be returned for each Ticker, because there are multiple properties for each Ticker. If one were to total these revenues, then they would be much larger than they should be. For example, AA went from 172,813 to 518,438, which is a multiple of three. AMAT grew by a multiple of two.

Note: Don't think that chasm traps always cause an integer multiple of an expected number. I have seen many people make this assumption, and if the multiple was not an integer, then they would refuse to believe that it is a chasm trap. To demonstrate this, all we need to do is delete the Ticker column. Then when the revenues are summed, they will not be an integer multiple larger, because some tickers have three properties and some have two properties.

Exercise: Chasm Trap Example

1. Drag the SIProperties table to the Classes and Objects section.
2. Save and Export the universe.
3. Use Web Intelligence or Desktop Intelligence to create the queries shown in the example.
4. After examining the results, delete the Siproperties class from the universe, as we will not need it.

Notes

Evolution of a Property Table

DOW_30 Table

TICKER	DOW_30
AA	Y
ACPW	N
AMCC	N
AMGN	N
AMR	N
AMZN	N
APWR	N
ATML	N

RISK_LEVEL Table

TICKER	RISK
AA	1
AAPL	2
ACPW	3
AMAT	2
AMCC	3
AMD	2
AMGN	1
AMR	2

BUY_SELL_REC Table

TICKER	BUYSELL
AA	1
AAPL	1
ACPW	0
AMAT	1
AMCC	1
AMD	1
AMGN	1
AMR	1

Combined Properties Table

TICKER	PROPERTY_ID	PROPERTY_DESC	PROPERTY_INT	PROPERTY_CHAR
AA	1	DOW30	0	Y
AA	2	RISKLEVEL	1	
AA	3	BUYSELL	1	
AAPL	2	RISKLEVEL	2	
AAPL	3	BUYSELL	1	
ACPW	1	DOW30	0	N
ACPW	2	RISKLEVEL	3	
ACPW	3	BUYSELL	0	
AMAT	2	RISKLEVEL	2	
AMAT	3	BUYSELL	1	
AMCC	1	DOW30	0	N
AMCC	2	RISKLEVEL	3	
AMCC	3	BUYSELL	1	
AMD	2	RISKLEVEL	2	
AMD	3	BUYSELL	1	
AMGN	1	DOW30	0	N
AMGN	2	RISKLEVEL	1	
AMGN	3	BUYSELL	1	
AMR	1	DOW30	0	N
AMR	2	RISKLEVEL	2	
AMR	3	BUYSELL	1	
AMZN	1	DOW30	0	N
AMZN	2	RISKLEVEL	2	
AMZN	3	BUYSELL	1	
AOL	2	RISKLEVEL	2	
AOL	3	BUYSELL	1	
APWR	1	DOW30	0	N
APWR	2	RISKLEVEL	3	
APWR	3	BUYSELL	0	
ATML	1	DOW30	0	N
ATML	2	RISKLEVEL	3	
ATML	3	BUYSELL	0	

Evolution of a Property Table

I remember when I rarely saw a property table. Usually, we just had a single property in each table and we joined all of the look-up tables to one table. But, database designers didn't like this strategy, because it required too much maintenance on the database side. So, the property table evolved to holding values for multiple properties. To demonstrate this evolution, I will describe a mock scenario.

One day the business people called the database designer and asked for a table that flagged the DOW 30 companies. So, the database person created a table called DOW_30 and joined it to the Company table. Now, if people were to make a query with Ticker and the DOW_30 column from the DOW_30 table, then all of the tickers will have a DOW_30 value of either 'Y' or 'N'. This made the business people very happy.

About a week goes by and the business people call the database person again. This time they request a table that will rank the risk of different companies. The database person becomes a little concerned, because he is beginning to realize that there may be many requests for such tables. Despite the concern, the database person creates a table called RISK_LEVEL. In this table there are two columns - TICKER and RISK. Risk will be a 1, 2, or a 3. This table is joined to COMPANY and now people can create queries with Ticker and Risk. The business people are again happy.

A week later and again the business people call the database person. They have a new request for a table. The database person inquires about the pervious tables and if they are still being used. The business people are not sure if they are being used or not, but this new table is very important. They need a table that will mark each company has a buy or a sell. The database person creates this table with two columns - TICKER and BUYSELL, and calls it BUY_SELL_REC. A sell will be a 0, and a buy will be a 1. This table is joined to COMPANY. All is well.

The database person realizes that there will be many calls and decides to create a single table. This table will be called PROPERTIES. This table will contain TICKER, as the three previous tables did. Next, a column must be added for the property value. This is difficult, because there numeric properties and character properties. No problem, just add a numeric column and call it PROPERTY_INT, and add a character column and call it PROPERTY_CHAR. Now, a column to identify the properties is added. This column is called PROPERTY_ID. There, now all three tables can be combined into one, with PROPERTY_ID identifying the three different properties.

Next, an interface is built. This interface allows the business people to manage the properties. They can alter existing values or create new properties. This frees the database person from ever having to create separate tables for each request.

Notes

Conditions on Objects (Chasm Trap Solution #1)

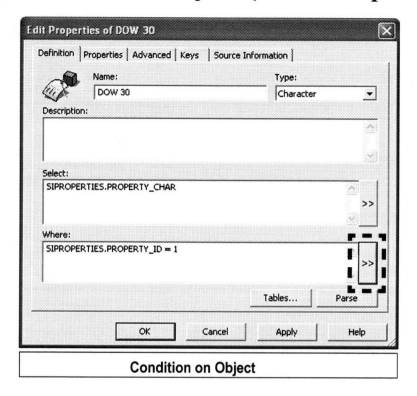

Condition on Object

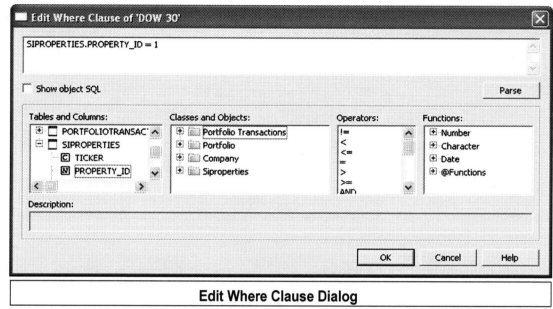

Edit Where Clause Dialog

DOW 30
 Select: SIPROPERTIES.PROPERTYCHAR
Where: SIPROPERTIES.PROPERTY_ID = 1

Risk Level
 Select: SIPROPERTIES.PROPERTY_INT
Where: SIPROPERTIES.PROPERTY_ID = 2

Buy Sell Rec
 Select: SIPROPERTIES.PROPERTY_INT
Where: SIPROPERTIES.PROPERTY_ID = 3

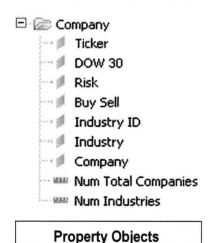

Property Objects

Conditions on Objects (Chasm Trap Solution #1)

The reason we have a chasm trap is that there are three properties for each ticker. If we were able to hold PROPERTY_ID constant, then there would only be one property per ticker. We can do this by adding a *Where Clause* to the object. To add a Where clause, we can click the >> button to the right of the Where edit on the Edit Properties dialog.

Exercise: Create the Three Property Dimension Objects

1. Open the Company class folder
2. Drag the PROPERTY_CHAR field from the SIPROPERTIES table and drop it on the Ticker dimension object.
3. Double-click on the Property Char object to open the Edit Properties dialog.
4. Change the object's name to DOW 30.
5. Click the >> button next to the Where edit field to open the Edit Where Clause dialog.
6. Scroll down the Tables and Columns list and double-click on the PROPERTY_ID field in the SIPROPERTIES table.
7. Edit the formula to: SIPROPERTIES.PROPERTY_ID = 1
8. Click OK. Click OK.
9. Drag the PROPERTY_INT field from the SIPROPERTIES table and drop it on the DOW 30 dimension object.
10. Double-click on the Property Int object to open the Edit Properties dialog.
11. Change the object's name to Risk.
12. Click the >> button next to the Where edit field to open the Edit Where Clause dialog.
13. Scroll down the Tables and Columns list and double-click on the PROPERTY_ID field in the SIPROPERTIES table.
14. Edit the formula to: SIPROPERTIES.PROPERTY_ID = 2
15. Click OK. Click OK.
16. Drag the PROPERTY_INT field from the SIPROPERTIES table and drop it on the Risk dimension object.
17. Double-click on the Property Int object to open the Edit Properties dialog.
18. Change the object's name to Buy Sell.
19. Click the >> button next to the Where edit field to open the Edit Where Clause dialog.
20. Scroll down the Tables and Columns list and double-click on the PROPERTY_ID field in the SIPROPERTIES table.
21. Edit the formula to: SIPROPERTIES.PROPERTY_ID = 3
22. Click OK. Click OK.

Notes

Property Dimension Behavior (Chasm Trap Solution #1)

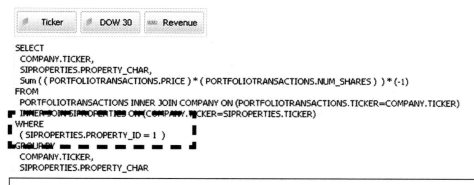

```
         Ticker        DOW 30     Revenue

SELECT
    COMPANY.TICKER,
    SIPROPERTIES.PROPERTY_CHAR,
    Sum ( ( PORTFOLIOTRANSACTIONS.PRICE ) * ( PORTFOLIOTRANSACTIONS.NUM_SHARES ) ) * (-1)
FROM
    PORTFOLIOTRANSACTIONS INNER JOIN COMPANY ON (PORTFOLIOTRANSACTIONS.TICKER=COMPANY.TICKER)
    INNER JOIN SIPROPERTIES ON (COMPANY.TICKER=SIPROPERTIES.TICKER)
    WHERE
    ( SIPROPERTIES.PROPERTY_ID = 1 )
    GROUP BY
    COMPANY.TICKER,
    SIPROPERTIES.PROPERTY_CHAR
```

Ticker	DOW 30	Revenue
AA	Y	172,813
ACPW	N	19,648
AMCC	N	8,465
AMGN	N	2,106
APWR	N	3,620
ATML	N	3,152
AXP	Y	(8,167)
BA	Y	69,375

One Property Object in the Query Returns Expected Results

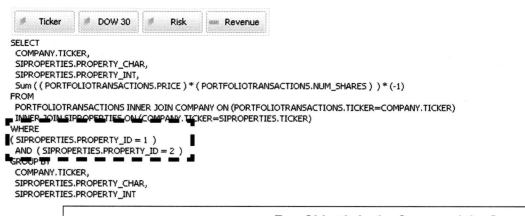

```
         Ticker        DOW 30         Risk        Revenue

SELECT
    COMPANY.TICKER,
    SIPROPERTIES.PROPERTY_CHAR,
    SIPROPERTIES.PROPERTY_INT,
    Sum ( ( PORTFOLIOTRANSACTIONS.PRICE ) * ( PORTFOLIOTRANSACTIONS.NUM_SHARES ) ) * (-1)
FROM
    PORTFOLIOTRANSACTIONS INNER JOIN COMPANY ON (PORTFOLIOTRANSACTIONS.TICKER=COMPANY.TICKER)
    INNER JOIN SIPROPERTIES ON (COMPANY.TICKER=SIPROPERTIES.TICKER)
WHERE
    ( SIPROPERTIES.PROPERTY_ID = 1 )
    AND ( SIPROPERTIES.PROPERTY_ID = 2 )
    GROUP BY
    COMPANY.TICKER,
    SIPROPERTIES.PROPERTY_CHAR,
    SIPROPERTIES.PROPERTY_INT
```

Ticker	DOW 30	Risk	Revenue

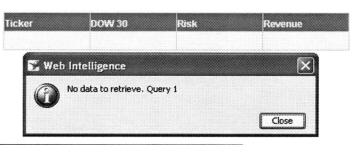

Web Intelligence

No data to retrieve. Query 1

Close

Two Object's in the Query and the Query Fails

Property Dimension Behavior (Chasm Trap Solution #1)

When one of our property objects is added to a query the results are as expected. Remember, we saw that AA's revenue is 172,813. That number is now consistent with our expectations. If we examine the SQL, we will see that Business Objects just added the where clause that was in the Edit Properties dialog, to the Where clause of our query. This means that any statements in the Where edit field of the Edit Properties dialog will be placed in the Where clause of any query in which the object is placed.

When we add two property objects to the same query, the query fails to return any rows. If we examine the SQL, we will see that the Where clause now has two conflicting conditions:

> **WHERE**
> **(SIPROPERTIES.PROPERTY_ID = 1)**
> **AND (SIPROPERTIES.PROPERTY_ID = 2)**

This is why there is no data returned. Many people will leave it like this and change the AND to an OR. I do not recommend doing this, because it just re-introduces the chasm trap, which is what we are trying to fix.

Notes

Detail Object Behavior (Chasm Trap Solution #1)

Ticker	DOW 30	Revenue

Ticker	DOW 30	Revenue

Ticker	Risk	Revenue

Ticker	DOW 30	Revenue
AA	Y	172,813
ACPW	N	19,648
AMCC	N	8,465
AMGN	N	2,106
APWR	N	3,620
ATML	N	3,152

Ticker	Risk	Revenue
AA	1	172,813
AAPL	2	(24,927)
ACPW	3	19,648
AMAT	2	12,667
AMCC	3	8,465
AMD	2	(7,322)

Two Queries Create Two Tables

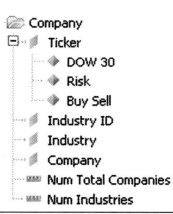

- 📁 Company
  - 📄 Ticker
    - ◆ DOW 30
    - ◆ Risk
    - ◆ Buy Sell
  - 📄 Industry ID
  - 📄 Industry
  - 📄 Company
  - ▦ Num Total Companies
  - ▦ Num Industries

Ticker	DOW 30	Risk	Revenue
AA	Y	1	172,813
AAPL		2	(24,927)
ACPW	N	3	19,648
AMAT		2	12,667
AMCC	N	3	8,465
AMD		2	(7,322)

If the Properties are Details, Then They Can Exist in the Same Table

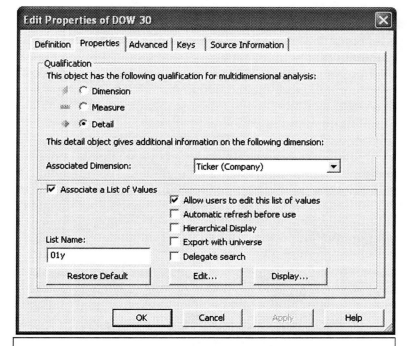

Properties Can Ba a Detail of Ticker

Detail Object Behavior (Chasm Trap Solution #1)

Earlier, we found that we cannot create a single query with two of our Property Dimension objects, because the conditions will conflict and cause no data to return. With Desktop Intelligence or Web Intelligence, we can have multiple queries in a document. If we create a query for Dow 30 and a query for Risk, as shown in the graphic, then Business Objects will create a separate table for each query. If we examine the tables, we can determine that the context of each table is Ticker. This means that each row can be identified by Ticker alone. The DOW 30 and Risk columns simply display a property of Ticker, and therefore have no effect on the context of the table. This means that we should be able to drag Risk from its table and drop it next to Dow 30 in the other table, as Risk will not affect the context of the Dow 30 table (In other words, Risk will not add any rows to the Dow 30 table that will cause Revenues to be multiplied). However, Business Objects will not allow Risk to be placed into the Dow 30 table, because it, and Dow 30, are both dimensions, and dimensions create and alter contexts. So, even though the objects will not alter the context in any way, Business Objects still believes that it could, because of the dimension qualification of the property objects.

Remember that if their parent dimension is in the report structure, then Details do not create contexts. This means that if we qualify our property objects as details of Ticker, then we could combine them in the same table, as long as Ticker was also in the table. We still need to create two queries - one for Risk and one for Dow 30. Business Objects will still create two tables. However, if the properties are defined as Details, then they can both be placed in the same table. This allows for one of the tables to be deleted.

Notice that qualifying the properties as Details has no effect on the SQL and we still need to create two different queries. Business Objects just treats details differently than it does dimensions. For example, suppose that you had a famous friend, and in Los Angeles, you could go anywhere with that friend. So, while with that friend, you could go and hang out with the celebrities. This would make you the detail friend of a dimension famous person. Now, suppose that you went out without your famous friend. Now, none of the celebrity hang outs will let you in. This is because you are only allowed in when accompanied by your dimension friend. I hope this analogy is okay.

One last note on this solution - This is not the best solution, because it requires that report developers create two queries. If they do not, and try to put multiple property objects in the same query, then the query will return no data. Once the queries are run, then one of the two tables created by the queries will have to be deleted. Then, the developer will have to drop the property objects into the same table. I think this is asking a lot of most developers, and I think that if you asked a room of 100 people to create a multiple property report, using this universe, then only about 10 people could do it. That's about a 10% success rate. The purpose of this solution was to demonstrate how conditions on objects behave and how details objects are used. The next solution will have a much higher success rate.

Notes

Aliasing Tables

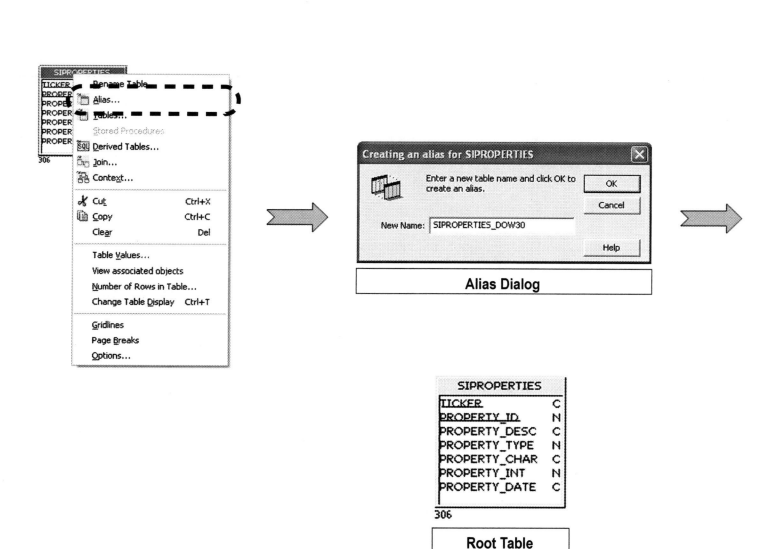

Alias Dialog

Root Table

Alias Tables

Aliasing Tables

An Alias of a table is a logical copy of another table. Aliases allow us to refer to the same table in logically different ways. For example, suppose that there was an Employee table, and in this table there was an employee id and a manager id. Both employees and managers are employees, so both will be identified in the Employee table. But how do you join a table to itself (Self Join)? If you try to join it to itself, as shown to the right, then the query will return only employees who are managers of themselves.

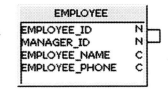

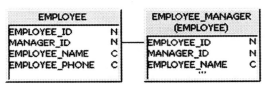

To solve this problem, we can alias the EMPLOYEE table and call the Alias the MANAGER table, and then we can join this alias to the EMPLOYEE table. Even though the data contained in both the alias and the root tables is exactly the same, they are logically different tables. For example, the join expression is: EMPLOYEE.MANAGER_ID=EMPLOYEE_MANAGER.EMPLOYEE_ID

To alias a table, we just right-click on it and select *Alias...* from the pop-up menu. Then assign a name to the new table. Most people leave the root table name and suffix it with a descriptive identifier, such as SIPROPERTIES_DOW30. Once a table has been aliased, we usually don't use the original in the structure. However, we cannot delete it since the aliases are using it as a base table. This poses a small problem for very organized people, because the universe will complain about the tables that are not joined to the structure.

Exercise: Alias the SIProperties Table

1. First, let's get rid of the objects and joins on the SIProperty table.
    • Delete the three SIProperty detail objects from the Company class.
    • Delete the join between the Company and SIProperties tables.
    You can accomplish each of these steps by first clicking on the object or join and then pressing the [Delete] key.
2. Now, let's alias the SIProperty table
    • Right-click on the SIProperties table and select | Alias... | from the pop-up menu.
    • Name the tables as shown in the graphic.
    • Repeat the above two steps until all three alias tables are created.

Notes

Aliasing Tables (Chasm Trap Solution #2)

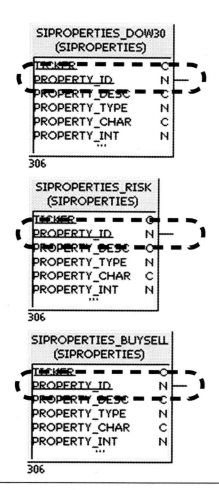

306

306

306

The Aliased Property Tables With Self Joins

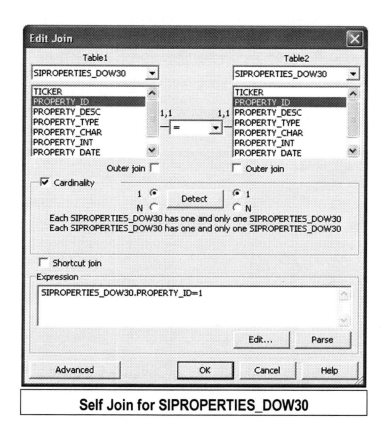

Self Join for SIPROPERTIES_DOW30

Aliasing Tables (Chasm Trap Solution #2)

The properties table evolved from three separate property tables - DOW_30, RISK, and BUY_SELL_REC. The chasm trap exists, because these three tables were used to populate a single table. The data from each table was given a property id to identify the table that it came from. For example, property id 1, represents the DOW_30 data, Property id 2, represents the RISK data, and property id 3, represents the BUY_SELL_REC data.

In solution #1, we used where conditions on the objects to hold the id constant, which did eliminate the chasm trap. However, if more than one property was placed in a query, the query would not return rows, because the where conditions pointed to the same table - SIPROPERTIES. Now, we have created three aliased tables that are logically separate from SIPROPERTIES. This will allow us to place the condition on the table itself, so each table can only return values for a single property. In essence, this will allow us to divide SIPROPERTIES into three individual tables again.

We are going to place the conditions on the tables using a self-join on PROPERTY_ID. Then, anytime data is returned from the table, the self-join condition will be included in the query.

Exercise: Create the Self-Joins

1. Create the SIPROPERTIES_DOW30 Join
   - Right-click on the SIPROPERTYIES_DOW30 table and select *Join...* from the pop-up menu.
   - Select SIPROPERTIES_DOW30 in each of the table drop lists.
   - Select PROPERTY_ID in both of the field lists.
   - Set the cardinality to 1-to-1.
   - Edit the Join Expression to:
     SIPROPERTIES_DOW30.PROPERTY_ID=1
2. Create the SIPROPERTIES_RISK Join
   - Right-click on the SIPROPERTYIES_RISK table and select *Join...* from the pop-up menu.
   - Select SIPROPERTIES_RISK in each of the table drop lists.
   - Select PROPERTY_ID in both of the field lists.
   - Set the cardinality to 1-to-1.

- Edit the Join Expression to:
  SIPROPERTIES_RISK.PROPERTY_ID=2
3. Create the SIPROPERTIES_BUYSELL Join
   - Right-click on the SIPROPERTYIES_BUYSELL table and select *Join...* from the pop-up menu.
   - Select SIPROPERTIES_BUYSELL in each of the table drop lists.
   - Select PROPERTY_ID in both of the field lists.
   - Set the cardinality to 1-to-1.
   - Edit the Join Expression to:
     SIPROPERTIES_BUYSELL.PROPERTY_ID=3

Notes

Outer Joins (Chasm Trap Solution #2)

Ticker	Revenue
AA	172,813
AAPL	(24,927)
ACPW	19,648
AMAT	12,667
AMCC	8,465
AMD	(7,322)

Correct Results (No Join to Properties)

Ticker	DOW 30	Revenue
AA	Y	172,813
ACPW	N	19,648
AMCC	N	8,465
AMGN	N	2,106
APWR	N	3,620
ATMI	N	3,152

Inner Join Loses Tickers

Ticker	DOW 30	Revenue
AA	Y	172,813
AAPL		(24,927)
ACPW	N	19,648
AMAT		12,667
AMCC	N	8,465
AMD		(7,322)

Outer Join Loses no Tickers

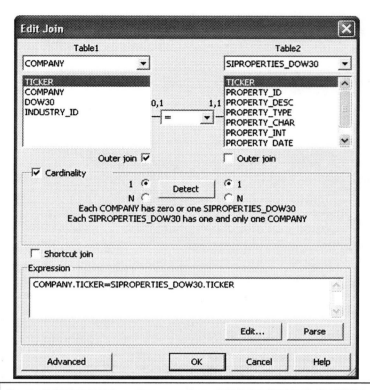

Each COMPANY has Zero or One SIPROPERTIES_DOW30

Ticker	Property Id	Property Desc	DOW 30
AA	1	DOW30	Y
ACPW	1	DOW30	N
AMCC	1	DOW30	N
AMGN	1	DOW30	N
AMR	1	DOW30	N
AMZN	1	DOW30	N

SIPROPERTIES DOW 30 Assignments

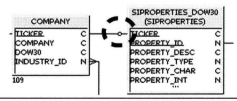

With ANSI92 a Bubble Will Be on the Non-Limiting Side

Outer Joins (Chasm Trap Solution #2)

The database designer created the property table for the business people to manage. Business people create properties and populate the values for the companies of interest. This does not mean that they will assign every company a given property. For example, maybe the media department will only assign media companies properties. They may not know the property values for companies outside of their department. This means that with most property tables, not all property values will be assigned.

When we join a table to another, a query on the two tables will return an intersection of data. It does this, because the tables are joined on a common key or common set of keys. Then, when a query is made on the tables, only matching keys are returned. If one table has an entry that the other does not, then this row cannot be returned. So with inner joins, a query should never return more rows then the larger of the two tables. If the query returns fewer rows, then it means that not all keys had a match in the joined look-up table, in this case SIPROPERTIES_DOW30.

If we examine the SIPROPERTIES_DOW30 table, we will see that there are no assignments for AAPL, AMAT, AMD, ... When Company is inner-joined to the SIPROPERTIES_DOW30 table, these unassigned companies are not returned in the data set. This can make people believe that there is no revenue for these companies, as seen in the graphic. When we outer-join COMPANY to SIPROPERTIES_DOW30, then queries will return the unassigned companies, also shown in the graphic.

To set the outer-join, we simply check the Outer-Join option in the Edit Join dialog. With ANSI92, we check the option under the table that we want to return all rows from, which, in this case is COMPANY. To make sure that we have chosen correctly, we can read the cardinality text - Each Company has Zero or One Property. This means that it is okay for a company to have no property assigned to it, and that all companies will be returned. The companies without properties will simply be assigned a NULL property value, which means that a property has not been assigned.

Exercise: Create the OuterJoins

1. Join TICKER from COMPANY to TICKER in SIPROPERTIES_DOW30.
2. Double-click on the join and check the *Outer Join* option under the COMPANY table.
3. Join TICKER from COMPANY to TICKER in SIPROPERTIES_RISK.
4. Double-click on the join and check the *Outer Join* option under the COMPANY table.
5. Join TICKER from COMPANY to TICKER in SIPROPERTIES_BUYSELL.
6. Double-click on the join and check the *Outer Join* option under the COMPANY table.

Notes

Dimension Objects (Chasm Trap Solution #2)

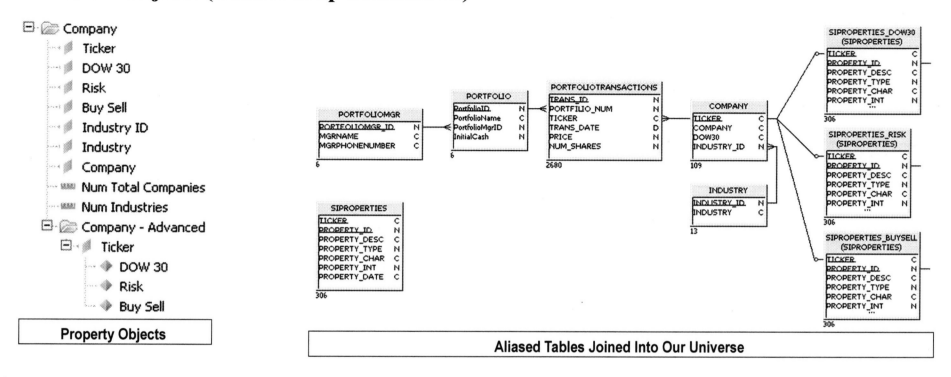

- Company
  - Ticker
  - DOW 30
  - Risk
  - Buy Sell
  - Industry ID
  - Industry
  - Company
  - Num Total Companies
  - Num Industries
- Company - Advanced
  - Ticker
    - DOW 30
    - Risk
    - Buy Sell

Property Objects

Aliased Tables Joined Into Our Universe

Ticker	DOW 30	Risk	Buy Sell	Revenue
Ticker	DOW 30	Risk	Buy Sell	Revenue

```
SELECT
COMPANY.TICKER,
SIPROPERTIES_DOW30.PROPERTY_CHAR,
SIPROPERTIES_RISK.PROPERTY_INT,
SIPROPERTIES_BUYSELL.PROPERTY_INT,
Sum ( ( PORTFOLIOTRANSACTIONS.PRICE ) * ( PORTFOLIOTRANSACTIONS.NUM_SHARES ) ) * (-1)
FROM
PORTFOLIOTRANSACTIONS INNER JOIN COMPANY ON (PORTFOLIOTRANSACTIONS.TICKER=COMPANY.TICKER)
  LEFT OUTER JOIN SIPROPERTIES  SIPROPERTIES_DOW30 ON (SIPROPERTIES_DOW30.PROPERTY_ID=1 AND COMPANY.TICKER=SIPROPERTIES_DOW30.TICKER)
  LEFT OUTER JOIN SIPROPERTIES  SIPROPERTIES_RISK ON (SIPROPERTIES_RISK.PROPERTY_ID=2 AND COMPANY.TICKER=SIPROPERTIES_RISK.TICKER)
  LEFT OUTER JOIN SIPROPERTIES  SIPROPERTIES_BUYSELL ON (SIPROPERTIES_BUYSELL.PROPERTY_ID=3 AND COMPANY.TICKER=SIPROPERTIES_BUYSELL.TICKER)
GROUP BY
COMPANY.TICKER,
SIPROPERTIES_DOW30.PROPERTY_CHAR,
SIPROPERTIES_RISK.PROPERTY_INT,
SIPROPERTIES_BUYSELL.PROPERTY_INT
```

Ticker	DOW 30	Risk	Buy Sell	Revenue
AA	Y	1	1	172,813
AAPL		2	1	(24,927)
ACPW	N	3	0	19,648
AMAT		2	1	12,667
AMCC	N	3	1	8,465
AMD		2	1	(7,329)

Reports Can Now Be Created with a Single Query

Dimension Objects (Chasm Trap Solution #2)

Now that we have joined the aliased tables to the table structure, we just need to pull over the property fields. But, should they be dimensions or details. One can argue that we will slice and dice the data on the properties. For example, group by DOW 30 Companies or Risk levels. If we slice and dice with the properties, then the properties are creating contexts and should be dimensions. Good argument, let's make them dimensions. Another person can argue that the business people create multiple query documents with feeds from many different sources. Some of these sources don't have these property values, but all of them have ticker. In order to include the properties in many of the reports, they must be details. Oh, also a good argument.

A single object cannot be both a dimension and a detail at the same time. Most people will create reports by simply selecting the objects and placing them in a query. This means that the objects can be dimensions. However, more advanced report developers need the objects to be details for their multiple query documents. So, let's make the objects dimensions in the main Company class. Then, let's create a subclass called Company - Advanced, and then copy the Ticker and property objects to this subclass. Then, we can make the properties details of Ticker in the subclass. We keep the Company name on the subclass, because we may want to have an advanced subclass in other classes, and Designer does not allow duplicate class names.

Exercise: Create the Property Objects

1. Drag the PROPERTY_CHAR field from SIPROPERTIES_DOW30 and drop it on the Ticker object in the Company class.
2. Rename the object to DOW 30. (Notice we do not need a condition on the object, because it now exists on the table.)
3. Drag the PROPERTY_INT field from SIPROPERTIES_RISK and drop it on the DOW 30 object in the Company class.
4. Rename the object to Risk.
5. Drag the PROPERTY_INT field from SIPROPERTIES_BUYSELL and drop it on the Risk object in the Company class.
6. Rename the object to Buy Sell.
7. Right-click on the Company class and select *Subclass...* from the pop-up menu.
8. Name the subclass: Company - Advanced.
9. Copy Ticker and the property objects from Company to Company - Advanced.
10. Qualify each property object as a detail of Ticker in the Company - Advanced subclass.

Notes

Derived Tables (Chasm Trap Solution #3)

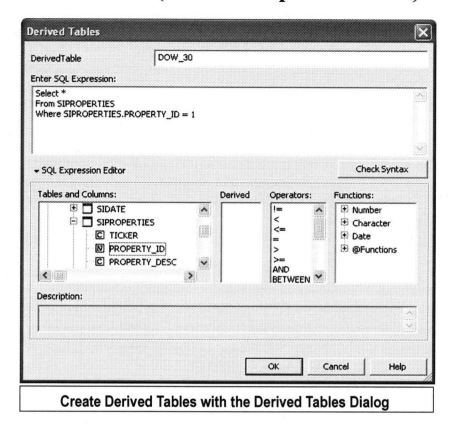

Create Derived Tables with the Derived Tables Dialog

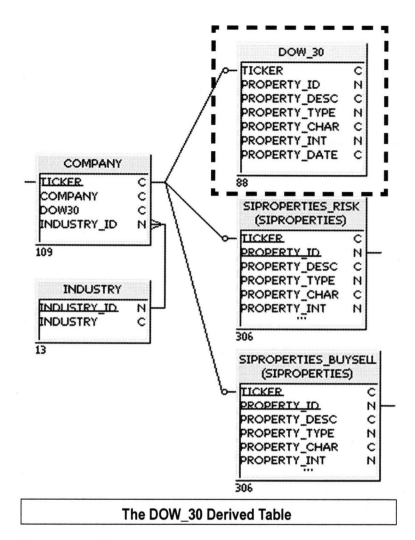

The DOW_30 Derived Table

SELECT
  DOW_30.PROPERTY_CHAR
FROM
  (
  *Select ***
  From SIPROPERTIES
  Where SIPROPERTIES.PROPERTY_ID = 1
) **DOW_30**

Derived Tables Create In-line SQL

Derived Tables (Chasm Trap Solution #3)

In the first chasm trap solution, we put the limiting condition on the object. With the next solution, we put the condition in a self join. With the Derived Table solution, we put the condition in the definition of the table. Notice that in the graphic, the DOW_30 table only has 88 rows, where the other property tables have 306. This means that the DOW_30 table only contains the DOW_30 rows from the property table.

To create a derived table, we select *Insert | Derived Tables...* from the menu. In the Derived Tables dialog, we provide a name and SQL definition for a derived table. We define derived tables with SQL. This SQL can contain tables in our connection or even other derived tables. In this example, we select * from the PRSIPROPERTIES table where PROPERTY_ID = 1. This SQL will return all rows for the DOW_30 property. Notice that when a query is made with the DOW_30 object, the Derived table's SQL is placed in the query, and then this SQL is aliased as DOW_30.

By the way, there is a forth solution to the chasm trap that is very similar to the derived table solution. A view can be made in the database, with the same SQL used to create the derived table. Then, this view can be used as any other table or view in the universe.

Now, we have four solutions to the chasm trap in this example. Many people ask me which one of the solutions is the best one. Well the first solution (Detail Objects) worked okay, but since we had to have multiple queries, it was difficult to create reports with. The second solution (Aliased Tables), works really well, since it takes advantage of the existing table structure and indexes. The third solution (Derived Tables), seems to be not that efficient, because it creates a data set that has no indexes, and since the definition is local to the universe, it would be hard to manage. The fourth solution (Database Views), is a good solution, but we don't always have access to the database, and in our case, the database person will not create views on a table that was created to be managed by the business people.

Exercise: Create the DOW_30 Derived Table

1. Select *Insert | Derived Tables...* from the menu.
2. Named the Derived Table DOW_30.
3. Create the SQL shown in the graphic, by typing and selecting components from the Tables and Columns section.
4. Click OK to create the table.
5. Double-click on the join between SIPROPERTIES_DOW30 and COMPANY.
6. In the Edit Join dialog, change the SIPROPERTIES_DOW30 table in the drop list, to DOW_30.
7. Click OK.
8. Double-click on the DOW 30 object, in the Company class, and change their *Select* field to DOW_30.PROPERTY_CHAR.
9. Delete the SIPROPERTIES_DOW30 table.

Notes

Summary Tables (Derived Tables)

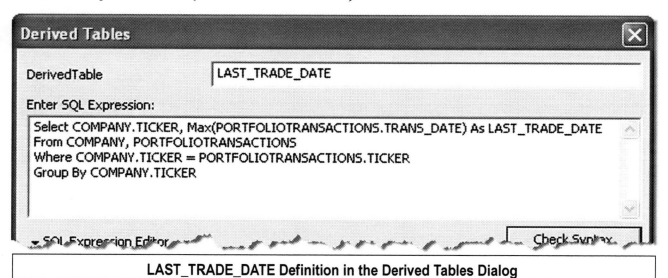

LAST_TRADE_DATE Definition in the Derived Tables Dialog

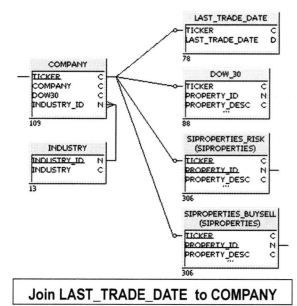

Join LAST_TRADE_DATE to COMPANY

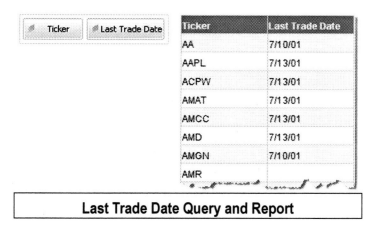

Last Trade Date Query and Report

Last Trade Date Object in Company Class

Summary Tables (Derived Tables)

Sometimes, we have a need to summarize an existing table. In this example, we want to return the last trade date for each ticker. We have PORTFOLIOTRANSACTIONS that has all of the trade dates for all of the companies traded. If we try to create a query with this table, then we will need to create subqueries that may not be very efficient.

To get a list of all of the last trade dates for the Tickers in Portfolio Transactions, we just need to create a derived table that returns the Max(TRANS_DATE) for each Ticker. Then we can join this table to the Company table. We should use an outer-join, because not all Tickers in the COMPANY table have a transaction. When a report is made, as in the graphic, the Tickers without transactions will have NULL last trade dates. This simply means that they have not been traded.

The Last Trade Date object belongs in the Company class, because Last Trade Date is a property of Company. It may not make sense to report developers, if we placed it in the Portfolio Transactions class.

Exercise: Create the LAST_TRADE_DATE Derived Table

1. Select *Insert | Derived Tables...* from the menu.
2. Named the Derived Table LAST_TRADE_DATE.
3. Create the SQL shown in the graphic, by typing and selecting components from the Tables and Columns section.
4. Click OK to create the table.
5. Join the LAST_TRADE_DATE table to the COMPANY table, as shown in the graphic. Remember to check the *Outer Join* option on the COMPANY side of the dialog.
6. Click OK.
7. Drag the LAST_TRADE_DATE field from the table and drop it on the Ticker object in the Company class.

Notes

Using the Case Statement to Decode Property Flags

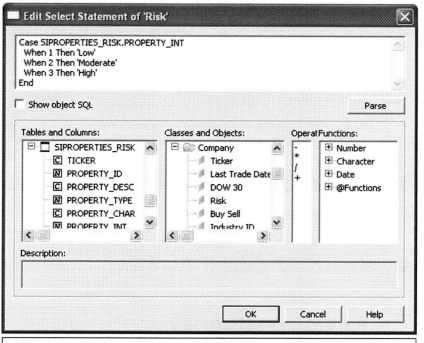

Edit Select Statement of 'Risk'

```
Case SIPROPERTIES_RISK.PROPERTY_INT
  When 1 Then 'Low'
  When 2 Then 'Moderate'
  When 3 Then 'High'
End
```

☐ Show object SQL   [Parse]

Tables and Columns:
- SIPROPERTIES_RISK
  - [C] TICKER
  - [N] PROPERTY_ID
  - [C] PROPERTY_DESC
  - [N] PROPERTY_TYPE
  - [C] PROPERTY_CHAR
  - [N] PROPERTY_INT

Classes and Objects:
- Company
  - Ticker
  - Last Trade Date
  - DOW 30
  - Risk
  - Buy Sell
  - Industry ID

Operat Functions:
- Number
- Character
- Date
- @Functions

Description:

[OK]   [Cancel]   [Help]

The Case Statement Can Decode Property Flags

Ticker	Risk	Buy Sell	Revenue
AA	1	1	172,813
AAPL	2	1	(24,927)
ACPW	3	0	19,648
AMAT	2	1	12,667
AMCC	3	1	8,465
AMD	2	1	(7,322)
AMGN	1		2,106

Integer Flags for Risk and Buy Sell

Ticker	Risk	Buy Sell	Revenue
AA	Low	Buy	172,813
AAPL	Moderate	Buy	(24,927)
ACPW	High	Sell	19,648
AMAT	Moderate	Buy	12,667
AMCC	High	Buy	8,465
AMD	Moderate	Buy	(7,322)
AMGN	Low	Buy	2,106

Text Desciptions for Property Values

Ticker	Risk	Buy Sell	Revenue
AA	0	Ÿ[□□	0
AAPL	0		----
ACPW	0		----
AMAT	0		----
AMGC			

Risk Improperly Typed as Number

```
Case SIPROPERTIES_RISK.PROPERTY_INT
  When 1 Then 'Low'
  When 2 Then 'Moderate'
  When 3 Then 'High'
End
```

Case Statement SQL

Using the Case Statement to Decode Property Flags

In the SIProperties table, we have two columns that have flag type data. This means that the information is represented by a numerical value. For example, in the Risk table a high risk company is flagged with a value of 3, moderate risk with a 2, and low risk with a 1. Some companies will have a dimension table that will join with the flag column and decode the numerical values. Such a table will resemble the following table:

FLAG_KEY	DESCRIPTION
1	Low
2	Moderate
3	High

In our case, this dimension table will not exist, because the database designer created the property table for the business people to manage. Therefore, we must decode the flags ourselves. In this example, we will use a case statement.

Note: The Case statement will return a character string. Before the Case statement, the property objects returned numeric values and were typed as Numbers. If their type is not changed to Character after the Case statement modification, then Web Intelligence will try to format the text as numbers. This will cause the report to look corrupted, as shown in the graphic. Some report functions will also cause this type-mismatch error.

Exercise: Use the Case Statement to Decode Risk and Buy Sell Recommendation

1. Double-click on the Risk dimension object.
2. Change the Select Statement to the following
   - Case SIPROPERTIES_RISK.PROPERTY_INT
     When 1 Then 'Low'
     When 2 Then 'Moderate'
     When 3 Then 'High'
   End
3. Change the Type to Character.
4. Click the Parse button to check the syntax.
5. Click *OK* to accept the change.

6. Double-click on the Buy Sell Rec dimension object.
7. Change the Select Statement to the following
   - Case SIPROPERTIES_BUYSELLREC.PROPERTY_INT
     When 1 Then 'Buy'
     When 0 Then 'Sell'
   End
8. Change the Type to Character.
9. Click the Parse button to check the syntax.
10. Click *OK* to accept the change.

Notes

Object Format to Decode Property Flags

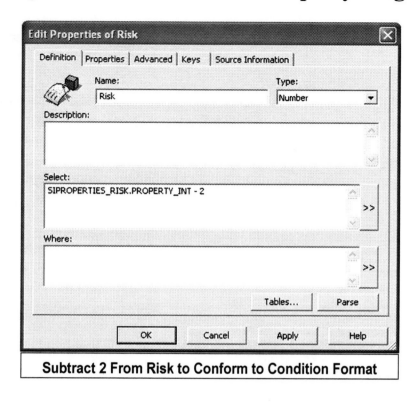

Subtract 2 From Risk to Conform to Condition Format

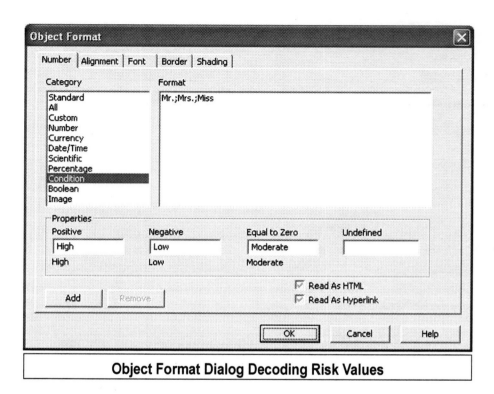

Object Format Dialog Decoding Risk Values

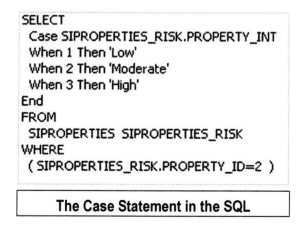

The Case Statement in the SQL

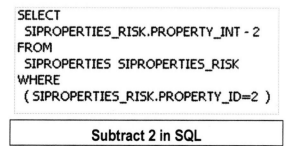

Subtract 2 in SQL

Object Format to Decode Property Flags

The Case statement that we used in the previous example, did decode the Risk and Buy Sell Recommendation flag values. However, the case statement physically replaced the values in the SQL with text strings. This has two effects on our report performance. First, it takes time for the Case statement to execute. I am not sure how long, but let's estimate at 15 clock-cycles. A clock cycle is one tick of the processor clock, so if you have a gigahertz system, a clock cycle is 1 nanosecond. So this would be 15 nanoseconds per row (Maybe not as bad as it was 15 years ago). The other ramification is that we lose the original integer values, which may not be too bad. However, if we wanted the property values to sort in their integer order, then we would lose this advantage, because the integers have been replaced with text.

One way to avoid these ramifications, is to not use the Case statement. We can try to replace the Case statement with the Object Format. For Buy Sell, this is not difficult. We simply choose the Boolean Category in the Object Format dialog, because the flag is binary - 0 for a sell, 1 for a buy.

The Risk property poses a slightly more challenging problem. It has three states - 1, 2, and 3. If we search the Categories in the Object Format dialog, we will find the Condition Category. This category expects three states - -1, 0, 1. We can make Risk conform to this expectation by subtracting 2 from the property value. Then we can use the format as shown in the dialog.

The object format has no effect on query time, nor the sort order of the integer flags. The reporter just formats the integer values with their assignments in the Object Format dialog.

Exercise: Use the Object Format to Decode Risk and Buy Sell Recommendation

1. Double-click on the Risk dimension object.
2. Change the Select Statement to the following
   • SIPROPERTIES_RISK.PROPERTY_INT - 2
3. Change the Type to Number.
4. Click *OK* to accept the change.
5. Right-click on Risk and select *Object Format...*
6. Select the Condition Category
7. Type High in the Positive field,
   Low in the Negative field,
   Moderate in the Equal to Zero field.
8. Click OK to accept the format.
9. Double-click on the Buy Sell Rec dimension object.
10. Change the Select Statement to the following
    • SIPROPERTIES_BUYSELLREC.PROPERTY_INT
11. Change the Type to Number.
12. Click *OK* to accept the change.
13. Right-click on Risk and select *Object Format...*
14. Select the Boolean Category
15. Type Buy in the True field, Sell in the False field
16. Click OK to accept the format.

Notes

Our Universe, So Far

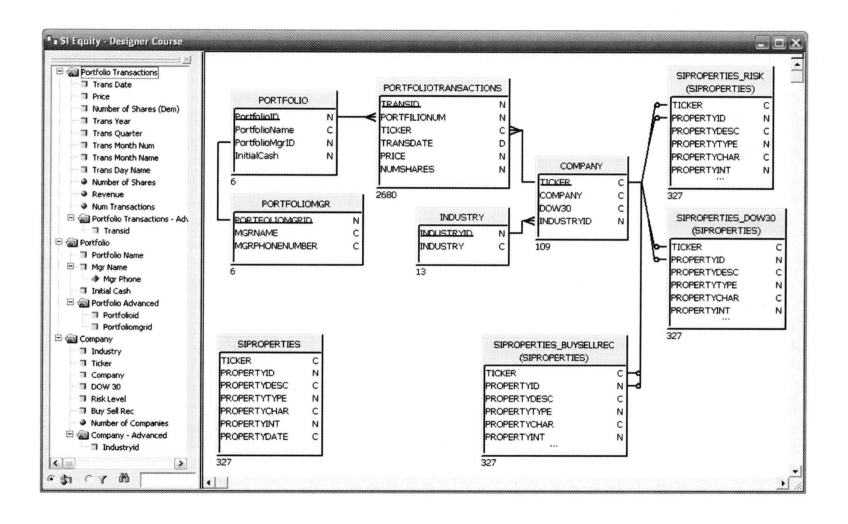

Our Universe, So Far

This is our universe so far. We have added the Portfolio Transactions fact table and all of the supporting dimension tables. We aliased the SIProperties table (one alias for each property) and joined the aliased tables to the structure using outer joins. We used outer joins, because we do not want to limit fact information that is not assigned a property. We created Dimension, Detail, and Measure objects. We know that Dimension objects define the contexts in reports. We also know that dimensions are used to link (merge) data providers, which is also known as synchronization. We learned that measures and details do not link data providers, therefore they are freer to move about a report.

We found out that measures will conform to any context, by aggregating with an aggregate function, such as Sum. This aggregating function is assigned to the measure on the Properties tab of the Edit Properties dialog for an object. There could (should) be an aggregation function as part of the select statement for the measure object, such as Sum(PORTFOLIOTRAMSACTIONS.NUM_SHARES). This aggregate has no effect on the objects behavior in the report. However, it does effect the data set that a query will return, by adding a Group By to the query, which causes the measure to sum to the objects in the Group By statement. These Group By objects are usually dimension objects.

We found that it is important that a detail object only have one value for each of its parent dimension's values. This is important, because Detail objects should never define a context - they can only accompany the context defining Dimensions. For example, Manager Phone should never define a context, because the Manager Dimension object should have that responsibility.

We also used derived tables to solve a chasm trap and to create a summary table. Derived tables are very helpful when trying to get tables to conform to the relationships in the table structure. For example, derived tables may also be used to de-normalize multiple tables, or to rid tables of inherent fan-traps. They can do this by using a Select Distinct and ignoring the columns that are creating the trap.

One more point. This universe only has six tables and 26 objects. I found this out by selecting *File | Parameters...* from the menu and then clicking on the Summary tab of the Parameters dialog. Some universes are much larger - hundreds of tables, and some are much smaller - one table. I am not going to say if universes should have more or less tables and objects. I am only going to say, do what you have to do, to get the job done. I've built universe of all sizes and guess what? They all worked fine.

Notes

Chapter 4: Working with Multiple Fact Tables

In this chapter we are going to address the issues that arise when we insert additional fact tables into a universe. We will discuss how defining a universe context will solve the possible chasm trap that occurs when adding an additional fact table. We are going to talk about how fact tables can share dimension tables within these defined contexts.

We are also going to discuss how to organize the objects in the universe after another fact table is introduced and contexts are defined. It is important that the people creating queries from the universe know which objects are in the contexts, so that their reports will be accurate.

We will also demonstrate how to create building-block universes and then link them together to create larger universes. We will do this by isolating the Company structure and creating an independent universe from it.

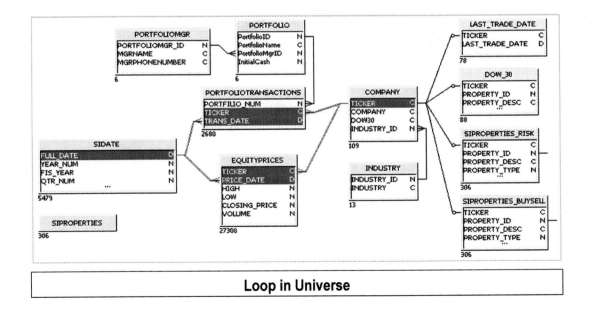

Loop in Universe

Add a Second Fact Table

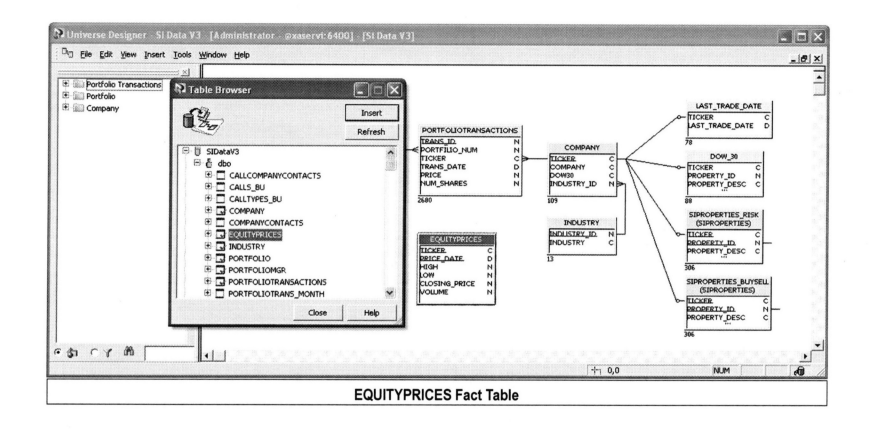

EQUITYPRICES Fact Table

Add a Second Fact Table

As is always the case, we just finish our universe and we are asked to insert another fact table. Of course, the argument is always - should we build a new universe or insert the fact table into an existing universe. To answer this question, we need to know how the data from the table will be used. If the data in the table will be unioned with data from a different fact table or if is to be used in subqueries for queries that use a different fact table, then it should be placed in the same universe as an existing fact table.

For example, a universe can contain both the Orders fact table and the Invoices fact table, because it is necessary to query which orders have been invoiced. The query would be something like Select Orders Where Orders Not In Invoices. You could also place Sales and Projected Sales in the same universe, because there is a need to union the actual data with the projected data to see if the projections are realistic. The query would be similar to Select Sales Union Select Projected Sales.

I think that there is no real reason to place all of your fact tables in a really large universe, unless they will be used in the same queries. In this case, we want to place the Equity Prices table in a universe. It seems that we may create queries from Portfolio Transactions that use the Equity Prices data. For example, did we sell at any highs or buy at any lows? How well did a manager synchronize with the highs and lows of an equity (stock)? We can probably answer both of these queries with some kind of a subquery or correlated logic. Therefore, we are going to place the EQUITYPRICES table in the SIEquity universe.

Exercise: Place EQUITY PRICES in the SIEquity Universe

1. Double-click on any white-space (open area) in the universe structure.
2. Locate EQUITYPRICES in the Table Browser and double-click on the table.

Notes

New Fact Table Chasm Trap

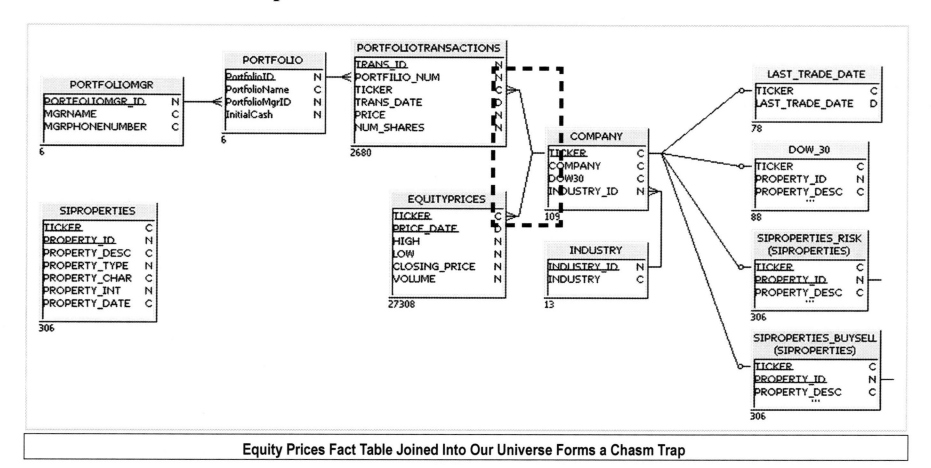

Equity Prices Fact Table Joined Into Our Universe Forms a Chasm Trap

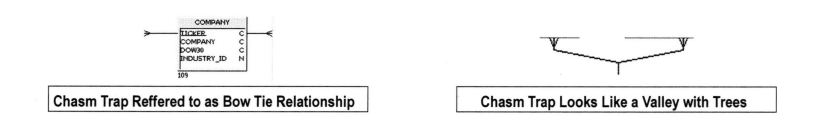

Chasm Trap Reffered to as Bow Tie Relationship

Chasm Trap Looks Like a Valley with Trees

New Fact Table Chasm Trap

We've added EquityPrices to our universe and joined it to the Company table via the Ticker index field. Next, we set the cardinality and notice that we have a chasm trap. Note that if you use the *Detect* button to set the cardinality, then it is backwards. Business Objects gets confused, because both EQUITYPRICES and COMPANY have primary keys. It's just that EQUITYPRICES has a composite key of Ticker and PriceDate. People can refer to chasm traps as Bow Tie relationships. I just call them arrow shooting back.

Since Ticker is a many join in EquityPrices and a many join in PortfolioTransactions, any join between the two tables will have a multiplying effect on any measure in either table (except Count Distinct). EQUITY PRICES will multiply the rows in PORTFOLIOTRANSACTIONS and PORTFOLIOTRANSACTIONS will multiply the rows in EQUITYPRICES. Since, both tables have summing measures, this multiplying effect will cause the results of queries to have much larger total than the actual totals.

Exercise: Join the EquityPrices table to Company

1. Click on the Ticker field in the EquityPrices table.
2. Drag the Ticker field to the Ticker field in Company.
3. Double-click on the join.
4. Set the Cardinality to Many (N) on the Equity Prices side and to One (1) on the Company side in the Edit Join dialog.
5. Click Ok to dismiss the dialog.

Notes

Chasm Trap Aliases (Solution #1)

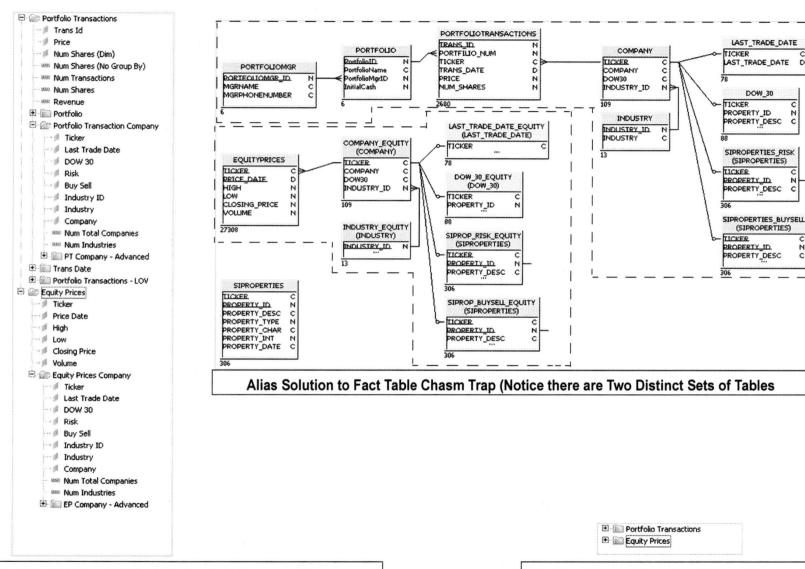

Alias Solution to Fact Table Chasm Trap (Notice there are Two Distinct Sets of Tables

With This Solution, We Have Redundant Company Classes

The Two Groups Keep the Objects Separate

Chasm Trap Aliases (Solution #1)

This solution is for discussion only. It is a valuable solution, but we are not going to use it in our universe that we are currently building.

We have a chasm trap, because both PORTFOLIOTRANSACTIONS and EQUITYPRICES want to share COMPANY. Earlier, when we had a chasm trap with SIPROPERTIES, we decided to alias our way out of the chasm trap. It probably would not make any sense to try and alias EQUITYPRICES, because we would end up with an alias for each date in the table, which would not be manageable. What if, we aliased the COMPANY, INDUSTRY, and the PROPERTIES tables? This could work, as shown in the graphic.

With the aliased solution, we create a class for Portfolio Transactions and a class for Equity Prices. This causes us to have two separate Company classes - one for Portfolio Transactions and one for Equity Prices. This is not totally undesirable, and sometimes we have to do it this way. However, this redundancy is hard to manage and sometimes confuses report developers, especially if the Company classes start to diverge, because of future modifications.

Another observation is that there are two distinct sets of tables - a group for EQUITYPRICES and a group for PORTFOLIOTRANSACTIONS. This means that if report developers choose objects from Equity Prices and Portfolio Transactions, then a Cartesian product will exist in the SQL. This is like a super chasm trap, because each table will completely multiply the rows in the other. EQUITYPRICES(Rows) * PORTFOLIOTRANSATIONS(Rows). Therefore, we didn't really fix the chasm trap, yet. So, if we did use this method, then we must tell report developers not to pick objects from both classes. How many report developers do you think will follow this rule? I hope you said not many.

So, if we can't depend on Report Developers to not select from each group, then maybe we can tell Business Objects to not let them. This we can do, by setting *Contexts*. Contexts will keep the two distinct groups of tables from creating a single query statement. This will prevent the Cartesian product from existing in a query.

Notes

Contexts to Keep Tables Separate (Solution #1)

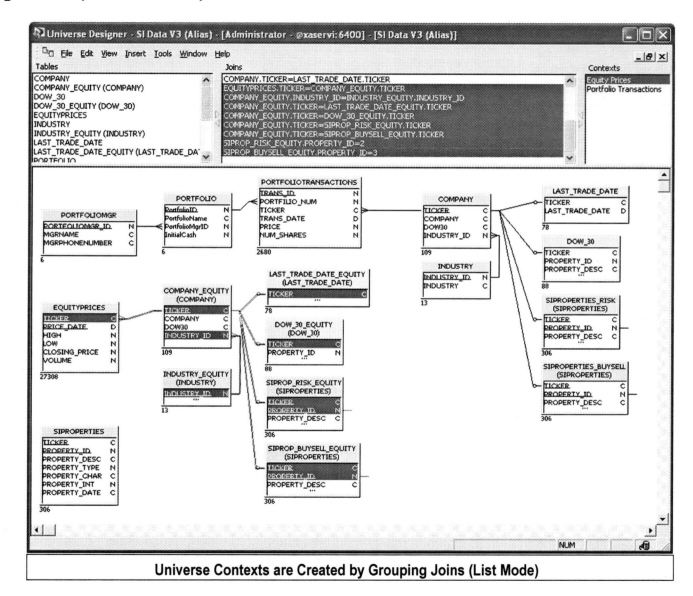

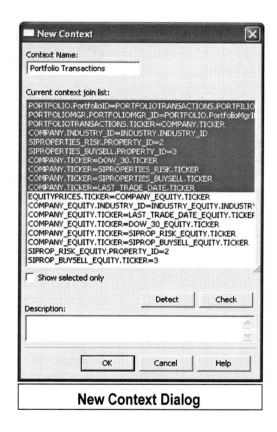

New Context Dialog

Universe Contexts are Created by Grouping Joins (List Mode)

Contexts to Keep Tables Separate (Solution #1)

Contexts can be created by first selecting all of the joins in a group of related tables, as in Equity Prices. Select multiple joins by holding down the [Ctrl] key while clicking on the joins. Be sure to include all of the self-joins on the Properties tables. Then, select *Insert | Context...* from the menu, which will launch the New Context dialog, with all of the selected joins highlighted in a list. Then, enter a name for the context in the *Context Name* field and click OK. A context should be created for each logical group of tables, which, in this case, is the Portfolio Transactions group and the Equity Prices group.

After creating a new context, the Designer will display the List Mode, as seen in the graphic. List mode lists all of the tables, joins, and contexts in a universe. To display the List Mode, select *View | List Mode* from the menu. Notice that we have two contexts listed in the List Mode - Equity Prices and Portfolio Transactions. If you click on either of them, then all of the joins in the context will be highlighted in the table structure.

Notice that List Mode also lists all of the tables in a universe. In large universes, it is convenient to use this list to find tables in the structure, because if you click on a name in the list, then the table will be selected in the structure.

Notes

Chasm Trap Contexts (Solution #2)

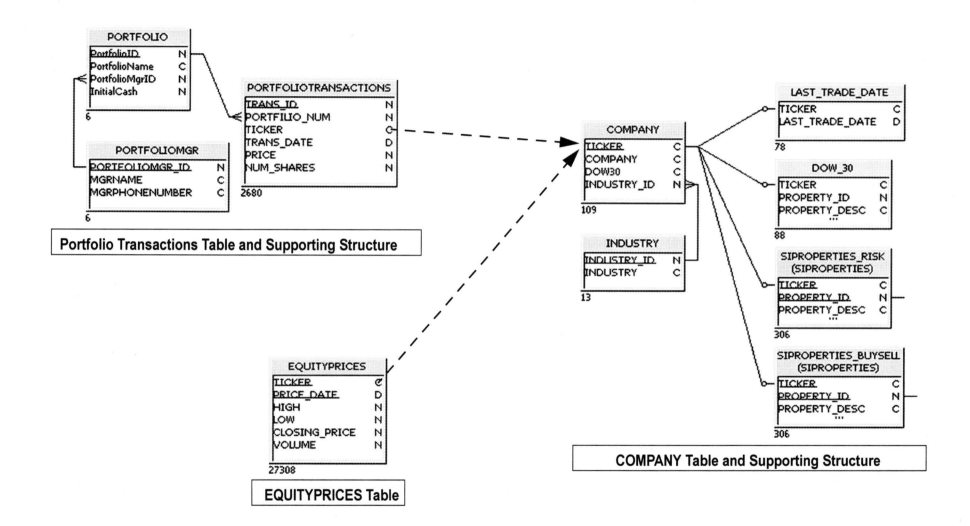

Portfolio Transactions Table and Supporting Structure

EQUITYPRICES Table

COMPANY Table and Supporting Structure

Chasm Trap Contexts (Solution #2)

This is the solution that we are going to use in our universe that we are building. We like this solution, because it allows us to have a single common Company class. It is also easier to maintain, as we expand our universe throughout the course of the book.

Both Portfolio Transactions and Equity Prices want to use the Company table and its supporting structure and objects, but neither one of them want to work with the other. Therefore, if we could allow Portfolio Transactions to have access to the Company structure, while disallowing it access to Equity Prices, then there would be no chasm-trap. We could also allow Equity Prices to have access to the Company structure, while disallowing it access to Portfolio Transactions. This will allow the two fact tables to share the Company table and its supporting structure. In other words, we could define valid paths through the tables, using the joins as a map. We can create these paths with Universe Contexts.

In solution #1, we used contexts to keep two distinct groups of table separate. In this solution, we want to use contexts to exclude unwanted joins. For example, if we select objects from any of the Portfolio tables, then we do not want people to join to EQUITYPRICES, as this will activate the chasm trap. So, in solution #1, we used contexts to avoid a Cartesian product, and in solution #2, we will use contexts to avoid the chasm trap.

So, now we know of two different types of contexts that can exist in Business Objects

1. Contexts that are defined by dimensions in a report. These contexts define to what level the measures in a report will aggregate. For, example, a report that has Region and Salesperson dimensions, will cause the measures to aggregate the salesperson's totals in each region.
2. Universe Contexts that define the paths through the tables via the joins in the universe structure. They make sure that there are no invalid paths, such as chasm traps or Cartesian products.

Notes

Defining a Universe Context (Solution #2)

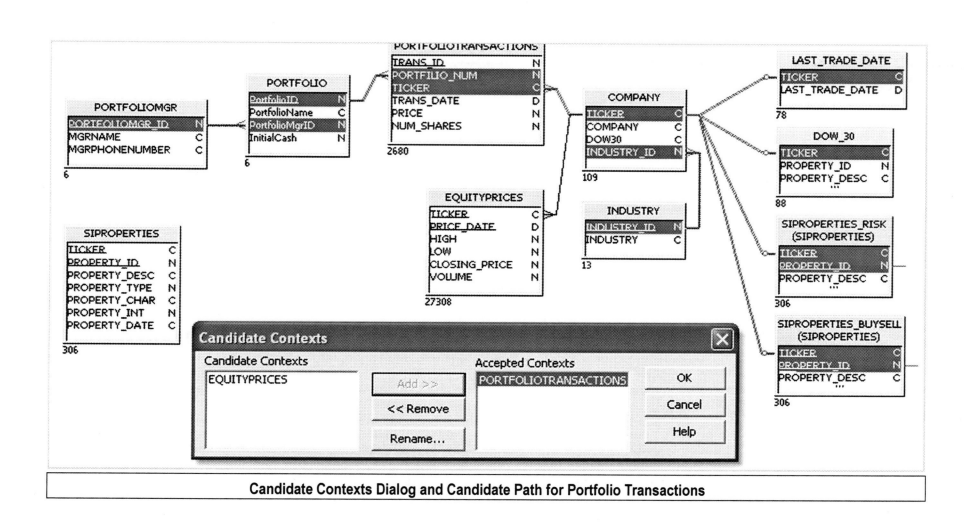

Candidate Contexts Dialog and Candidate Path for Portfolio Transactions

Defining a Universe Context (Solution #2)

Basically, when we define contexts, we observe the cardinalities in the joins. A valid path should be something like - One-to-Many (or One-to-One), One-to-Many, Many-to-One, Many-to-One and so on. The reversal of cardinalities happens at a fact table. This is not always the case, but most of the time it is true. Since we use such an algorithm, then it is possible to create a context detection tool. This tool will traverse the joins in a structure and recommend valid contexts, these valid context recommendations are called Context Candidates.

To access the Candidate Contexts dialog, select *Tools | Automated Detection | Detect Contexts...* from the menu. Context detection can only be accurate if all cardinalities in the structure are defined. If they are not, then Business Objects will warn that the detection may not be accurate.

Notice that all of the joins in the structure are highlighted, except for the Equity Prices join to Company. It is not highlighted, because it will not be part of the Portfolio Transactions context. To accept this recommendation, click the *Add >>* button to send the candidate context to the Accepted Contexts list. To select any candidate context, click on it in the list.

Exercise: Automatically Detect Contexts in Our Universe

1. Make sure all cardinalities in the universe are set.
   - When setting the SIProperty cardinalities, do not use the *Detect* button in the Edit Join dialog, because it will probably be incorrect. Manually set it one-to-one in the Edit Join dialog.
2. Click the Detect Contexts button in the Editing toolbar.
3. Highlight each of the Candidate Contexts and then click the *Add >>* button to accept the recommendation.

Notes

Viewing Defined Contexts (List Mode)

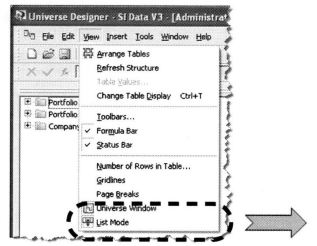

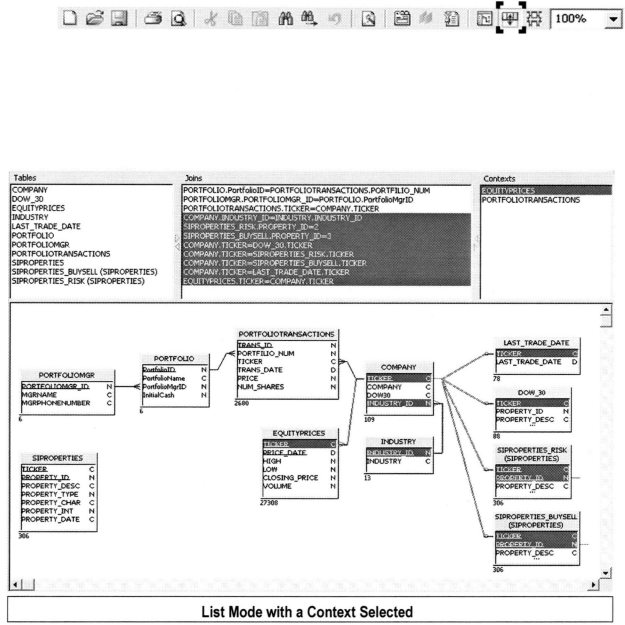

List Mode with a Context Selected

Viewing Defined Contexts (List Mode)

Once a universe contains a context, it becomes a little more complicated, because sometimes we have to know what contexts exist. To view existing contexts, we view the universe in List Mode. To view the universe in list mode, select *View | List Mode* from the menu. List mode displays three new sections at the top of the Universe Structure - Tables, Joins, and Contexts.

Click on any table in the list and the table in the structure is highlighted. This is a convenient way to locate tables in the structure. Looking for joins in the list can be a bit cumbersome, but if you click on a join in the structure, then the join statement will be highlighted in the list. To view all of the joins and tables in a context, simply click on the label in the Contexts section. This will cause all of the join statements in the context to be highlighted in the Joins section and also, all of the context joins in the structure.

Exercise: View the Universe in List Mode

1. Select | View | List Mode| from the menu.
2. Click on each of the two contexts and observe the joins in the structure.
   Notice that each context usually contains one fact table.

Notes

Deleting and Manually Inserting Contexts

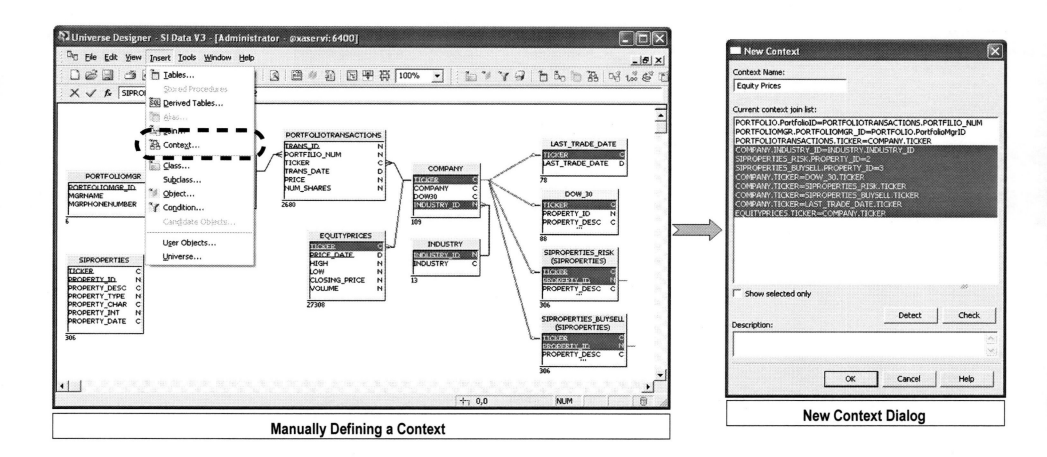

Manually Defining a Context

New Context Dialog

Deleting and Manually Inserting Contexts

We can delete context definitions from a universe, by first selecting the context label in the Contexts list and then by pressing the [Delete] key. Deleting a context in this manner will not delete any of the universe structure. It will just delete the context definition from the universe.

Sometimes we cannot, or will not, use the Automation Detection method for defining contexts. We cannot automatically define the context, if the cardinalities do not match the expected pattern. Sometimes, we know that the cardinalities are not conventionally arranged - one-to-many, one-to-many, many-to-one,..., but we know that our universe will act the way we want it to. In these cases, we cannot use automatic detection, because it will incorrectly define them.

Therefore, we have to manually define the contexts. We do this, by first selecting all of the joins that will be in the context. To select all of the joins, we can click on any join in the structure and then, while holding down the [Ctrl] key, click on the rest of the joins to be in the context. Once all of the joins are selected, then we select *Insert | Context...* from the menu. These actions will bring up the New Context dialog with all of the selected joins highlighted in the list. Now, all we have to do is name our new context and type a description in the Description field. We repeat this process for all of the contexts in the universe.

Exercise: Delete Portfolio Transaction Context and Manually Redefine It

1. If your Designer is not in List Mode, then select | *View | List Mode* | from the menu.
2. Click on the PORTFOLIOTRANSACTIONS context in the Contexts list and then press the [Delete] key to delete it.
3. Click on the join between PORTFOLIOMGR and PORTFOLIO to select it.
4. Hold down the [Ctrl] key and click on the following joins
   • PORTFOLIO - PORTFOLIOTRANSACTIONS
   • PORTFOLIOTRANSACTIONS - COMPANY
   • COMPANY - INDUSTRY
   • COMPANY - SIPROPERTIES_BUYSELL
   • COMPANY - DOW_30, COMPANY - SIPROPERTIES_RISK, COMPANY - SIPROPERTIES_BUYSELL
5. Select | *Insert | Context...* | from the menu.
6. Name the Context - Portfolio Transactions and click *OK*.

Notes

The Fact Table Class (Equity Prices)

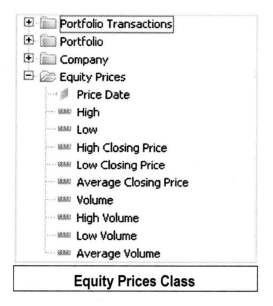

Equity Prices Class

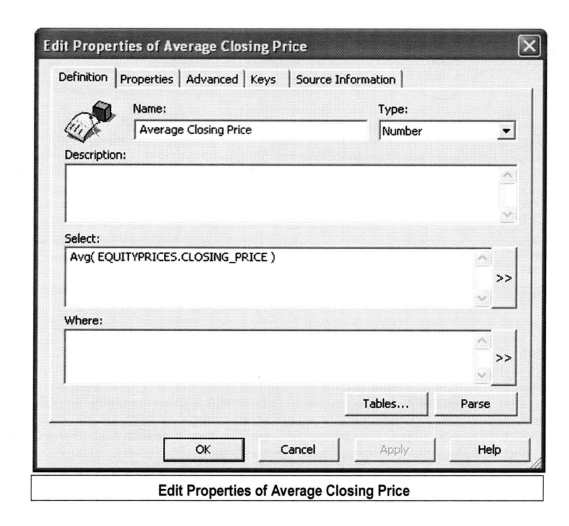

Edit Properties of Average Closing Price

The Fact Table Class (Equity Prices)

Now that we have integrated the EQUITYPRICES table into our universe, using Chasm Trap Solution #2, we now need to create a class and objects, so that the data will be accessible to report developers. Note, most objects from a fact table should be measures or keys.

First, we delete Ticker. Ticker is joined to Ticker in the COMPANY table, if we need ticker in a report, we will use Ticker from the Company class. Next, we look at High. High is the highest price that a stock hit during a day. So reporters will ask questions like, "What was the high price yesterday?" They can also ask what the high price was last week, last month, last quarter, or last year. This means that it should be a measure that uses the Max function. The same argument for Low, but with the Min function. The Closing Price is the price of a stock at the end of the day. So, people can ask what the high closing price was, the low closing price, and even the average closing price. This is why we have High, Low, and Average Closing Price measures. The Volume is similar to Closing Price, but Volumes can sum. For example, what was the volume last week, last year, and so forth. This is the reason we have Volume (Total Volume), High, Low, and Average Volume.

Exercise: Create Objects and Class Structure

1. Drag the EQUITYPRICES table into the Classes and Objects section.
2. Rename the Class Equity Prices.
3. Delete Ticker from Equity Prices (Foreign Key).
4. Double-click on High and change the formula to
   Max(EQUITYPRICES.HIGH)
5. Double-click on Low and change the formula to
   Min(EQUITYPRICES.LOW)
6. Make two copies of Closing Price.
7. Double-click on Closing Price
   • Change its name to: High Closing Price
   • Change its formula to: Max(EQUITYPRICES.CLOSING_PRICE)
8. Double-click on a copy of Closing Price
   • Change its name to: Low Closing Price
   • Change its formula to: Min(EQUITYPRICES.CLOSING_PRICE)
9. Double-click on a copy of Closing Price
   • Change its name to: Average Closing Price
   • Change its formula to: Avg(EQUITYPRICES.CLOSING_PRICE)
10. Make three copies of Volume
11. Double-click on Volume
   • Sum(EQUITYPRICES.VOLUME)
12. Double-click on a copy of Volume
   • Change its name to: High Volume
   • Max(EQUITYPRICES.VOLUME)
13. Double-click on a copy of Volume
   • Change its name to: Low Volume
   • Min(EQUITYPRICES.VOLUME)
14. Double-click on a copy of Volume
   • Change its name to: Average Volume
   • Avg(EQUITYPRICES.VOLUME)

Notes

Working With Contexts

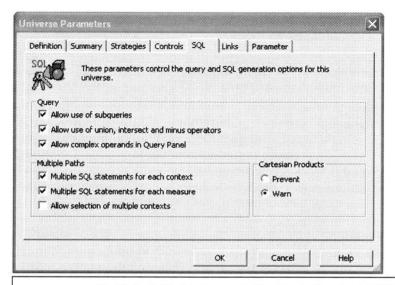

Ticker	Trans Year	Revenue		Ticker	High	Low
AA	2000	(259,238)		AA	45.71	23.13
AA	2001	432,050		AAPL	64.13	13.63
AAPL	2000	(103,094)		ACPW	79.75	12.7
AAPL	2001	78,167		AMAT	94.5	34.13
ACPW	2000	(17,569)		AMCC	109.75	11.25
ACPW	2001	37,217		AMD	47.5	13.56
AMAT	2000	(10,013)		AMGN	80.44	45.44
AMAT	2001	22,680		AMR	43.94	27.63
AMCC	2000	(50,575)		AMZN	49.63	8.1
AMCC	2001	59,040		AOL	63.25	31.5

Multiple SQL Statements For Each Context Will Cause Multiple Queries and Multiple Report Structures

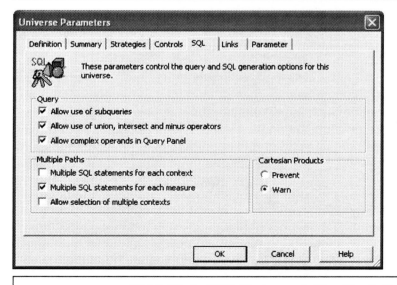

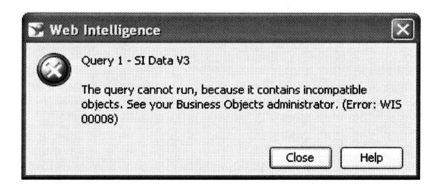

If *Multiple SQL Statements For Each Context* is Not Checked, Then the Query Will not Run

Working with Contexts

Earlier, we set contexts in our universe to keep the Fact tables from creating a Chasm Trap in our queries. The contexts tell Business Objects to keep the tables (joins) separate, so that our reports will be accurate. Business Objects keeps the sets of data separate two different ways, and the way that it chooses depends on the option *Multiple SQL Statements For Each Context* on the SQL tab of the Universe Parameters dialog.

If this option is checked, then Business Objects will create a separate query for each context involved with the objects in the Query. These multiple queries can cause a table for each query to be created when the report is executed for the first time. Notice that the context of the two tables in the graphic is different, in one table the context is Ticker - Year. In the other, the context is just Ticker. This is why the two tables are separate, because there dimensions from both queries that are not in common with the other.

If the *Multiple SQL Statements For Each Context* option is not checked, then Business Objects will not let the query execute. It does this by displaying the message box shown in the graphic, which notifies the report developer that the query contains *incompatible objects*. The objects are incompatible, because there are objects from two or more different contexts.

Notes

Multiple SQL Statements for Each Context

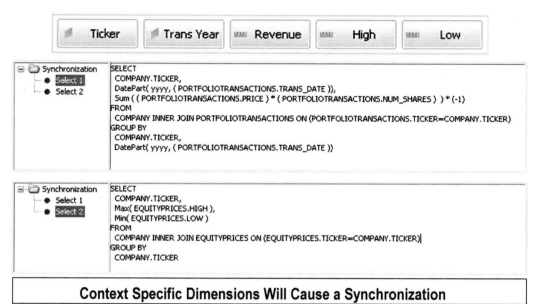

Ticker	Trans Year	Revenue
AA	2000	(259,238)
AA	2001	432,050
AAPL	2000	(103,094)
AAPL	2001	78,167
ACPW	2000	(17,569)
ACPW	2001	37,217
AMAT	2000	(10,013)
AMAT	2001	22,680
AMCC	2000	(50,575)
AMCC	2001	59,040

Ticker	High	Low
AA	45.71	23.13
AAPL	64.13	13.63
ACPW	79.75	12.7
AMAT	94.5	34.13
AMCC	109.75	11.25
AMD	47.5	13.56
AMGN	80.44	45.44
AMR	43.94	27.63
AMZN	49.63	8.1
AOL	63.25	31.5

Buttons: Ticker | Trans Year | Revenue | High | Low

Synchronization / Select 1 / Select 2:
```
SELECT
    COMPANY.TICKER,
    DatePart( yyyy, ( PORTFOLIOTRANSACTIONS.TRANS_DATE )),
    Sum ( ( PORTFOLIOTRANSACTIONS.PRICE ) * ( PORTFOLIOTRANSACTIONS.NUM_SHARES ) ) * (-1)
FROM
    COMPANY INNER JOIN PORTFOLIOTRANSACTIONS ON (PORTFOLIOTRANSACTIONS.TICKER=COMPANY.TICKER)
GROUP BY
    COMPANY.TICKER,
    DatePart( yyyy, ( PORTFOLIOTRANSACTIONS.TRANS_DATE ))
```

Synchronization / Select 1 / Select 2:
```
SELECT
    COMPANY.TICKER,
    Max( EQUITYPRICES.HIGH ),
    Min( EQUITYPRICES.LOW )
FROM
    COMPANY INNER JOIN EQUITYPRICES ON (EQUITYPRICES.TICKER=COMPANY.TICKER)
GROUP BY
    COMPANY.TICKER
```

Context Specific Dimensions Will Cause a Synchronization

Context Specific Dimensions Will Cause Multiple Tables

Buttons: Ticker | High | Low | Revenue | Num Transactions

Join / Select 1 / Select 2:
```
SELECT
    COMPANY.TICKER,
    Max( EQUITYPRICES.HIGH ),
    Min( EQUITYPRICES.LOW )
FROM
    COMPANY INNER JOIN EQUITYPRICES ON (EQUITYPRICES.TICKER=COMPANY.TICKER)
GROUP BY
    COMPANY.TICKER
```

Join / Select 1 / Select 2:
```
SELECT
    COMPANY.TICKER,
    Sum ( ( PORTFOLIOTRANSACTIONS.PRICE ) * ( PORTFOLIOTRANSACTIONS.NUM_SHARES ) ) * (-1),
    Count( DISTINCT PORTFOLIOTRANSACTIONS.TRANS_ID)
FROM
    COMPANY INNER JOIN PORTFOLIOTRANSACTIONS ON (PORTFOLIOTRANSACTIONS.TICKER=COMPANY.TICKER)
GROUP BY
    COMPANY.TICKER
```

Ticker	High	Low	Revenue	Num Transactions
AA	45.71	23.13	172,813	52
AAPL	64.13	13.63	(24,927)	18
ACPW	79.75	12.7	19,648	16
AMAT	94.5	34.13	12,667	14
AMCC	109.75	11.25	8,465	20
AMD	47.5	13.56	(7,322)	12
AMGN	80.44	45.44	2,106	25
AMR	43.94	27.63		
AMZN	49.63	8.1		

Measures and and Common Dimensions will Cause a Join

No Context Specific Dimensions Results in a Single Table

Multiple SQL Statements for Each Context

If we allow *Multiple SQL Statements For Each Context*, then Business Objects can behave in two different ways. When objects in the Result Objects section of the Reporter come from two different contexts, then two different data sets will be created. Business Objects must then work with these two sets of data, and the types of objects selected dictate this behavior.

If a dimension object from a specific context is included in the query, such as Trans Year, then Business Objects cannot simply join the two data sets together. The reason for this is that Business Objects wants to join the two sets of data on the common dimensions. These common dimensions are treated much like keys and all of the dimensions in a data set define the key. This means that if two data sets have identical keys, then they can simply be joined together. However, if a dimension from one context is included in the query, then it will not be possible for both queries to have identical keys. Therefore, they cannot be joined and must be synchronized on the common dimensions.

If no context-specific dimension objects are included in the query and there is at least one common dimension, such as Ticker, then the datasets can join on the common dimensions. This allows for a single table to be created when the query is ran for the first time. The common dimensions come from the noncontext-specific tables, such as COMPANY, INDUSTRY, LAST_TRADE_DATE, and the Property tables.

Since the *Multiple SQL Statements For Each Context* option can cause two different behaviors and requires knowledge of object behavior and definition, I don't usually check this option. It does provide an advantage, but one must understand the advantage in order to take advantage of it. Also, report developers understand that they can create two queries and merge the data sets in the document. This gives them more control over how the queries create SQL and how the objects behave on a report.

Exercise: Clear the Multiple SQL Statements For Each Context Option

1. Select *File | Parameters ...* from the menu.
2. Click on the SQL tab to activate it.
3. Clear all of the Multiple Paths check boxes.

Notes

Organizing Classes with Contexts

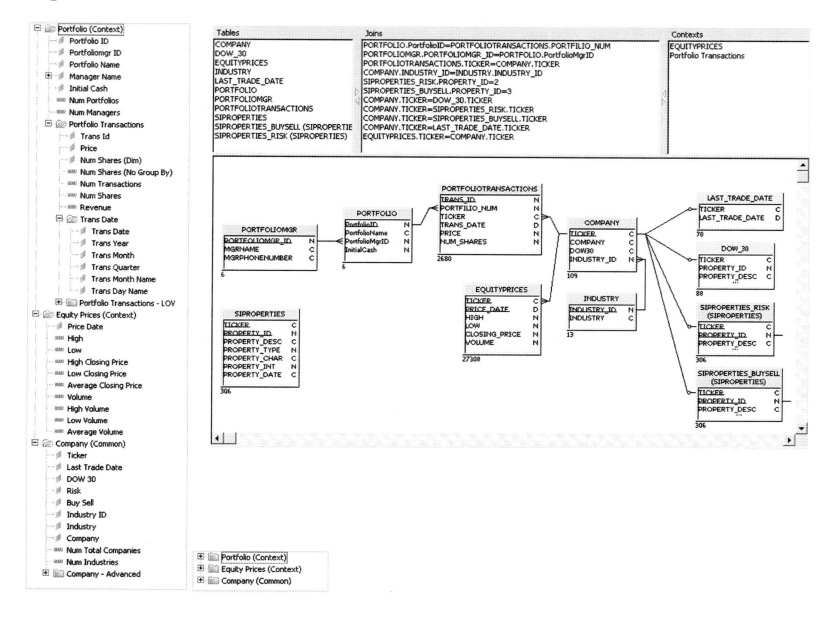

Organizing Classes with Contexts

I have been training Business Objects for over ten years and I really want my students to learn, so that they can have great careers. This is why I am always so surprised when they call me and ask me to create reports for them. I usually ask them why they are not creating the reports, and the most common answer is that they don't know what objects to use. They say, "If I select these two objects, then the reporter creates two different tables. Then when I try to put the objects together, I receive an incompatible error." At this point, they just want me to come and do it for them.

They don't know what objects to use, because the contexts in the universe are not identifiable through the Query interface. In addition, in the worse cases, Universe Designers have taken objects from different contexts and placed them in the same class. This makes it almost impossible for report developers to create reports.

Therefore, it is very important not to mix objects from different contexts within a single class. It is also important to label classes to let report developers know that a class is context specific or if it common to all contexts. In the graphic, we have moved all Portfolio classes into a single Portfolio class. We did this, because they all represent objects that come from the Portfolio Transactions context. We then suffixed the class with a Context label. We also suffixed Equity Prices with a Context label.

The Company class contains objects that can be used with both Portfolio Transactions and Equity Prices contexts. So, we label this class as Common. Now, people know what the contexts are and how they will affect the reports that they want to create. If all universes were created similar to this, then consultants would get much less opportunity to create your reports.

Exercise: Organize Folders

1. Open the Portfolio Class.
2. Drag the Portfolio Transactions class into the Portfolio class.
3. Rename the Portfolio Class to - Portfolio (Context)
4. Drag the Equity Prices class and place it under the Portfolio (Context) class.
5. Rename Equity Prices to - Equity Prices (Context)
6. Rename Company to - Company (Common)

Notes

Database Delegated Measures

Ticker	High Closing Price	Low Closing Price	Average Closing Price
AA	45.36	23.5	34.19
AAPL	63.44	14	27.66
ACPW	73.56	13.61	29.19
AMAT	94	35.38	54.16
AMCC	107	11.31	54.21
AMD	45.63	13.69	25.57
AMGN	78	51.51	65.63

High, Low, Average Price

High Closing Price	Low Closing Price	Average Closing Price
243	1.19	4,657.61

Average is Wrong

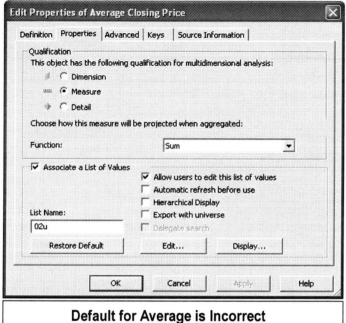

Default for Average is Incorrect

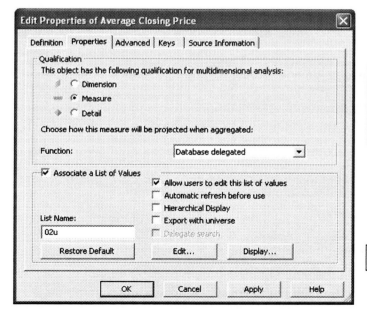

High Closing Price	Low Closing Price	Average Closing Price
243	1.19	#TOREFRESH

High Closing Price	Low Closing Price	Average Closing Price
243	1.19	43.16

Database Delegated is Correct

Database Delegated Measures

If we make a query with High, Low, and Average Closing Price for each ticker, then we should notice that the average price is always somewhere between high and low. The highest high price from table is $243. The lowest low price is $1.19. If this is true and we delete the Ticker column, then the average price should be somewhere between 243 and 1.19. However, when we delete the Ticker column, then the result Average Price is much larger than 243! What happened? To answer this, I'll start with an example and then return to this problem.

Suppose that the average price of 100,000 houses in California is $1,000,000. Let's also suppose that the price of 1 house in Virginia is $500,000. If someone was to ask me what the average price of all the house is, then would I answer $750,000 which is (1,000,000 + 500,000)/2? Or, would I answer $999,995, which is (1,000,000*100,000 + 1*1,000,000)/(100,000 + 1). The latter must be true, since most of the houses cost $1,000,000.

After studying the above example, we realize that when the Ticker column is deleted, then Business Objects cannot get the correct answer without re-running the query for the new context, which is the table minus the Ticker column. The next thing we should notice is that when we deleted the Ticker column the average was not between the highest high and the lowest low, as $750,000 and $999,995 were from the example. So why is it so wrong?

The default was incorrect because Business Objects defaulted to Sum for the Average function on the Properties tab of the Edit Properties dialog. I believe that Business Objects defaults to Sum, because it is obviously incorrect. In my opinion, they do this, because defaulting to the Average function would also be incorrect, but maybe only subtly incorrect, which would cause confusion. Sum has been the default since earlier versions of Business Objects. However, with the release of V3, there is a new function to choose for report level aggregation. This new function is Database Delegation, which means that if the context for a calculated measure changes, then Business Objects will only display the new level of aggregation, after it is able to run a query to calculate it. Database Delegation should be used with Averages and most counts (Because Fan Traps often exist in counts). For example, if you went to one store and bought oranges, then you bought 1 fruit. If you go to another store and buy oranges again, then you bought 1 fruit. If you sum these counts, which is the default for count, then you will get 2 fruits, which is not the case. You still only bought 1 fruit, just 2 different stores.

Exercise: Change Measure Report Level Aggregation to Database Delegation

1. Double-click on Average Closing Price and, on the Properties tab, change its Report Level aggregation to Database Delegation.
2. Do the same for Average Volume.

Notes

Adding a Date Table

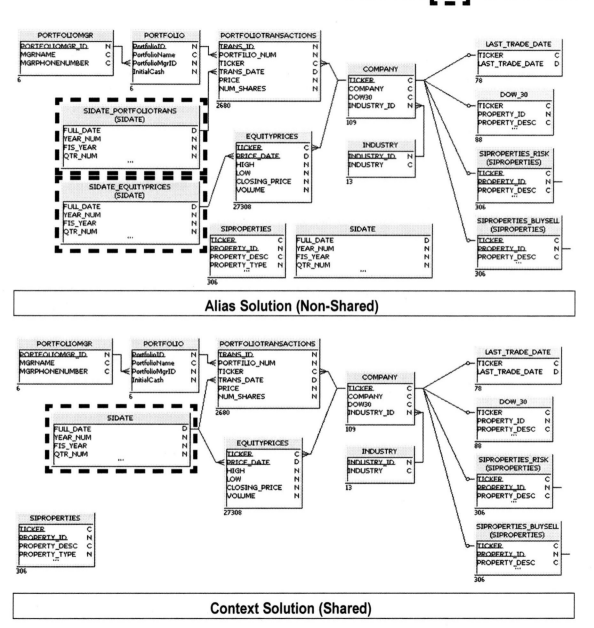

Alias Solution (Non-Shared)

Context Solution (Shared)

Adding a Date Table

Date tables are tables that have Date or a Date Key as a primary key. Date Tables have many columns that contain Date Derivatives, such as Year, Quarter, Month, Week, Previous Year, First of Year, and so forth. Earlier, we created date derivatives using formulas and database functions. We saw that these formulas can vary with different databases, which makes them difficult to use. Date tables already contain all of the date derivatives, so they do not need to be calculated. This keeps the derivatives consistent between databases and universes.

In our example, we can use one of two options to add the date table. We can alias it for each date, as seen the top graphic. This method works well, but we must have a different group of dates for each date that uses the table. In this example, we would have to have a date folder in Portfolio Transactions and Equity Prices. This is not the most desirable solution, because it creates redundancy that must be managed. By the way, some tables have two or more important dates, such as Invoice Date and Order Date in the Invoice table, which require the Alias solution.

In our example, we are going to join SIDATE to both the PORTFOLIOTRANSACTIONS and EQUITYPRICES table. This will allow us to create one common date class that is similar to the Company class, which is also common to both contexts. This will allow us to manage only one date class. In either solution, we will have to add the new joins to the existing contexts.

Exercise: Add the SIDate Table to the Structure

1. Click the *Table Browser* toolbar button. Locate SIDate in the Browser and drag it to the Structure section of the Designer.
2. Click on TRANS_DATE in the PortfolioTransactions table and drag it to the FULL_DATE field in the SIDate table (This will create a join).
3. Double-click on the new join and define the cardinality as 1 to n (one SIDate to many TransDate).
4. Click on PRICE_DATE in the EquityPrices table and drag it to the FULL_DATE field in the SIDate table (This will create a join).
5. Double-click on the new join and define the cardinality as 1 to n (one SIDate to many PriceDate)
6. Double-click on the Equity Prices context to open the Edit Context dialog. Find the join - SIDATE.FULL_DATE=EQUITYPRICES.PRICEDATE, in the list and click on it to select it.
7. Click *OK* to accept the addition of the new join to the Equity Prices context.
8. Double-click on the Portfolio Transactions context to open the Edit Context dialog. Find the join - SIDATE.FULL_DATE=PORTFOLIOTRANSACTIONS.TRANSDATE, in the list and click on it to select it.
9. Click *OK* to accept the addition of the new join to the Portfolio Transactions context.
   • Notice that the two new joins were located at the bottom of the join list, as joins are listed in chronological order.

Notes

Add Date Class

Dates Common
- Full Date
- Year Num
- Fis Year
- Qtr Num
- Fis Qtr
- Month Num
- Fis Period
- Month Name
- Day Name
- First Of Year
- End Of Year
- Days In Year
- Days Into Year
- Workdays In Year
- Workdays Into Year
- Fis First Of Year
- Fis End Of Year
- Days In Fis Year
- Days Into Fis Year
- Workdays In Fis Year
- Workdays Into Fis Year
- First Of Qtr
- End Of Qtr
- Days In Qtr
- Days Into Qtr
- Workdays In Qtr
- Workdays Into Qtr
- Fis First Of Qtr
- Fis End Of Qtr
- Days In Fis Qtr
- Days Into Fis Qtr
- Workdays In Fis Qtr
- Workdays Into Fis Qtr
- First Of Month
- Days In Month
- Days Into Month
- Workdays In Month
- Workdays Into Month
- First Of Week
- Days Into Week
- Rolling 90 Days

- Prev Year Full Date
- Prev Year
- Prev Fis Year
- Prev First Of Year
- Prev End Of Year
- Days In Prev Year
- Days Into Prev Year
- Workdays In Prev Year
- Workdays Into Prev Year
- Prev Fis First Of Year
- Prev Fis End Of Year
- Days In Prev Fis Year
- Days Into Prev Fis Year
- Workdays In Prev Fis Year
- Workdays Into Prev Fis Year
- Prev Year First Of Qtr
- Prev Year End Of Qtr
- Prev Year Days In Qtr
- Prev Year Days Into Qtr
- Prev Year Wdays In Qtr
- Prev Year Wdays Into Qtr
- Prev First Of Qtr
- Prev End Of Qtr
- Day Offset Into Prev Qtr
- Wday Offset Into Prev Qtr
- Prev Qtr Days In Qtr
- Prev Qtr Wdays In Qtr
- Prev Qtr Wdays Into Qtr
- Prev Year First Of Fis Qtr
- Prev Year End Of Fis Qtr
- Py Fis Year Days In Qtr
- Py Fis Year Wdays In Qtr
- Prev First Of Fiscal Qtr
- Prev End Of Fiscal Qtr
- Prev Fis Year Days In Qtr
- Prev Fis Year Wdays In Qtr
- Prev Year First Of Month
- Prev Year End Of Month
- Prev Year Days In Month
- Prev Year Wdays In Month
- Prev First Of Month
- Prev End Of Month
- Prev Days In Month
- Prev Wdays In Month
- Prev First Of Week

Transactions Dates

- Portfolio Transactions
  - Trans Id
  - Price
  - Num Shares (Dim)
  - Num Shares (No Group By)
  - Num Transactions
  - Num Shares
  - Revenue
  - Trans Date
    - Trans Date
    - Trans Year
    - Trans Month
    - Trans Quarter
    - Trans Month Name
    - Trans Day Name

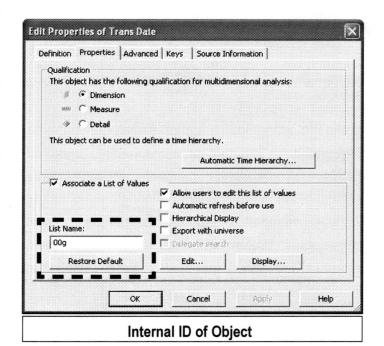

Internal ID of Object

> **Date Tables Can Contain
> Many Useful Fields.
> Most of Them Will Contain
> Current and Previous
> Date Derivatives.
> Ours Contains Abot82 Fields.**

Add Date Class

Date tables can contain many fields that can be used in many ways. In the graphic, we just dragged the SIDate table over to create the class and renamed the class to Dates (Common). The fields became dimension objects, as many of them should be. However, many of them can also be measures. For example, Sum (Days in Month). We will not do this, because it will cause built-in fan traps that report developers will have to understand. For example, there are 31 days in December. This means that each Date row for December will have 31 days associated with it. Then, if someone was to select Month and Number of Days (the measure), then the number of days would be 31 * 31.

We do have a slight problem - We have Trans Dates in Portfolio Transactions that has been in the universe for some time. We do not want these dates, as we want people to use the dates in the new Dates (Common) class. However, we just cannot delete the Trans Dates, because we will probably break any existing reports that use these objects.

It is important to realize that Business Objects can refer to objects using either their name or internal ID. If we realize that each object has an internal ID, then we can move objects without breaking reports. So we will move the existing Trans Date objects into the new Dates (Common) class and delete their counterparts that are currently in the Dates (Common) class. Then, we can rename and point the objects to the SIDate table.

One other note - It is important to realize that once we rename and point Trans Date to the SIDate table, then all of the other Trans Date derivatives will work, even if we do not change their formulas. The reason for this, is that they do not point directly to any table, because they point to Trans Date using the @Select function. Here is the formula for Trans Year with the @Select in bold: DatePart(yyyy, **@Select(Trans Date\Trans Date)**). This is why it is better to use objects in formulas and not the fields directly. We will still point the objects to the SIDate table, because we want to rid ourselves of database specific date functions, and we also want to work with dates in a consistent manner.

Exercise: Move the Date Dimensions

1. Drag the Trans Date object from Trans Date and drop it below Full Date. Then, delete the Full Date object.
2. Double-click on Trans Date
   • Change its formula to: SIDATE.FULL_DATE
3. Drag the Trans Year object from Trans Date and drop it below Year Num. Then, delete the Year Num object.
4. Double-click on Trans Year
   • Change its formula to: SIDATE.YEAR_NUM
5. Do the same for Trans Month, Trans Quarter, Trans Month Name, and Trans Day Name.
6. **Delete Price Date** from Equity Prices.

Notes

The Date Conditions

Date Range Condition

Date Range

@Select(Dates (Common)\Full Date) BETWEEN
@Prompt('Enter Begin Date', 'D', 'Trans Date\Trans Date',,) AND
@Prompt('Enter End Date', 'D', 'Trans Date\Trans Date',,)

To Date Conditions

Year to Date

@Select(Dates (Common)\Full Date) <= @Prompt('Enter Date', 'D', 'Dates (Common)\Full Date',,) AND
@Select(Dates (Common)\Full Date) >=
(Select *SIDATE.FIRST_OF_YEAR* From SIDATE Where SIDATE.FULL_DATE = @Prompt('Enter Date', 'D', 'Dates (Common)\Full Date',,))

Quarter to Date

@Select(Dates (Common)\Full Date) <= @Prompt('Enter Date', 'D', 'Dates (Common)\Full Date',,) AND
@Select(Dates (Common)\Full Date) >=
(Select *SIDATE.FIRST_OF_QTR* From SIDATE Where SIDATE.FULL_DATE = @Prompt('Enter Date', 'D', 'Dates (Common)\Full Date',,))

Month to Date

@Select(Dates (Common)\Full Date) <= @Prompt('Enter Date', 'D', 'Dates (Common)\Full Date',,) AND
@Select(Dates (Common)\Full Date) >=
(Select *SIDATE.SIDATE.FIRST_OF_MONTH* From SIDATE Where SIDATE.FULL_DATE = @Prompt('Enter Date', 'D', 'Dates (Common)\Full Date',,))

Week to Date

@Select(Dates (Common)\Full Date) <= @Prompt('Enter Date', 'D', 'Dates (Common)\Full Date',,) AND
@Select(Dates (Common)\Full Date) >=
(Select *SIDATE.FIRST_OF_WEEK* From SIDATE Where SIDATE.FULL_DATE = @Prompt('Enter Date', 'D', 'Dates (Common)\Full Date',,))

The Date Conditions

Earlier, we made our date conditions using SQL Server or Oracle functions and formulas. The functions and formulas can be difficult to understand and may be incorrect. For example, suppose the formula to calculate first of the month failed for the last month of the year? I have worked in many companies, and one of my biggest challenges has always been figuring out how their date logic works. To overcome this, I now put first of periods in my date table. This allows me a consistent structure for calculating to Date conditions. If you look at the graphic, then you will see that each to date condition only differs by one field - the first of the period field.

When I first came up with this idea, many database designers thought I was nuts, because, for example, I would ask them to put *first of the year* in the date table. They would say, the first of the year is the 1st, why do you need this? Then, I would show them the condition formulas in the graphic and many of them would yield and put the first of the periods in the date table. Notice that I even have first of previous periods, so I can calculate, for example, Previous Year to Date. This logic is highly efficient and offers a consistent structure for to date conditions.

Exercise: Remove all Date Objects and Replace with Common SIDate Objects

1. Locate the three date conditions that are in the Portfolio Transactions class and drag them into the Dates (Common) class.
2. Modify each of the formulas to the formulas shown in the graphic.
3. Add the Week to Date and the Quarter to Date conditions.
4. If you want to experiment, try to create Previous Year to Date.
   The Answer is below.

@Select(Dates (Common)\Full Date) <=
  (Select SIDATE.PREV_YEAR_FULL_DATE From SIDATE Where SIDATE.FULL_DATE = @Prompt('Enter Date', 'D', 'Dates (Common)\Full Date',,))
AND
@Select(Dates (Common)\Full Date) >=
  (Select SIDATE.PREV_FIRST_OF_YEAR From SIDATE Where SIDATE.FULL_DATE = @Prompt('Enter Date', 'D', 'Dates (Common)\Full Date',,))

Notes

Loops in a Universe

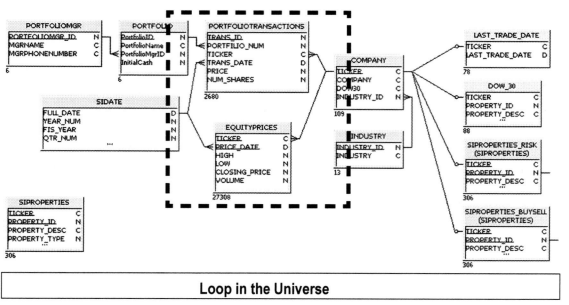

Loop in the Universe

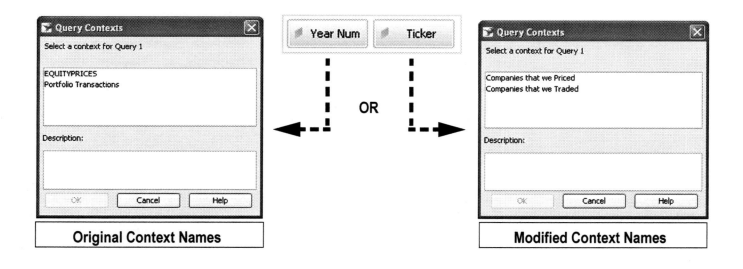

Original Context Names   OR   **Modified Context Names**

Loops in a Universe

If we look at the center of our universe, then we should see a loop created by COMPANY and SIDATE being shared with EQUITY PRICES and PORTFOLIOTRANSACTIONS. Loops generally have to be solved by assigning a context to each half of the loop, which we already did. The Portfolio Transactions context includes the upper path through the PORTFOLIOTRANSACTIONS table and the EQUITYPRICES context includes the lower path through the EQUITYPRICES table. However, we did not create theses contexts to solve the loop. We created them to solve the chasm-trap created by the Fact tables sharing the SIDATE and COMPANY tables, and we created the contexts long before any loop existed. This means that universe without loops can, and often do, have contexts.

What do I mean by the context solved the loop? Well, if we were to select objects from Dates (Common), Portfolio (Context), and Company (Common), then there would be no problem and the query will run as usual. However, what if we just selected from the two Dimension classes - Dates (Common) and Company (Common)? Now, Business Objects would be confused and not know which context it should use. Should it use the path through PORTFOLIOTRANSACTIONS or the path through EQUITY PRICES? Since it does not know, it will ask the report developer through a prompt, as shown in the lower part of the graphic.

When we created our contexts, we did not worry too much about naming the contexts, because we did not have a loop at the time. So, we just accepted the default names. Now that there is a loop, Business Objects will prompt report developers to select a context, and many people will not recognize the default context names. Therefore, when we have a loop in the universe, we should always try to give our contexts meaningful names. In this case, I chose to name the contexts - *Companies that we Priced* and *Companies that we Traded*. These names make sense and let the report refresher know exactly what data they will be retrieving. For example, if they choose Companies that we Traded for the query in the graphic, then they would get a list of companies that were traded for each year num in the data set returned. By the way, this could be very different from a list of companies that were priced for those years, which is what would be returned, if Companies that we Priced were selected.

Exercise: Rename the Contexts

1. Open the List Mode panel, by selecting *View | List Mode* from the menu.
2. Double-click on the EQUITY PRICES context and rename it to - Companies that we Priced.
3. Double-click on the Portfolio Transactions context and rename it to - Companies that we Traded.

Notes

Detect Loops Button

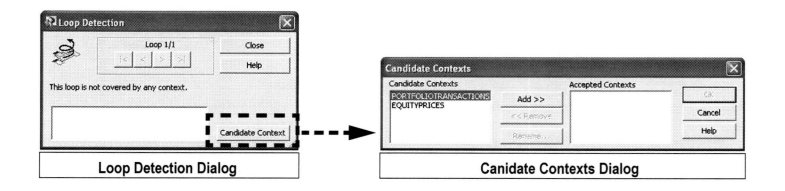

Loop Detection Dialog	Canidate Contexts Dialog

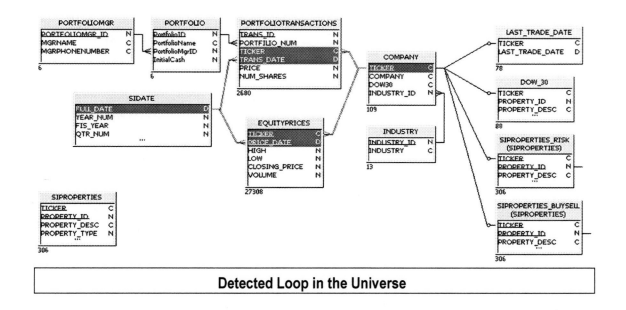

Detected Loop in the Universe

Detect Loops Button

There is a button on the toolbar called Detect Loops and there is a menu item called *Tools | Automatic Detection | Detect Loops....* This command will locate loops in the universe. If there is a loop that is not assigned to contexts, then the dialog will have the following message - This loop is not covered by any context. This means that we should click the Candidate Context button, which will launch the Automatic Context Detection dialog, also known as the Candidate Contexts dialog. We used this dialog earlier, when we automatically assigned our contexts.

The existence of the button reinforces the belief that contexts were created to solve for loops, which is not true. We will never have to click this button during out universe creation, because we need to solve for our chasm traps, before any loop even exists. Also, in the first Fact Table chasm trap solution (Where we aliased the dimension tables), we didn't even have a loop, but we needed the contexts to keep the Cartesian product from happening. In fact, I believe that out of the thousands of universes that I have ever created that I have never clicked on this button to create contexts in my universe. Why? Because, I must solve for the chasm traps before the loops exist.

So why is the button there? I believe it is here, because people used to want to design universes the same way that they designed their databases. This would mean dumping all of their tables into the workspace and then joining all the tables. This would create loops that one may not be aware of. But if each table is individually added, then the ramifications of the addition can be considered as they are added. This is probably a better way to design, and is the method that we are using in this book.

Notes

Our Universe (So Far)

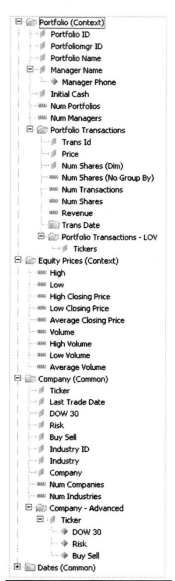

Objects and Classes

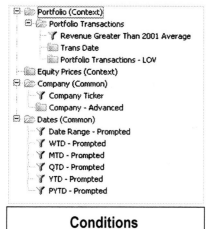

Conditions

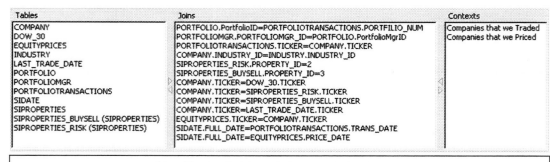

List Mode (Tables, Joins, and Contexts)

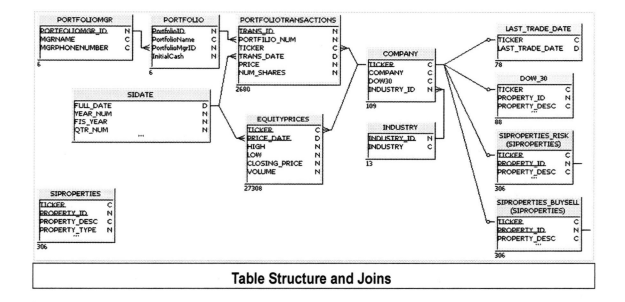

Table Structure and Joins

Our Universe (So Far)

Our universe now contains two fact tables and a date table. When we added the new fact table, we needed to create contexts to solve for the Chasm Trap created when both fact tables joined to COMPANY. The SIDATE table allowed us to have a common dates class, because the tables in both contexts have access to it. This will make our queries between the two different fact tables more consistent, because they will both have access to the same date derivatives and conditions. When we added the SIDATE table, we created a loop. The loop was of little matter to us, because we already added the new joins to their respective contexts to solve for the chasm traps created by the joins. However, with the formation of a loop, Business Objects must prompt report developers for which context they are interested in. Since Business Objects must use the names of the contexts in the prompt, we went back and gave our contexts more functional names. There is also a space for descriptions, but if you name them properly, then you may not need a description.

I hope that you understand how I created the to-date conditions. This is a method that I developed, because of the confusion that usually accompanies to-date conditions in most companies. For example, do an internet search on SQL Server Month to Date and see how many different solutions that people are offering. The method that I presented provides a very straight forward and consistent solution to most to-date conditions.

By the way, most universes that I create have this form. It is very easy to use and most report developers have few problems when designing documents. Of course, not all universes are so conveniently designed, so in the next chapter we will introduce some complications.

When your universe is in a stable state, you should save and export it. This places a copy in a universe domain that is protected by the database administrators. When we want to work on it again, we should always import a fresh copy. This way we will always be working with an accepted stable state of the universe.

Exercise: Save and Export Universe

1. Select | *File* | *Save* | from the menu.
2. Export the Universe
    • Select | *File* | *Export* | from the menu.
    • Select a Group in the Groups list.
    • Select the domain in the Domains drop list.
    • Click *OK*.

Notes

Universe Linking (Separate Company Universe)

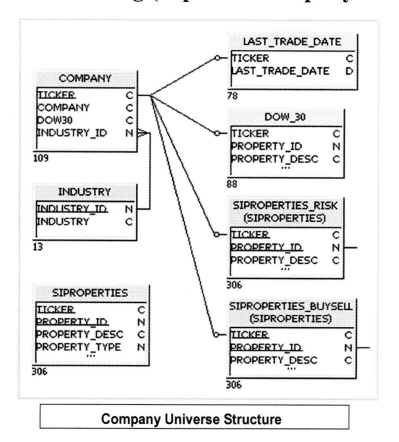

Company Universe Structure

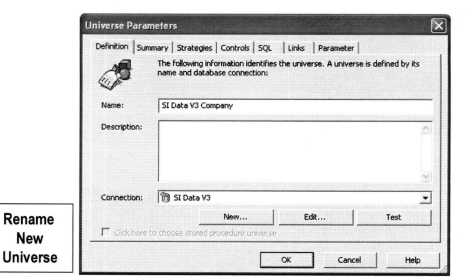

Rename New Universe

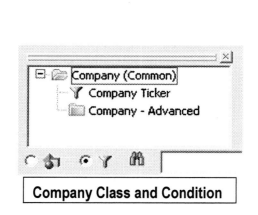

Company Class and Condition

Company Class and Objects

Create a Separate Company Universe

Many times, after creating your first universe, you will notice that pieces of the universe can be used in other universes. At this point, you can just copy the needed pieces into the other universes. However, this may pose a maintenance problem, because the copies and the originals may diverge in definition. Then, in some universes the copies may behave differently than in others. If this happens, people will begin to question the accuracy of your universes. Once they start questioning, it is very hard to get their confidence back.

Therefore, it may be better to create a universe from the logical groupings of components that may be repeated in the other universes. Then, the separate universes can be individually maintained, without diverging from copies of themselves. In this universe, you could create two groupings - One for Portfolio and one for Company. In this chapter, we will create the Company Universe.

Exercise: Create Separate Company Universe

1. Save and Export our Universe (To protect it).
2. Save our Universe as (SI Data V3 (Linked))
   • Select | *File SaveAs...* | from the menu.
   • Type *SI Data V3 (Linked)* in the File Name field.
   • Click *OK.*
   • Select *File | Parameters...* from the menu.
   • Enter *SI Data V3 (Linked)* into the Name field.
   • Enter *Linked Universe* into the Description field.
   • Click *OK.*
3. Export SI Data V3 (Linked). We'll Use this copy in our example. Then we will go back to our original that we exported in step #1.
4. Save SI Data V3 (Linked) as SI Data V3 Company. We will create the Company universe from this copy and link it to SI Data V3 (Linked).
   • Select | *File SaveAs...* | from the menu.
   • Type *SI Data V3 Company* in the File Name field.
   • Click *OK.*
   • Select *File | Parameters...* from the menu.
   • Enter *SI Data V3 Company* into the Name field.

   • Enter *Company universe* in the Description field.
   • Click *OK.*
5. Close and select all of the classes, except the Company (Common) class.
6. Delete the selected folders, by pressing the [Delete] key.
7. Select all tables that are to the left of Company and press the [Delete] Key (**Do not delete SIPROPERTIES**, as all of the Aliases will fail).
8. Save and Export the universe.
9. Close the universe.

Notes

Linking the Universe

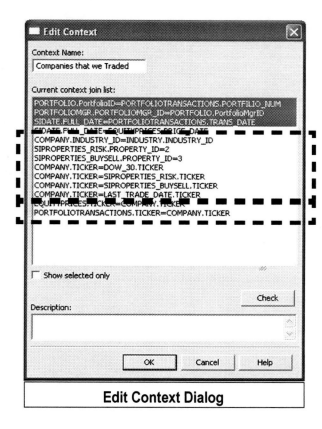

Edit Context Dialog

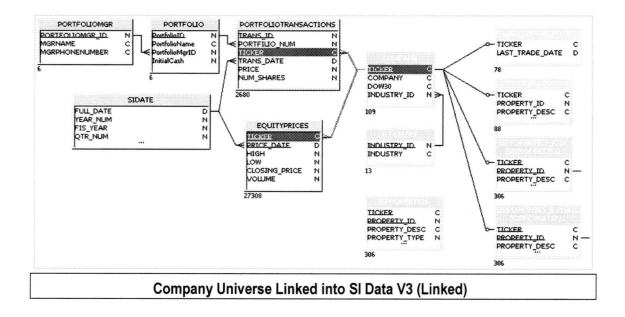

Company Universe Linked into SI Data V3 (Linked)

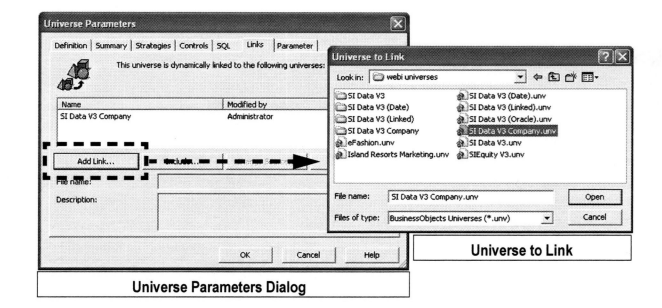

Universe Parameters Dialog

Universe to Link

Linking the Universe

Now that we've created the Company Universe, it is time to put it to work. We can do this by linking it into the SI Data V3 (Linked) universe that we saved in the previous exercise. We link universes on the Links tab of the Universe Parameters dialog. We can link as many universes as we need, but in this chapter, we are only going to link one.

Once we have linked a universe into another, the structure, classes, and objects will appear in the Universe Designer. The objects from the linked universes will be dimmed (grayed), as shown in the graphic. Once the objects are in the structure, we will have to logically join the tables and add the joins to any contexts in the universe. We may even have to create new contexts.

We cannot edit or alter any linked (grayed) objects in a universe. We must always open the root universe that was linked in. This stops us from creating new definitions that may diverge from the originals. It also guarantees that any universe that is using the link universe will have the exact same objects and definitions that any other universe will have.

Exercise: Link the Company Universe to the SI Equity Universe

1. Open SI Data V3 (Linked).
2. Delete the Company structure from SI Data V3 (Linked).
   - Select and delete the Company (Common) class.
   - Click on all of the Joins and Tables that are with the Company group (Company, Industry, SIProperties_*) and press the [Delete] key.
   - Click *Yes* in the Confirm Join Delete dialog.
3. Link the Company Universe into SI Data V3 (Linked)
   - Select | *File* | *Parameters...* | from the menu.
   - Activate the Link tab in the Universe Parameters dialog.
   - Click the *Add Link...* button.
   - Open the SI Data V3 Company universe.
     (If it is not in the list, then you may not of exported it.)
   - Click the *OK* button.
4. Arrange the tables so that they are not on top of each other.

5. Join Ticker from Equity Prices to Ticker in Company.
6. Join Ticker from Portfolio Transactions to Ticker in Company.
7. Adjust the Contexts.
   - Select | View | List mode | from the menu.
   - Double-click on the Portfolio Transactions context.
     Notice that in the Edit Context dialog all of the company universe joins and the joins to Company are list last in the list. This is because joins are listed in chronological order. Therefore, it is rather easy to find and select the needed joins to complete the context.
   - Repeat the previous two bullets for Equity Prices.

Notes

Chapter Summary

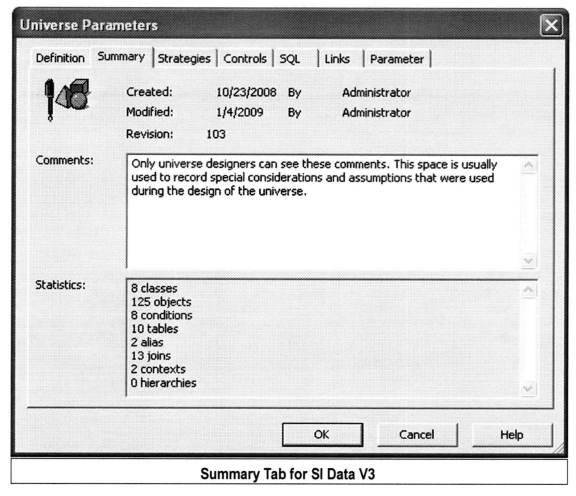

Summary Tab for SI Data V3

8 Classes
125 Objects
8 Conditions
10 Tables
2 Alias
13 Joins
2 Contet

Chapter Summary

This was a very important chapter, because it taught us how to deal with multiple fact tables, contexts, and loops. We saw that there were multiple solutions to many of the problems that we face when creating universes. For example, we could have aliased the SIDATE table and linked each copy to their respective fact table, or we could simply join the SIDATE table to both fact tables and use contexts to solve the resulting chasm traps. Notice that I did not say the contexts solved the resulting loop. I did not say loop, because even though the SIDATE table did cause a loop, we already had the contexts to solve the chasm trap created by joining the COMPANY table to both fact tables.

Another point that I want to make is that either the aliased or the shared solution would have worked. The Aliased solution did not create a loop and the Shared solution did create a loop. The loop had little effect on our decision making process, as we went with the shared solution so that we can have a single class to represent dates in the universe. I point this out because I often hear people say that you solve chasm traps with contexts and fan traps with aliases, which is not a good rule of thumb to have (Actually, it is not correct, as we proved here).

We also explored how to make to-date conditions using a date table. These to-date conditions are very easy to create, if the first of the period of interest is included in the date table. So, always try to insist that the first of periods are in the date table, when they are designed. Also, it is a good idea to have as many previous date derivatives as possible.

We learned that Average and Count measures will function correctly in a query, but if they are re-aggregated on the report, then the result could be incorrect. For example, averaging averages, is not correct. The average must be calculated using the entire population, as the house example demonstrated. We also found that if we sum counts, then we can be introducing fan traps into the calculation. Therefore, Business Objects has added a new report level aggregation for measures, which is Database Delegation.

We also created a linked universe. We did this on a universe that we called SI Data V3 (Linked), because we didn't want the linked file to distract from future lessons. Linked universes are great, because they allow us to create universe building blocks. However, many large companies will not link universes, because if one of the components breaks, then every universe linked to it will also break.

On the Summary graphic, we see that we have 10 tables and 125 Objects. This could be 5 Tables or 500 Tables, and it really would not matter to me. Universes have little control over the number of tables that are included in them, because Designers can only work with what the Database Designers have created. I have heard people try to put limits on the number of elements in a universe. This is not realistic, unless the Database and Universe designers work closely together.

Notes

Chapter 5: Data Complications

In this chapter, we are going to examine how data relationships in tables can affect the information returned to reports. We are going to discuss joining our fact tables, add aggregate tables, and consider fan-traps - both acceptable and not acceptable versions. This is a very important chapter, because these are the types of challenges that we face when building universes.

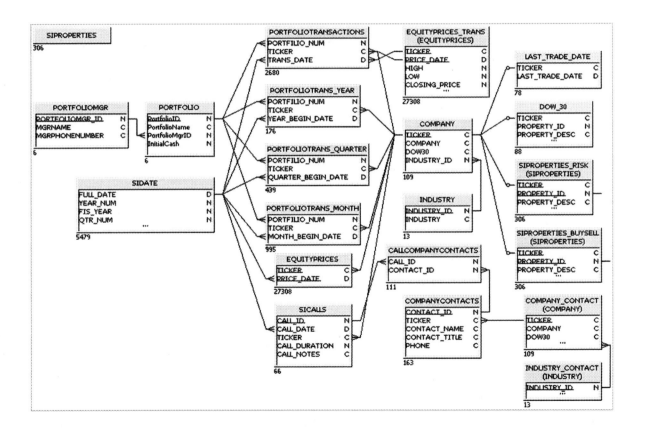

Aggregated Tables

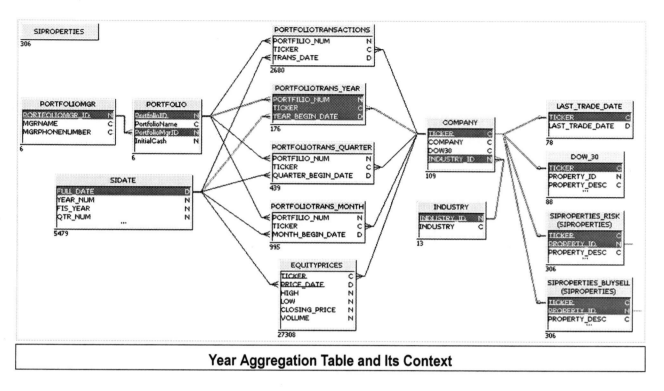

Year Aggregation Table and Its Context

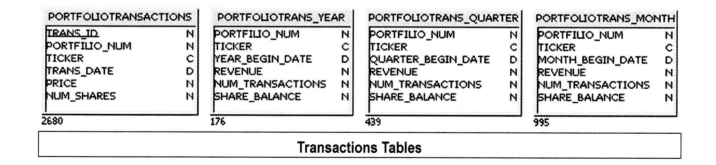

Transactions Tables

Aggregated Tables

The PORTFOLIOTRANSACTIONS table has 2680 rows. It contains the details of all the trades made each day. If a report developer wanted to create a Yearly report, then they would not be interested in the daily details. However, if all they had was the PORTFOLIOTRANSACTIONS daily table, then they would have to use this table, and the SQL would have to create yearly summaries from the detail data.

What if there was a Yearly table that already had all of the daily data aggregated to the yearly resolution? If a developer was to use this table, instead of the daily table, then the query would be much faster, because it would have much less rows to work with. In our example, this yearly table is PORTFOLIOTRANS_YEAR, which has only 176 rows, which is 92.5% less than PORTFOLIOTRANSACTIONS.

In our database, we have three aggregated tables - PORTFOLIOTRANS_YEAR, PORTFOLIOTRANS_QUARTER, and PORTFOLIOTRANS_MONTH. These tables summarize Revenue, Number of Transactions, and Share Balance. The date for the period is represented by the beginning date of the period. This will allow us to join the summary tables to the date table.

Exercise: Add the Aggregated Tables

1. Insert the SIDate table
   - Select | *Insert* | *Tables...* | from the menu.
   - Locate select PORTFOLIOTRANS_YEAR, PORTFOLIOTRANS_QUARTER, and PORTFOLIOTRANS_MONTH in the list.
   - Drag the selected taables to the Structure.
2. Create the Joins (For each of the Summary tables)
   - Drag the Date field in the Summary table to Full_Date in SIDate.
   - Drag the Ticker field to the Ticker field in Company.
   - Drag the PORTFOLIO_NUM field to PortfolioID in PORTFOLIO.
   - Set the cardinalities of the joins (n-to1).
3. Create a Context for each new table
   - Best way to do this, is to first open List Mode - Select View | List Mode from the menu.

- Select the Companies that we Traded context. This will select all of the joins for that context in the structure.
- Unselect the joins to the PORTFOLIOTRANSACTIONS table, by holding down the [Ctrl] key and clicking on the three joins.
- Select the three joins attached to any Summary table, by down the [CTRL] key and clicking on the joins.
- Select | *Insert* | *Context...* | from the menu and name the context Yearly, Quarterly, or Monthly Transaction.
- Click *OK* to accept the context.
- Repeat for the other two Aggregation tables.

Notes

Aggregate Objects (Solution #1)

Aggregate Classes

First Of Year	Yearly Revenue	Yearly Transactions	Yearly Share Balance
1/1/00	(6,933,784)	1,225	155,900
1/1/01	8,510,980	1,455	(155,900)
Sum:	1,577,196	2,680	0

First Of Qtr	Quarterly Revenue	Quarterly Num Transactions	Quarterly Share Balance
7/1/00	(4,278,686)	588	96,00(
10/1/00	(2,655,098)	637	59,90(
1/1/01	349,438	645	17,20(
4/1/01	2,750,713	643	(45,800
7/1/01	5,410,828	167	(127,300
Sum:	1,577,195	2,680	(

First Of Month	Monthly Revenue	Monthly Num Transactions	Monthly Share Balance
7/1/00	(3,008,431)	148	55,400
8/1/00	(1,832,371)	233	38,000
9/1/00	562,116	207	2,600
10/1/00	(1,275,482)	231	28,800
11/1/00	(583,157)	204	14,400
12/1/00	(796,460)	202	16,700
1/1/01	911,394	215	(8,900)
2/1/01	609,760	189	(6,700)
3/1/01	(1,171,716)	241	32,800
4/1/01	113,306	193	2,600
5/1/01	2,924,905	232	(56,500)
6/1/01	(287,497)	218	8,100
7/1/01	5,410,828	167	(127,300)
Sum:	1,577,195	2,680	0

Aggregate Reports

First Of Year	Quarterly Revenue	Quarterly Num Transactions	Quarterly Share Balance
1/1/00	(6,933,784)	1,225	155,900
1/1/01	8,510,980	1,455	(155,900)
Sum:	1,577,196	2,680	0

Year Object Used with Quarter Aggregation

Aggregate Objects (Solution #1)

We are not going to use this solution in our on-going example universe, but we will discuss this solution to help us understand alternative solutions.

This solution simply creates a subclass, in the Portfolio class, for each level of aggregation. All of the measures are sum measures from their respective tables. These classes can be used to create reports with Portfolio, Company, and Date information.

This solution works well, as can be seen by the middle group of Report Tables. However, it can become confusing when dates at different resolutions than the level of aggregation are used with the objects. For example, the report table on the right has the First of the Year column and the Quarterly aggregate measures. The information is correct for the year totals, because the quarters will add up to the yearly totals. However, it is confusing to look at, because the measure columns state that they are quarterly values. Also, since the report is at the yearly level, the yearly measures, from the Portfolio Trans Yearly class, should have been used. The way the report is structured it processed four times more data than it should have.

Notes

Aggregate Awareness (Solution #2)

Revenue

Function:	@Aggregate_Aware (
Year Level:	Sum(PORTFOLIOTRANS_YEAR.REVENUE),
Quarter Level:	Sum(PORTFOLIOTRANS_QUARTER.REVENUE),
Month Level:	Sum(PORTFOLIOTRANS_MONTH.REVENUE),
Daily Level:	Sum (PORTFOLIOTRANSACTIONS.PRICE *PORTFOLIOTRANSACTIONS.NUM_SHARES) * (-1))

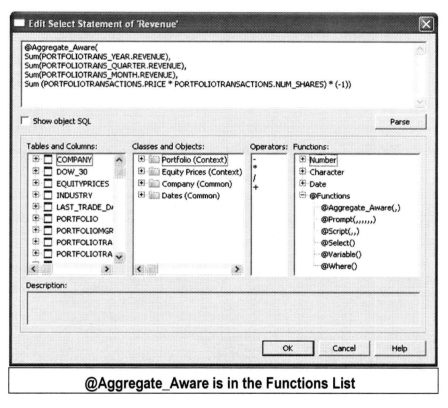

@Aggregate_Aware is in the Functions List

Num Shares

@Aggregate_Aware (
Sum(PORTFOLIOTRANS_YEAR.SHARE_BALANCE),
Sum(PORTFOLIOTRANS_QUARTER.SHARE_BALANCE),
Sum(PORTFOLIOTRANS_MONTH.SHARE_BALANCE),
Sum(PORTFOLIOTRANSACTIONS.NUM_SHARES))

Num Transactions

@Aggregate_Aware (
Sum(PORTFOLIOTRANS_YEAR.NUM_TRANSACTIONS),
Sum(PORTFOLIOTRANS_QUARTER.NUM_TRANSACTIONS),
Sum(PORTFOLIOTRANS_MONTH.NUM_TRANSACTIONS),
Count(Distinct PORTFOLIOTRANSACTIONS.TRANS_ID))

Aggregate Awareness (Solution #2)

We have four different levels of aggregation for Revenue, Num Transactions, and Num Shares. In the previous solution, we created a class of measures for each level, but we found out that report developers could still use a lower level of aggregation than they need to. This didn't make the reports wrong, but it made them less efficient. Somehow, we need to synchronize the level of aggregations with the date dimension objects in a query. If we could do this, then we could instruct Business Objects to select the proper level of aggregated measure for the dimensions in a query. We will do this with Aggregate Awareness.

The first step is to realize all of the ways that revenue can be calculated, which are:

> **Yearly**: Sum(PORTFOLIOTRANS_YEAR.REVENUE)
> **Quarterly**: Sum(PORTFOLIOTRANS_QUARTER.REVENUE)
> **Monthly**: Sum(PORTFOLIOTRANS_MONTH.REVENUE)
> **Daily**: Sum (PORTFOLIOTRANSACTIONS.PRICE * PORTFOLIOTRANSACTIONS.NUM_SHARES) * (-1)

These formulas are listed in the desired order for consideration. For example, we would like the Yearly formula to be considered first, because its Aggregation table contains fewer rows than the other tables being considered. We tell Business Objects that it has multiple choices of formulas with the @Aggregate_Aware function, which takes formulas for arguments. I believe that there is no reasonable limit on the number of formulas that it can take as arguments.

Exercise: Use the @Aggregate_Aware function

1. Double-click on Revenue in Portfolio Transactions.
2. Click the >> button to open the Edit Select dialog.
3. Modify the Revenue formula to the formula shown in the Graphic.
4. Repeat for Num Transactions and Num Shares.

Notes

Aggregate Navigation (Solution #2)

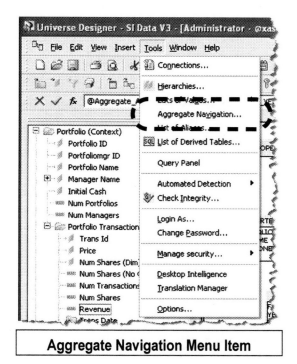

Aggregate Navigation Menu Item

Aggregate Navigation Dialog

Aggregate Navigation Dialog

Aggregate Navigation allows you to set up alternate aggregate tables.
Check the objects and/or conditions to be defined as incompatible with the selected table.

Universe Tables:
- COMPANY
- DOW_30
- EQUITYPRICES
- INDUSTRY
- LAST_TRADE_DATE
- PORTFOLIO
- PORTFOLIOMGR
- PORTFOLIOTRANSACTIONS
- PORTFOLIOTRANS_MONTH
- PORTFOLIOTRANS_QUARTER
- PORTFOLIOTRANS_YEAR
- SIDATE
- SIPROPERTIES
- SIPROPERTIES_BUYSELL
- SIPROPERTIES_RISK

Associated Incompatible Objects:
- Portfolio (Context)
- Equity Prices (Context)
- Company (Common)
- Dates (Common)
  - ☑ Trans Date
  - ☐ Year Num
  - ☑ Fis Year
  - ☑ Quarter Num
  - ☑ Fis Qtr
  - ☑ Month Num
  - ☑ Fis Period
  - ☑ Month Name
  - ☑ Day Name
  - ☐ First Of Year
  - ☐ End Of Year
  - ☐ Days In Year
  - ☑ Days Into Year
  - ☐ Workdays In Year
  - ☑ Workdays Into Year
  - ☑ Fis First Of Year
  - ☑ Fis End Of Year
  - ☑ Days In Fis Year
  - ☑ Days Into Fis Year
  - ☑ Workdays In Fis Year
  - ☑ Workdays Into Fis Year
  - ☑ First Of Qtr
  - ☑ End Of Qtr
  - ☑ Days In Qtr
  - ☑ Days Into Qtr
  - ☑ Workdays In Qtr
  - ☑ Workdays Into Qtr
  - ☑ Fis First Of Qtr
  - ☑ Fis End Of Qtr
  - ☑ Days In Fis Qtr
  - ☑ Days Into Fis Qtr
  - ☑ Workdays In Fis Qtr
  - ☑ Workdays Into Fis Qtr
  - ☑ First Of Month
  - ☑ Days In Month
  - ☑ Days Into Month
  - ☑ Workdays In Month

☐ With incompatibles only   Incompatibles only ☐

Detect Incompatibility   OK   Cancel   Help

Aggregate Navigation (Solution #2)

Now that we told Business Objects that it has a choice of formulas to use, we must tell it how to choose. We want to tell it if a query contains a daily object, then it cannot use the Year, Quarter, or Month aggregation tables. If a query contains monthly objects, then Business Objects cannot use the Year or Quarter aggregation tables. If a query contains a Quarterly object, then Business Objects cannot use the Yearly aggregation table. If a query has a Yearly object, then Business Objects can use any of the aggregation tables, but should use the Yearly aggregation table.

We will do this with Aggregate Navigation. With Aggregate Navigation, we first select a table in the Universe Tables list in the Aggregate Navigation dialog. Then, we select objects in the Associated Incompatible Objects list that would cause formulas from the selected tables to be incorrect. For example, if we are looking at PORTFOLIOTRANS_YEARLY, then we don't want any objects that are a lower resolution than year, such as Quarter, Month, Week, or Day. This is why in the graphic that almost all of the objects are selected, because most of them are at a lower resolution than year.

Suppose that a query had a day resolution object, such as Full Date and Business Objects was considering the following measure formulas:

> Yearly: Sum(PORTFOLIOTRANS_YEAR.REVENUE)
> Quarterly: Sum(PORTFOLIOTRANS_QUARTER.REVENUE)
> Monthly: Sum(PORTFOLIOTRANS_MONTH.REVENUE)
> Daily: Sum (PORTFOLIOTRANSACTIONS.PRICE * PORTFOLIOTRANSACTIONS.NUM_SHARES) * (-1)

Business Objects would navigate in the following order: The Yearly Formula cannot be used, because Full Date is incompatible with PORTFOLIOTRANS_YEAR. The Quarterly Formula cannot be used, because Full Date is incompatible with PORTFOLIOTRANS_QUARTER. The Monthly Formula cannot be used, because Full Date is incompatible with PORTFOLIOTRANS_MONTH. The Daily Formula can be used, because Full Date is compatible with PORTFOLIOTRANSACTIONS, as PORTFOLIOTRANSACTIONS should have no incompatibilities.

Notes

Incompatibilities (Solution #2)

PORTFOLIOTRANS_MONTH

Full Date	Prev Fis Year Days In Qtr
Fis Year	Prev Fis Year Wdays In Qtr
Fis Qtr	Prev First Of Week
Fis Period	
Day Name	
Fis First Of Year	
Fis End Of Year	
Days In Fis Year	
Days Into Fis Year	
Workdays In Fis Year	
Workdays Into Fis Year	
Fis First Of Qtr	
Fis End Of Qtr	
Days In Fis Qtr	
Days Into Fis Qtr	
Workdays In Fis Qtr	
Workdays Into Fis Qtr	
First Of Week	
Days Into Week	
Rolling 90 Days	
Prev Year Full Date	
Prev Fis Year	
Prev Fis First Of Year	
Prev Fis End Of Year	
Days In Prev Fis Year	
Days Into Prev Fis Year	
Workdays In Prev Fis Year	
Workdays Into Prev Fis Year	
Prev Year First Of Fis Qtr	
Prev Year End Of Fis Qtr	
Py Fis Year Days In Qtr	
Py Fis Year Wdays In Qtr	
Prev First Of Fiscal Qtr	
Prev End Of Fiscal Qtr	
Prev Fis Year Days In Qtr	

PORTFOLIOTRANS_QUARTER (Compatible)

Year Num
Quarter Num
First Of Year
End Of Year
Days In Year
Days Into Year
Workdays In Year
Workdays Into Year
First Of Qtr
End Of Qtr
Days In Qtr
Workdays In Qtr
Prev Year
Prev First Of Year
Prev End Of Year
Days In Prev Year
Days Into Prev Year
Workdays In Prev Year
Workdays Into Prev Year
Prev Year First Of Qtr
Prev Year End Of Qtr
Prev Year Days In Qtr
Prev Year Wdays In Qtr
Prev First Of Qtr
Prev End Of Qtr
Prev Qtr Days In Qtr
Prev Qtr Wdays In Qtr

PORTFOLIOTRANSACTIONS
No Incompatibilities

PORTFOLIOTRANS_YEAR (Compatible)

Year Num
First Of Year
End Of Year
Days In Year
Workdays In Year
Prev Year
Prev First Of Year
Prev End Of Year
Days In Prev Year
Workdays In Prev Year

Year Num	Revenue

```
SELECT
  SIDATE.YEAR_NUM,
  Sum(PORTFOLIOTRANS_YEAR.REVENUE)
FROM
  SIDATE INNER JOIN PORTFOLIOTRANS_YEAR ON (SIDATE.FULL_DATE=PORTFOLIOTRANS_YEAR.YEAR_BEGIN_DATE)
GROUP BY
  SIDATE.YEAR_NUM
```

Month Num	Revenue

```
SELECT
  SIDATE.MONTH_NUM,
  Sum(PORTFOLIOTRANS_MONTH.REVENUE)
FROM
  SIDATE INNER JOIN PORTFOLIOTRANS_MONTH ON (SIDATE.FULL_DATE=PORTFOLIOTRANS_MONTH.MONTH_BEGIN_DATE)
GROUP BY
  SIDATE.MONTH_NUM
```

Full Date	Revenue

```
SELECT
  PORTFOLIOTRANSACTIONS.TRANS_DATE,
  Sum (PORTFOLIOTRANSACTIONS.PRICE * PORTFOLIOTRANSACTIONS.NUM_SHARES) * (-1)
FROM
  PORTFOLIOTRANSACTIONS
GROUP BY
  PORTFOLIOTRANSACTIONS.TRANS_DATE
```

Incompatibilities (Solution #2)

From the Graphic, we can see that any object that is at a lower level of resolution than the aggregate table is not compatible with the aggregate table. For example, if we examine the PORTFOLIOTRANS_QUARTER list of incompatibilities, then we would see that anything that quarters cannot add up to is incompatible. For example, Year would not be incompatible, because four quarters add up to a year. However, Month would be incompatible, because quarters do not add up to months.

We don't have to set Year incompatible with Month for the reason stated above. However, if the Year object is in a query, then we want the PORTFOLIOTRANS_YEAR formula to be used and not the PORTFOLIOTRANS_QUARTER formula. We are sure that it will not use the PORTFOLIOTRANS_QUARTER formula, because the PORTFOLIOTRANS_YEAR formula is listed first in the @Aggregate_Aware function. This means that PORTFOLIOTRANS_YEAR will be selected before PORTFOLIOTRANS_QUARTER has a chance to be considered. This is why we list the formulas from most summarized (or Desirable) to most detailed (or Less Desirable).

Notice the Queries and their resulting SQL in the graphic. The correct aggregate table is being used for each query. With really large tables aggregate awareness can dramatically speed up query times.

Exercise: Set the Aggregate Navigation

1. Select *Tools | Aggregate Navigation...* from the menu.
2. Select the PORTFOLIOTRANS_MONTH table in the Universe Tables list.
3. Check the objects listed in the graphic for this table.
4. Do the same for PORTFOLIOTRANS_QUARTER.
5. Select PORTFOLIOTRANS_YEAR.
6. Check any object that Years cannot add up to. Remember that Year and Fiscal Year are different, and therefore Year cannot add up to Fiscal Year.
   Also, remember to add the Trans Id, Price, Num Shares (Dim), and Num Shares (No Group By) objects from Portfolio Transactions.

Notes

Fact Table as a Look-up

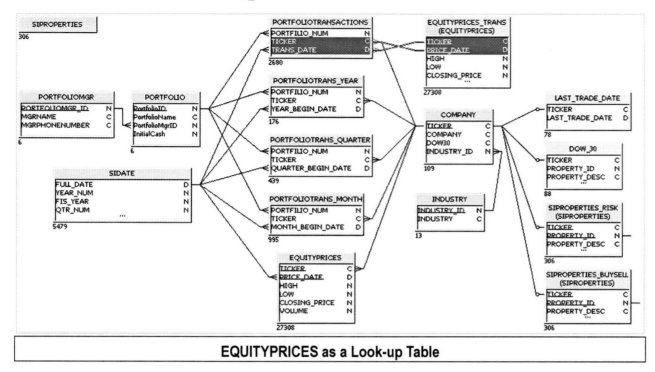

EQUITYPRICES as a Look-up Table

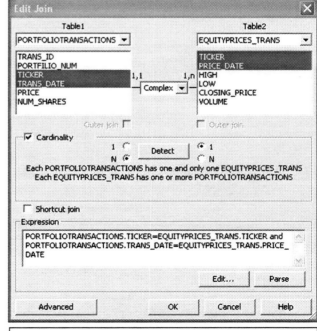

Edit Join Dialog

Join Expression
PORTFOLIOTRANSACTIONS.TICKER=EQUITYPRICES_TRANS.TICKER
AND
PORFLIOTRANSACTIONS.TRANS_DATE=EQUITYPRICES_TRANS.PRICE_DATE

Fact Table as a Look-up

In the previous chapter, we added the EQUITYPRICES table to our universe. We treated this table like a fact table, because it had transactions from each day and people wanted to analyze stock prices over time. But, what if people wanted to see the stock price information along with the trade transaction information? This will allow analysts to study the purchase price relative to the market price action on the day that the stock (equity) was purchased. This would mean treating EQUITYPRICES as a look-up table.

The primary key into EQUITYPRICES is Ticker and PriceDate. Every row in the table can be uniquely identified with these two keys. These two keys are also available in the PORTFOLIOTRANSACTIONS table. Therefore, we can join EQUITYPRICES to PORTFOLIOTRANSACTIONS through Ticker and PriceDate, which would be a 1-to-many cardinality. Therefore, no chasm or fan trap.

To join EQUITYPRICES, we first need to Alias it. In this example, we name the Alias, EQUITYPRICES_TRANS. The join expression is shown in the graphic, along with the join dialog. Notice that we created one join and And'ed the two equalities. It is best to create one join with all of the join logic, rather than dragging multiple fields to create multiple separate joins between two tables. After joining the tables, don't forget to add it to the *Companies that we Traded* context.

In this example, we are using an inner-join as opposed to an outer-join, because we are assuming that we only trade companies that we are tracking the prices of. This may be a dangerous assumption, because if we trade companies that are not in the EQUITYPRICES_TRANS table, then it could eliminate valid trades from a report.

Exercise: Join EQUITYPRICES to PORTFOLIOTRANSACTIONS

1. Alias EQUITYPRICES, name the alias: EQUITYPRICES_TRANS.
2. Join EQUITYPRICES_TRANS to PORTFOLIOTRANSACTIONS
    * Drag Ticker to Ticker, then double-click the resulting join.
    * Hold [Ctrl] and Click PRICE_DATE on the EQUITYPRICES side.
    * Hold [Ctrl] and Click TRANS_DATE in PortfolioTransactions.
      Notice that the Outer Join option is now disabled. It was to be an Outer Join, then you need to select that option before modifying the expression.
    * Click OK.

3. Add the new joins to the *Companies that we Traded* context.
    * Select *View | List Mode* from the menu.
    * Double-click on the *Companies that we Traded* context.
    * Select the new join in the Edit Context dialog
      It should be the last join in the list, since it was the last created.
    * Click OK.

Notes

Objects From Fact to Fact

Edit Properties Dialog for High

Daily Price Objects

Trans Id	Ticker	Price	High	Low	Closing Price
2	MO	25	25.31	24.63	24.88
3	MCD	31.5	32.44	31	31.5
4	AA	33.13	32.75	31.75	32.56
5	T	33.13	33.94	31.88	33.69
6	HON	36.5	36.63	35.63	35.81
7	CAT	36.63	36.63	35.88	35.94
8	IP	36.5	36.75	35.81	36.31
9	DIS	37.63	37.69	36.25	37.13

Report Table with Transacin Price and Market Price

Objects From Fact to Fact

Once the EQUITYPRICES_TRANS table is joined in, we need to create the daily price objects. Since the EQUITYPRICES_TRANS table is joined to PORTFOLIOTRANSACTIONS, we need to place the new objects within the Portfolio Transactions class, as these objects will be incompatible with the aggregated transaction tables. We will do this by creating a subclass within Portfolio Transactions. We may not need the subclass, but it may help developers realize that these are special objects that may need extra consideration.

Since these new objects are not compatible with the Aggregation tables, we must add them to the Aggregate Navigation list of incompatible objects for these tables. If we forget to do this, then any report that contains these measures and one of the aggregate aware measures, may try to use the PORTFOLIOTRANS_YEAR table, since it is the first to be considered. This will cause an incompatible object error.

In this example, we are going to create a High Closing Price and a Low Closing Price. However, we are using EQUITYPRICES_TRANS at a daily resolution, since it is joined to PORTFOLIOTRANSACTIONS. This means that we may not need both a high and a low, because they will be equal most of the time. Many Designers will just use either the max or the min and call it Closing Price. The danger with this is that Report Developers may use the table to create reports with a greater resolution than day, and this would cause the Closing Price to span more than one day, which would show either the minimum or the maximum closing price for the time range. I think that if an aggregate is to be used in an object's definition, than the aggregate should be reflected in the object's name. This will eliminate confusion and allow report developers to avoid studying the SQL to determine an object's behavior.

Exercise: Create Daily Price Objects

1. Create the Daily Transactions Subclass within Portfolio Transactions.
   • Right-click on Portfolio Transactions class and select *Subclass...*
   • Name subclass Daily Price and Volume
2. Drag High, Low, Closing_Price, and Volume to Daily Transactions.
3. Double-click on High and change the formula to: Max(EQUITYPRICES_TRANS.HIGH).
4. Double-click on Low and change the formula to: Min(EQUITYPRICES_TRANS.LOW).
5. Double-click on Closing Price and
   • Name: High Closing Price
   • Formula: Max(EQUITYPRICES_TRANS.CLOSING_PRICE).
6. Make a copy of High Closing Price, then double-click on it
   • Name: Low Closing Price
   • Formula: Min(EQUITYPRICES_TRANS.CLOSING_PRICE).
7. Double-click on Volume and change the formula to: Sum(EQUITYPRICES_TRANS.VOLUME).

Notes

Add a Third Fact Table

SICALLS Context Definition

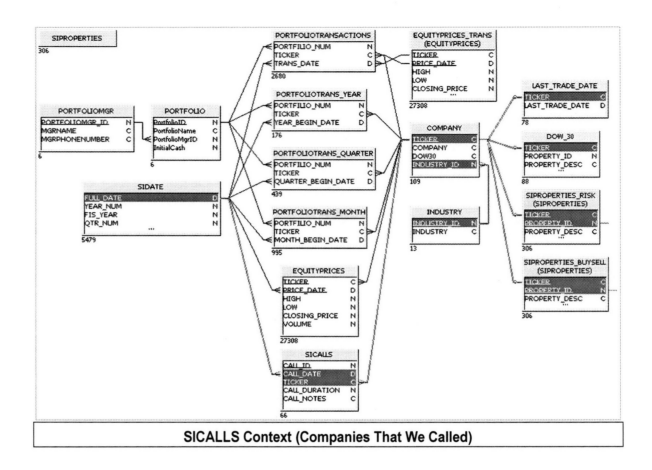

SICALLS Context (Companies That We Called)

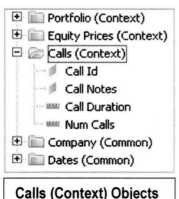

Calls (Context) Objects

Call Duration
Sum(SICALLS.CALL_DURATION)

Num Calls
Count(DISTINCT SICALLS.CALL_ID)

Add a Third Fact Table

Okay, now we will add just one more fact table to the universe. To do this, we insert the table via the Table Browser. After inserting the table, we then join it to the structure and define the join cardinalities. Next, we drag the table to the Universe (Classes and Objects) section to create the default objects. Next, we modify the default Call Duration dimension object to have the formula *Sum(SICALLS.Call_Duration)*, which will cause it to turn to a measure. We create another measure object called *Num Calls* and set its formula to *Count(Distinct SICALLS.CALL_ID)*. The last thing that we do is to create a new context to accommodate the addition of another fact table (Notice that the universe now has three loops). There you go, the addition of a fact table in less than ten minutes.

With this new fact table, we can query the dates that companies were called. We can also see the properties of the companies, so we'll know the effort applied to High Risk companies, DOW 30 companies, and Buy Sell Recommendation companies. With the Call Duration measure object, we'll know the number of minutes spent on each call or even the number of minutes made on calls each month of the year. There is a lot of great information that we can derive from our ten minute addition to our universe.

Exercise: Add the SICALLS Table

1. Insert the SIDate table
   - Select | *Insert* | *Tables...* | from the menu.
   - Locate the SICalls table in the list and drag it to the Structure.
2. Create the Joins
   - Drag the Call_Date field to the Full_Date field in SIDate.
   - Drag the Ticker field to the Ticker field in Company.
   - Set the cardinalities of these two joins.
3. Create the Companies That We Called Context
   - Select *View* | *List Mode* from the menu.
   - Click on the *Companies that we Priced* context.
   - Hold the [Ctrl] key and click the two joins off of EQUITYPRICES. Deselect these two joins.
   - Hold the [Ctrl] key and click the two joins off of SICALLS. Select these two joins.
   - Select | *Insert* | *Context...* | from the menu and name the context.

4. Create the default SICalls class and objects
   - Drag the SICalls table into the Universe (Classes and Objects) section to create the class and default dimension objects.
5. Create the Call Duration measure
   - Double-click on the Call Duration object.
   - Change the formula to: Sum (SICALLS.CALL_DURATION).
6. Create the Num Calls object
   - Copy CALL_ID and double-click on the copy.
   - Name: Num Calls.
   - Select: Count(DISTINCT SICALLS.CALL_ID).
7. Delete the default Ticker and Call Date dimension objects.

Notes

Fan Traps

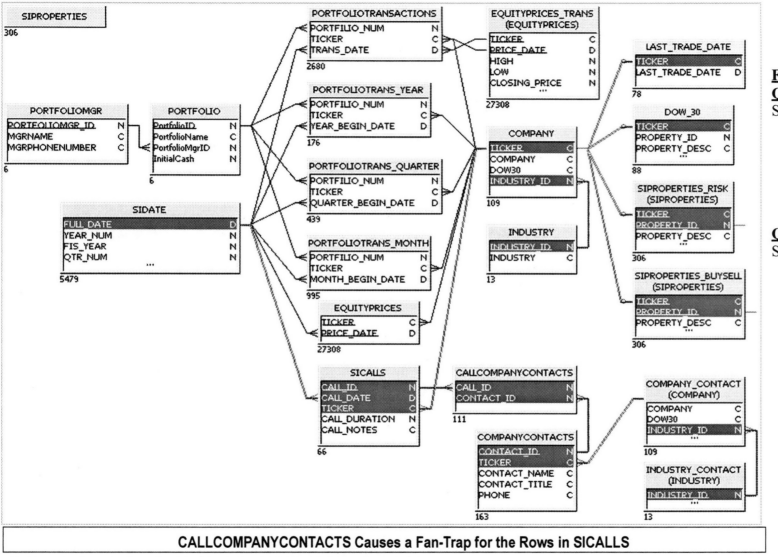

Fan-Trap

Query 1

Select Job, Count(Applicant)

Job 1	50
Job 2	50
Job 3	50
Total	150

Query 2

Select Count(Applicant)

Total	50

CALLCOMPANYCONTACTS Causes a Fan-Trap for the Rows in SICALLS

SICALLS.CALL_ID=CALLCOMPANYCONTACTS.CALL_ID
CALLCOMPANYCONTACTS.CONTACT_ID=COMPANYCONTAT.CONTACT_ID
COMPANYCONTACTS.TICKER=COMPANY_CONTACT.TICKER
COMPANY_CONTACT.INDUSTRY_ID=INDUSTRY_CONTACT.NUSTRY_ID

Fan Traps

I know you were wondering, why in the world did we add another fact table? While adding the SICalls table to the universe did add a great deal of valuable information to our universe, it did not add much in new universe design knowledge. This will change right now, because we are going to add a new table that will cause a *Fan-Trap*.

Remember that every table in a relationship diagram multiplies the rows in the other tables that are related to it. Usually, this multiplication is directional - multipliers of 1 or greater going away from the fact table and multipliers of 1 or 0 going back to the fact table, which can be seen by the arrows shooting away from the fact table. This means that a query should return no more rows than are in the fact table.

A Fan-Trap is created when a table joined to the universe multiplies the rows in the fact table. It does this by fanning the fact table's rows across a repeating key, in this case the key is CALL_ID. Notice that the CALLCOMPANYCONTACTS table now looks like the fact table, because it has only many joins associated with it. Business Objects cannot detect fan-traps, as it does Chasm-traps, because the offending join appears correct.

Here is an example of a fan-trap that I recently saw on a job. A customer was counting the number of people applying to jobs. The report developer created a query that had Job, Count(Applicants). They told me that 150 people were applying to 3 jobs. Okay, so 150 applicants. Later, I created a query on just applicant, Count(Applicant), and it returned only 50 applicants. So, how could they get 150, and I get only 50. Well, it turned out that there were 50 different applicants all applying to the same three jobs. The applicants were getting *Fanned* across the 3 jobs.

In our structure, the Fan-Trap is caused by the join CALLCOMPANYCONTACTS to SICALLS. Notice that the arrow is shooting back at the fact table. This means there could be more than one contact on a phone call, such as a conference call. These multiple contacts will fan the call duration.

Exercise: Add the CallCompanyContacts tables to the Universe Structure

1. Insert the CallCompanyContacts tables
   • Select | *Insert | Tables...* | from the menu.
   • Insert CALLCOMPANYCONTACTS and COMPANYCONTACTS.
2. Alias COMPANY and INDUSTRY
   • Call them COMPANY_CONTACT and INDUSTRY_CONTACT.

3. Join the four tables, then join CALLCOMPANYCONTACTS to the SICalls table.
   • Join Expressions are shown in the graphic.
4. Set the Cardinalities for the Joins, as shown in the graphic.
5. Add the new join to the Calls context.
6. Double-click on the Companies tha we Called context and select the new joins (Probably the last four in the list).

Notes

Fan Trap Ramifications

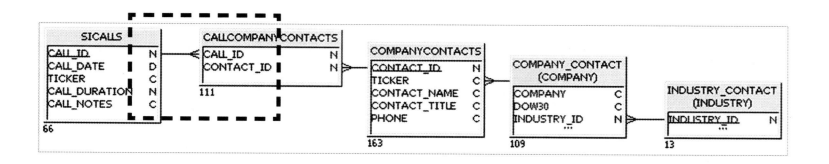

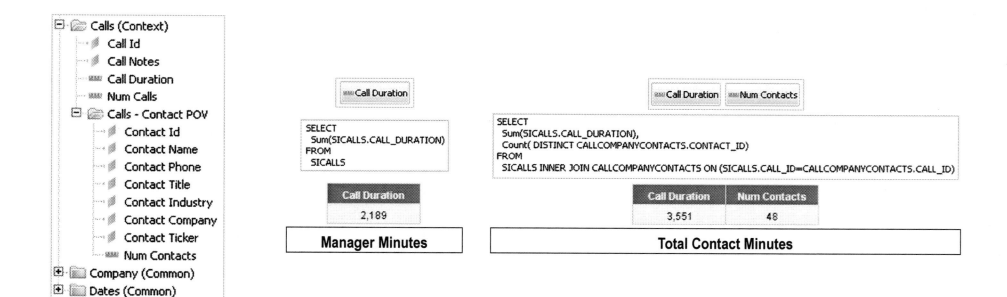

Fan Trap Ramifications

If you were to build a universe with just the tables shown in the graphic, and then, select *Tools | Automated Detection | Detect Contexts...* from the menu, then Business Objects would show a dialog stating that no new contexts are needed. This means that Business Objects doesn't realize that there is a Fan-Trap in the relationship. Remember, when we had a Chasm-Trap, Business Objects did suggest a context to fix the chasm-trap. Both fan-traps and chasm-traps multiply the rows in the tables that are involved in the relationship. However, fan-traps are more sneakier than chasm-traps, because everything appears to be fine.

Sometimes, fan-traps are not a problem and other times they are a problem. We may not care if there is a fan-trap, if there are no measures involved, because Business Objects will only display unique combinations of Dimensions and Details. Also, we can simply do Select Distinct queries and all will be fine. However, if there are measures, then the results of these measures will be multiplied by the number of times that the row gets fanned, as in our job applicant example.

So, is our fan-trap bad? Well, we do have a measure involved - Call Duration. And, Call Duration is fanned across the contacts on a call. However, this is a healthy fan, because the result is not really incorrect. Without the fan, we get to see how many minutes the managers were on the phone, which was 2189 minutes. With the fan, we get to see how many minutes of contact exposure the manager had, which was 3,551 minutes. For example, I usually do virtual classroom training, where I am on the phone for 8 hours. If there are 10 students on the conference call and all students came from the same company, then the company had 80 hours of employee training (8 hours * 10 students). So the fan is not incorrect, it is just a different point of view. The error is when report developers assume that the manager minutes are the contact minutes or vice versa. This is similar to when the company counted 150 applicants when there were only 50.

Exercise: Add the CallCompanyContacts objects

1. Create the Calls - Contact POV subclass
   • Right-click on Calls (Context) and select *Subclass...*
   • Name the class: *Calls - Contact POV*
2. Add CONTACT_ID from CALLCOMPANYCONTACTS
3. Copy CONTACT_ID and create the Num Contacts measure.
4. Add CONTACT_NAME, CONTACT_TITLE, and PHONE from COMPANYCONTACTS.
5. Add COMPANY and TICKER from COMPANY_CONTACT.
6. Add INDUSTRY from INDUSTRY_CONTACT.

Notes

Multiple SQL Statements for Each Measure

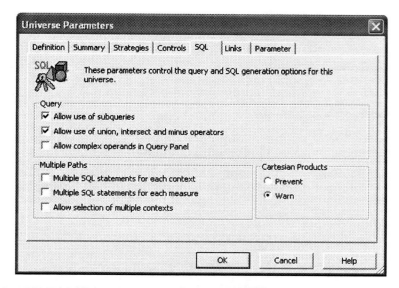

Call Duration	Num Calls	Num Contacts	Num Companies
3,551	66	48	25

```
SELECT
  Sum(SICALLS.CALL_DURATION),
  Count( Distinct SICALLS.CALL_ID),
  Count( DISTINCT CALLCOMPANYCONTACTS.CONTACT_ID),
  Count( DISTINCT COMPANY.TICKER)
FROM
  COMPANY INNER JOIN SICALLS ON (SICALLS.TICKER=COMPANY.TICKER)
    INNER JOIN CALLCOMPANYCONTACTS ON (SICALLS.CALL_ID=CALLCOMPANYCONTACTS.CALL_ID)
```

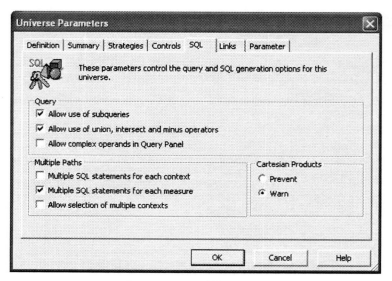

Call Duration	Num Calls	Num Contacts	Num Companies
2,189	66	48	109

Synchronization
- Select 1
- Select 2
- Select 3

```
SELECT
  Sum(SICALLS.CALL_DURATION),
  Count( Distinct SICALLS.CALL_ID)
FROM
  SICALLS
```

Synchronization
- Select 1
- Select 2
- Select 3

```
SELECT
  Count( DISTINCT CALLCOMPANYCONTACTS.CONTACT_ID)
FROM
  CALLCOMPANYCONTACTS
```

Synchronization
- Select 1
- Select 2
- Select 3

```
SELECT
  Count( DISTINCT COMPANY.TICKER)
FROM
  COMPANY
```

Multiple SQL Statements for Each Measure (Revisited)

The reports in the center of the graphic were both created from the query in the upper-right corner. When the Multiple SQL Statements for each Measure option is not checked, a single query that joins all of the tables involved will be created to return the data set. This will force the relationships to behave as they were designed to do, which means that we had 3,551 minutes of contact time, 66 Calls, talked 48 Contacts, and called 25 different companies.

When the option is checked, Business Objects may create a separate query for each measure's respective table. In this example, this means three queries - Call Duration and Num Calls from SICalls, Num Contacts from CALLCOMPANYCONTACTS, and Num Companies from COMPANY. Since each measure is queried from its own table, then all relationships are ignored and the effects of any joins are removed. This means that the query is placed solely on the table. So, there are a total of 2,189 minutes and 66 Distinct Calls in the SICall table, 48 Distinct Contacts in the CALLCOMPANYCONTACTS table, and 109 Companies in the COMPANY table.

Some people use this option to fix their fan-trap, but only part of it, and this option introduces new errors. For example, we only called 25 companies, not 109. 109, is the total companies in the COMPANY table. Also, depending on which other objects are included in the query, these numbers can change. Therefore, in my opinion, it is best not to check this option and to rely on the SQL that we have become so familiar with.

Exercise: If you have a Reporting Tool Create the Query With and Without the Option

1. Clear the *Multiple SQL Statements for Each Measure* Option and save the universe.
2. Select | Tools | Desktop Intelligence | from the menu.
3. Create a query with Call Duration, Num Calls, Num Contacts, and Num Companies.
4. Click the *SQL* button in the Query Panel and observe the SQL statement.
5. Run the query.
6. Return to Designer and set the *Multiple SQL Statements for Each Measure* Option and save the universe.
7. Repeat steps 2 through 5 above.

Notes

Database Delegation and Fan Traps

Call Id	Contact Id	Call Duration
2	1	15
2	2	15
3	1	31
3	2	31
4	1	60
5	1	23
5	2	23
64	112	40
65	112	45
66	111	6
67	111	41
67	112	41
68	115	18
		#TOREFRESH

Delegation Duration Total

Call Id	Contact Id	Call Duration
64	112	40
65	112	45
66	111	6
67	111	41
67	112	41
68	115	18
		2,189

Total Independent of Fan

Call Id	Contact Id	Call Duration
2	1	15
2	2	15
3	1	31
3	2	31
4	1	60
5	1	23
5	2	23
64	112	40
65	112	45
66	111	6
67	111	41
67	112	41
68	115	18
		3,551

Fanned Total

```
SELECT
  0 AS GID,
  NULL,
  NULL,
  Sum(SICALLS.CALL_DURATION)
FROM
  SICALLS
UNION
  SELECT
  1 AS GID,
  SICALLS.CALL_ID,
  CALLCOMPANYCONTACTS.CONTACT_ID,
  Sum(SICALLS.CALL_DURATION)
FROM
  SICALLS INNER JOIN CALLCOMPANYCONTACTS ON (SICALLS.CALL_ID=CALLCOMPANYCONTACTS.CALL_ID)
GROUP BY
  SICALLS.CALL_ID,
  CALLCOMPANYCONTACTS.CONTACT_ID
```

Database Delegation and Fan Traps

Sometimes, the fanned total is never important. Okay, maybe not never, but almost never important. For example, I worked in an investment bank for a while. In this bank they had different departments, such as Media and Technology. These departments represented companies within these industries. So, if the bank did a deal with AMD, then the technology department would get credit for the revenues. The bank was set up this way, so that departments would not go outside their industry to make deals, as all industry specific deals would go to its respective department.

Okay, then what happens if Microsoft makes a deal with the bank that generates $1,000,000 for the bank? Microsoft is both a Technology company and a Media company. Therefore, both the Media and Technology claim the $1,000,000. In a report listing the departments and their revenues, it would appear to be $2,000,000 if the fan was totaled. To avoid this fanned total, the Database Delegated aggregation function can be chosen on the Properties tab of the Revenue measure.

In our universe, if we set Call Duration to Database Delegation, then when we totaled the durations, we would get 2,189, even we summed across the fan, as shown in the graphic. This shows that the database delegation projection can be used with almost any aggregate function and not just averages and counts. In our Microsoft example, the total would be $1,000,000.

One note here, many people expect the total of a column to equal the total of each row in the column. So, when they expect 3,551, and they get 2,189, then we should label the total appropriately. We are also expecting the report designers to realize that the total won't necessarily equal the sum of the row values, which may be confusing to some. I normally just sum across the fan, then make a new query independent of the fan for the non-fanned total. Then, I show both totals. In the Microsoft example, this would be: $2,000,000 (Shared Revenue Total), $1,000,000 (Total Bank Revenue).

Notice that I included the SQL to show you how database delegation works. There are two SQL statements Unioned together. The second SQL statement, is the default created by the objects in the query. It has a GID of 1 and contains the fan object (CONTACT_ID). The first query was created to accommodate a context change for the delegated measure, which happened when we totaled the Call Durations. The new context is independent of Call ID and Contact ID. Its GID is 0. So Call Duration is involved in two different contexts: GID: 0 and GID: 1. The query is created when the context is added, but will not be refreshed until the document is refreshed. This is why the #TOREFRESH place holder is in the total cell on the report.

Notes

Invoice Type Fan Traps

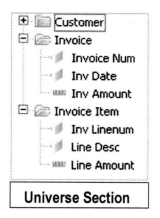

Universe Section

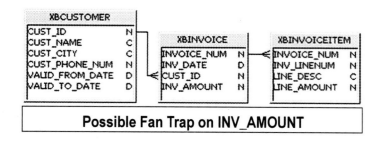

Possible Fan Trap on INV_AMOUNT

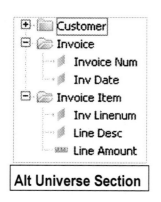

Alt Universe Section

Invoice Num	Inv Date	Inv Amount
101	9/25/06	500
102	9/25/06	1,000
103	9/26/06	2,000
104	9/27/06	2,500
	Sum:	6,000

Invoice Num	Inv Date	Inv Amount

No Fan

Invoice Num	Inv Linenum	Line Desc	Line Amount
101	1	Paintballs	300
101	2	Pads	200
102	1	Fast Marker	500
102	2	Paintballs	300
102	3	Hopper	200
103	1	Accurate Marker	1,000
103	2	Faser Barrel	500
103	3	E Hopper	500
104	1	Best Marker	1,500
104	2	Best Paintballs	500
104	3	Googles	500
		Sum:	6,000

Invoice Num	Inv Linenum	Line Desc	Line Amount

No Fan

Invoice Num	Inv Linenum	Line Desc	Inv Amount
101	1	Paintballs	500
101	2	Pads	500
102	1	Fast Marker	1,000
102	2	Paintballs	1,000
102	3	Hopper	1,000
103	1	Accurate Marker	2,000
103	2	Faser Barrel	2,000
103	3	E Hopper	2,000
104	1	Best Marker	2,500
104	2	Best Paintballs	2,500
104	3	Googles	2,500
		Sum:	17,500

Invoice Num	Inv Linenum	Line Desc	Inv Amount

Fans Inv Amount Across Linenum

Invoice Type Fan Traps

The fan-trap in the previous example was created by two different Points of View (POV) - Manager minutes and Contact minutes. These POV's made both totals legitimate. In this example, the fan-trap is more destructive, because the fan creates an inaccurate total by fanning a summary amount across detail rows. In the graphic, the two reports on the left are correct, because one totals summary amounts with summary information (Invoice), and the other sums detail amounts with detail information (Invoice Line Numbers). The table on the right is incorrect, because it sums summary amounts (Invoice) across details rows (Invoice Line Numbers).

The automatic context detection utility would report that no contexts are needed, because the cardinalities do not show cause for concern. However, if you look at the data in the XBINVOICE, then you will notice that there is an amount (INV_AMOUNT) stored in the table. This means that INV_AMOUNT will be multiplied by the many side of the join between the two tables, and thus the fan-trap is formed.

One solution to this problem is to not make a measure on INV_AMOUNT, and always use the LINE_AMOUNT stored in XBINVOICEITEM. This would get rid of the fan-trap and all reports will be accurate, if the details do add up to the invoice amount. However, this will make summary reports less efficient, because they would have to sum detail information to arrive at the summary information.

Another solution would be to leave both measures in the universe and simply tell all report developers to use the detail measure for detail reports and to use the summary measure for summary reports. If we relied on this solution, then we will have a bunch of confused report developers and business people, because there is no way to enforce that developers are actually adhering to the rule.

Exercise: Create a Universe with XBCustomer, XBINVOICE, and XBINVOICEITEM

1. Select *File | New...* from the menu.
2. Name the universe XBInvoice, select the SI Data V3 connection.
3. Click OK to create the universe.
4. Select *Insert | Tables...* from the menu.
5. Insert XBCUSTOMER, XBINVOICE, and XBINVOICEITEM.
6. Join the three tables, as shown in the graphic.
7. Set the cardinalities, as shown in the graphic.
8. Drag each of the tables into the Universe section to create classes.

9. Xbinvoice class
   - Rename class to Invoice
   - Delete Cust Id
   - Inv Amount formula: Sum(XBINVOICE.INV_AMOUNT).
10. Xbinvoiceitem class
    - Rename class to Invoice Item
    - Line Amount formula: Sum(XBINVOICEITEM.LINE_AMOUNT).

Notes

Aggregate Aware Solution

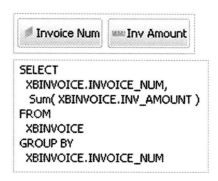

```
SELECT
  XBINVOICE.INVOICE_NUM,
  Sum( XBINVOICE.INV_AMOUNT )
FROM
  XBINVOICE
GROUP BY
  XBINVOICE.INVOICE_NUM
```

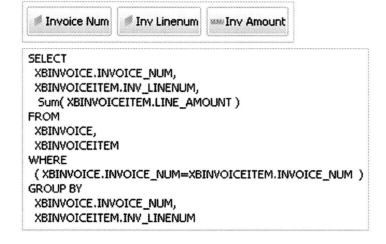

```
SELECT
  XBINVOICE.INVOICE_NUM,
  XBINVOICEITEM.INV_LINENUM,
  Sum( XBINVOICEITEM.LINE_AMOUNT )
FROM
  XBINVOICE,
  XBINVOICEITEM
WHERE
  ( XBINVOICE.INVOICE_NUM=XBINVOICEITEM.INVOICE_NUM )
GROUP BY
  XBINVOICE.INVOICE_NUM,
  XBINVOICEITEM.INV_LINENUM
```

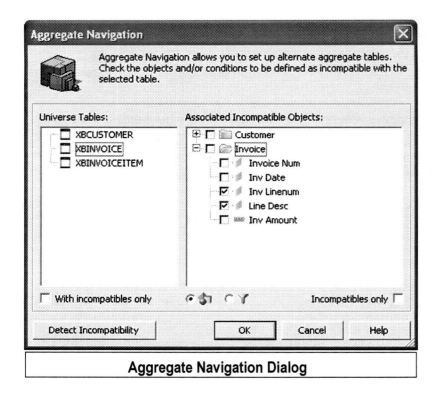

Aggregate Navigation Dialog

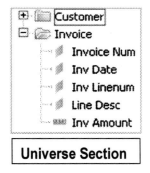

Universe Section

(Inv Amount)

@Aggregate_Aware(Sum(XBINVOICE.INV_AMOUNT), Sum(XBINVOICEITEM.LINE_AMOUNT))

Aggregate Aware Solution

In the previous example, we left it up to the query designer to choose the correct measure for the query resolution. This does leave some room for error, but most query designers will know which measure to use and how to use them. That being said, what if we wanted to guarantee that the query designer will never pick the incorrect measure? We could guarantee this with *Aggregate Awareness*.

Aggregate awareness allows us, the Universe Designer, to decide which aggregate formulas should be used in queries constructed from our universe. Or, really, which measures formulas are incompatible with the detail tables. In this example, we have two levels of aggregation - the invoice level and the invoice line item level. The invoice level calculation is incompatible with the line item objects, because the line item table is a multiplier for it.

To instruct Business Objects to realize that there is more than one formula available, we use the @Aggregate_Aware function. This function allows us to list all of the formulas as arguments. These formula arguments should be listed from most summarized to most detailed. In this example, the first argument is the invoice level formula, and then the line item level.

The next step is to define the objects that are incompatible with the summary tables. In this case the summary table is Invoice and the detail objects are Inv Linenum and Line Desc. If either of these two objects is used in a query with Inv Amount, then the summary formula cannot be used. If the summary formula cannot be used, then next formula in the @Aggregate_Aware formula will be used - Sum(XBINVOICEITEM.LINE_AMOUNT). This is called Aggregate Navigation.

Exercise: Create Aggregate Awareness in Paintball Invoice Universe

1. Create @Aggregate_Aware Measure Object
   - Double-click on Inv Amount and change its Select statement to
   - @Aggregate_Aware(Sum(XBINVOICE.INV_AMOUNT), Sum(XBINVOICEITEM.LINE_AMOUNT))
2. Move Inv Linenum and Line Desc from the XB Invoice Item class to the XB Invoice class.
3. Delete the XB Invoice Item class and the objects in it.

4. Define Aggregate Navigation
   - Select | Tools | Aggregate Navigation... | from the menu.
   - Click on the XBInvoice table in the Universe Tables list.
   - Open the XB Invoice class and check Inv Linenum and Line Desc.
   - Click OK.

Notes

Universe Heirarchies

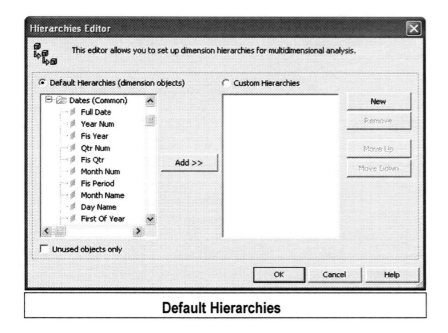

Default Hierarchies

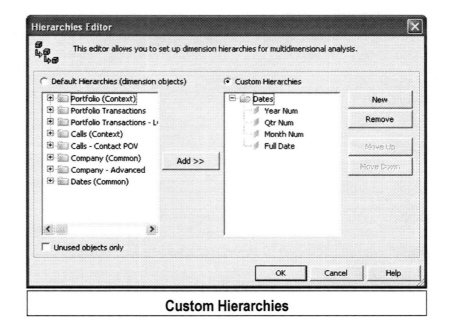

Custom Hierarchies

Universe Hierarchies

Many of the applications that use Business Objects' Universes to build queries allow people to drill down object hierarchies. This means that if they drill into a year object, then the column may be replaced by the quarter object. This drilling allows people to view summary reports and then, when interested, they can drill down into more detailed levels. This is one of the great advantages of Business Objects' applications.

By default, every dimension object in a class forms a hierarchy. This is not a very good idea, unless you have organized your universe in such a way that every object in every class goes from most general to most specific (detailed). I could not imagine anybody doing this, but I am sure that someone, somewhere has done just this. In our case, we will not do this. We will simply select *Tools | Hierarchies...* from the menu and use the Hierarchy Editor to define custom hierarchies for our universe.

The Hierarchies Editor allows us to create new custom hierarchies from the dimension objects in our universe. In our case, we can make a date hierarchy that drills through the date objects - Year Num, Quarter Num, Month Num, and Full Date. Notice that it goes from most general to most detail.

Exercise: Create a Custom Hierarchy

1. Select | *Tools | Hierarchies...* | from the menu.
2. Select the *Custom Hierarchies* option.
3. Click the *New* button and name the new hierarchy *Dates*.
4. Open the Dates (Common) class in the Default Hierarchies list.
5. Double-click on Year Num, Quarter Num, Month Num, and Full Date. This will move the objects into the new Dates hierarchy in the same order as they were double-clicked.
6. Click the *OK* button to accept the new hierarchy.

Notes

Chapter Summary

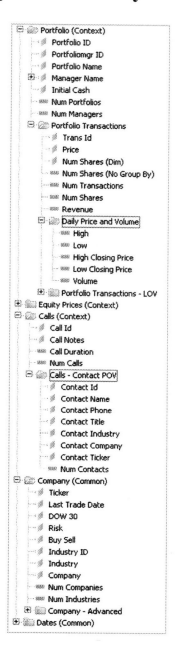

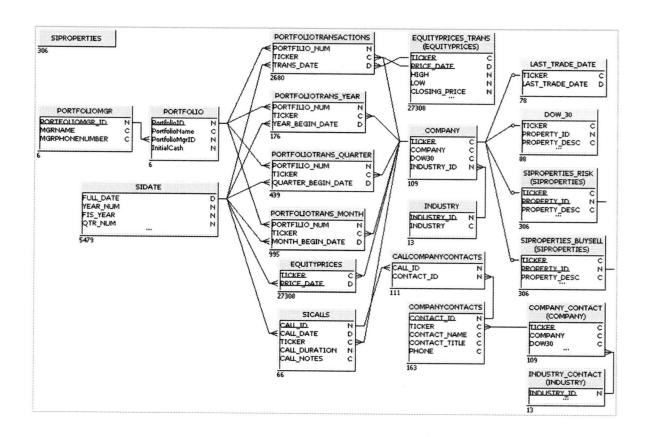

Chapter Summary

This chapter introduced us to the Fan Trap and how it can affect the results of our queries. We learned that these traps can be solved on the Report or the Designer level. We also learned that we may not be able to prevent some fan traps from delivering skewed results. We thought about making the measure in the summary table, in our case Invoice, a dimension. This will prevent it from being multiplied when columns are deleted from a table containing detail objects, such as removing invoice line number from a table.

We learned about Aggregate Awareness and how it could solve our fan trap problem. It did this by selecting the correct measure formula for the resolution of the dimensions in the query. For example, if invoice line number is in the query, then aggregate awareness will select the formula that uses the invoice item amount and not the formula that uses the invoice amount.

We also learned how to add Aggregated tables to our universe. The example shown in this chapter is not the only way to add aggregated tables, and for another solution, you can open the eFashion universe that ships with the Business Objects application. This solution uses aggregated tables that are not related to the existing dimension tables in the universe. Therefore, there are three discrete sets of tables that the Aggregate Navigation navigates.

In addition, we turned our EQUTIYPRICES fact table into a look-up table. This cannot always be done with fact tables, and some will even argue that EQUITYPRICES is not a fact table at all. However, it is interesting to see that we can use the table in two different ways in our universe, and hopefully, the example will help you decide on how to use similar tables in your universes.

We discussed Hierarchies in the universe and found out that if we do not define any, then Business Objects will assume that every class contains a hierarchy. This is probably unacceptable in most cases. So, we discussed how to create Custom Hierarchies.

Notes

Chapter 6: Additional Topics

This is the final chapter of the course. Here, we will learn a few more tricks and how to print our universe definitions. We will start with creating custom list of values for objects in our universe. These lists of values will make it easier for people to locate values in the list. I have noticed that one of the most popular complaints about Business Objects is that people cannot find the values in the lists quick enough. If we solve this problem, then we have made a large step towards making our clients satisfied.

Next, we will talk about hiding objects in the universe. Then, another join topic, where we are going to discuss how to join tables to dimension tables that have valid date ranges. In today's demanding world, many dimension tables have such ranges.

Lastly, we are going to discuss how to print the universe definitions. We will find out that we can customize the printing so we can print only the aspects that we are interested in.

Universe Parameters

Definition
Name:	SI Equity - Designer Course
Description:	Connection to SIData on SIMother. Used in the Designer class.
Connection:	SIEQUITY_XI

General information
Created:	9/19/2006 by bo_service
Modified:	10/6/2006 by bo_service
Comments:	

Statistics:	10 Classes
	40 Objects
	10 Tables
	3 Aliases
	13 Joins
	3 Contexts
	1 Hierarchies
	5 Conditions

Strategies
Join strategy:	Edit Manually (none)
Table strategy:	(Built-in) Standard
Object strategy:	(Built-in) Standard Renaming

Controls
Limit size of result set to:	unchecked
Limit size of long text objects to:	1000 characters
Limit execution time to:	unchecked
Warn if cost estimate exceeds:	unchecked

SQL parameters
Query
Allow use of subqueries:	yes
Allow use of union, intersect and minus operators:	yes
Allow complex conditions in Query Panel:	yes
Cartesian products:	prevent

Multiple paths
Generate several SQL statements for each context:	yes
Generate several SQL statements for each measure:	yes
Allow selection of multiple contexts:	no

Links

SI Company - Designer Course

List of Values

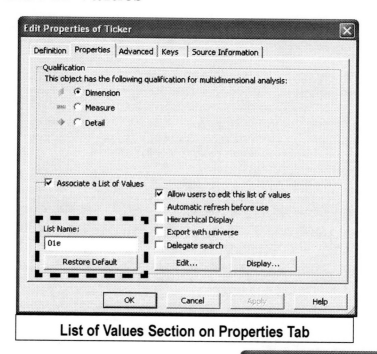

List of Values Section on Properties Tab

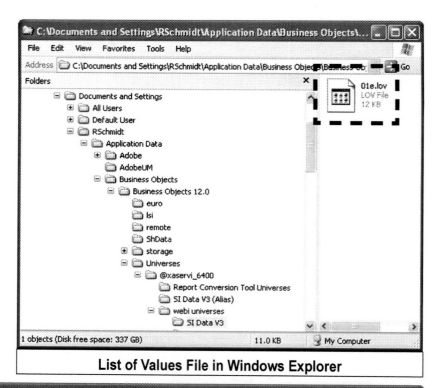

List of Values File in Windows Explorer

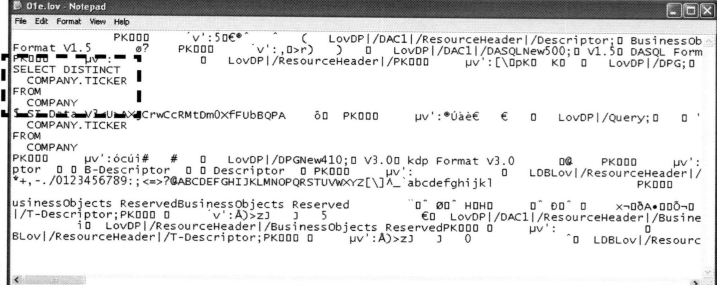

Encrypted List of Values File

List of Values

When we use the @Prompt function, we can allow report refreshers to select a value from a list of values. The *List of Values* is the third argument in the @Prompt function. When we made the List of Values assignment, we simply identified an object through the class\object identifier, such as 'Dates (Common)\Full Date'. Now we will discuss what the list of values is and why we referred to it with this syntax.

Every object can have a list of values associated with it, although it really only makes sense for non-aggregated objects. This means that by default every Dimension and Detail will have a list of values associated with it. Then when report developers create conditions, they can refer to the list to place values in the operands of their conditions. The default SQL for a list is simply a Select Distinct statement, which can be seen in the graphic.

Business Objects creates a file for every List of Values that has been used on a machine. This means that if the List of Values was viewed, then there will be a file on the hard drive of the machine. For Web Intelligence, this will be on the server, since reports are executed on the server. Web Intelligence Rich Client, will create the files locally. The LOV (List of Values) file contains the SQL definition of the list and the values from the previous refresh. The values are encrypted, as shown in the graphic. By default, LOV's will only refresh automatically the first time they are used, then each additional use will just read the values from the file. This is why LOV's display quicker after the first viewing.

On the Properties tab, there is a *List Name* field. This field contains the default name of the LOV, which is also the internal ID of the object. This why it is best not to delete existing objects. Notice that the name of the file in the graphic is the same as the name on the Properties tab.

Since the LOV file contains the SQL definition of the LOV values, we can modify this definition to create custom lists. We can do this on two levels: Locally and Enterprise wide. If we do it locally, then only the local applications Desktop Intelligence and Web Intelligence Rich Client can take advantage of the lists. If we want to use the list Enterprise wide or with Web Intelligence thin client, then we will have to export the List of Values with the universe, which is also an option on the Properties tab.

Exported lists take up storage in the repository, and in earlier versions, sometimes even the entire document domain. For this reason, we don't make custom lists for every object and then export them with the universe. If you do require many LOV's then you can purge them of data and export only the definition. I will show how to do this later.

Notes

Editing Lists of Values

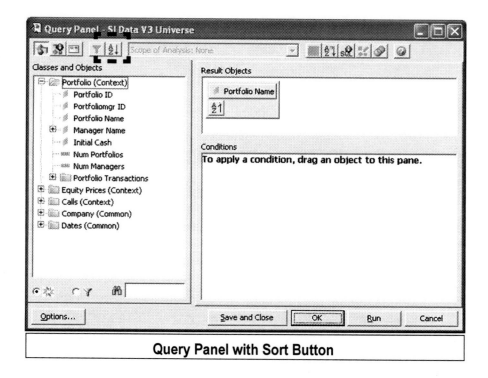

Query Panel with Sort Button

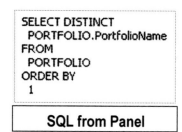

```
SELECT DISTINCT
  PORTFOLIO.PortfolioName
FROM
  PORTFOLIO
ORDER BY
  1
```

SQL from Panel

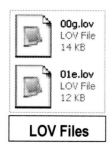

00g.lov
LOV File
14 KB

01e.lov
LOV File
12 KB

LOV Files

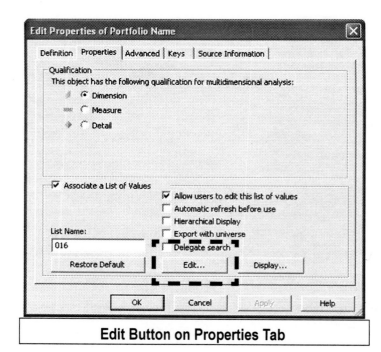

Edit Button on Properties Tab

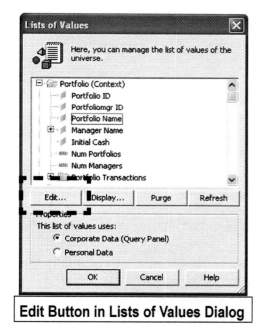

Edit Button in Lists of Values Dialog

Editing Lists of Values

Every Dimension and Detail object gets a basic default query for its List of Values, which is simply a Select Distinct... From... SQL statement. There is no sort, no conditions, or any other logic. This extra logic is left to us to implement.

We can edit a List of Values by clicking on the *Edit* button on the Properties tab, in the Edit Properties dialog for any object. We can also access all lists of values through the Lists of Values dialog, which is accessed by selecting *Tools | Lists of Values | Edit a List of Values...* from the menu.

Clicking the Edit button launches the Query Panel for the LOV. This is the same Query Panel that is available in Desktop Intelligence, so if you are familiar with that application, then this panel will be very familiar. It is also very similar to the Web Intelligence query panel. With this dialog, we can add objects and conditions to the query, we can sort and/or filter the list, and we can also place various query options, such as limiting the number of rows.

When you have finished modifying the query, you can press Run to save the List with values, or you can click OK or Save and Close to save the List without values. The later is the preferred method, if you are exporting the lists. A LOV file is usually about 12 KB with no data. The file 00g.lov, in the graphic, contains values, and its size is 14 KB.

Exercise: Sort the LOV for Portfolio Name

1. Select *Tools | Lists of Values | Edit a List of Values* from the menu.
2. Select the Portfolio Name object in the Portfolio (Context) class.
3. Click the *Edit* button to display the Query Panel for the object.
4. Click on the Portfolio Name object in the Result Objects section.
   - Click the *A-Z* button on the left side of the Query Panel toolbar. Notice that there is now a sort icon on the Portfolio Name object.
   - Click the *Run* button.
5. Click OK to exit the Lists of Values dialog.

SELECT DISTINCT
  PORTFOLIO.PortfolioName
FROM
  PORTFOLIO
ORDER BY
  1

Notes

List of Values Options

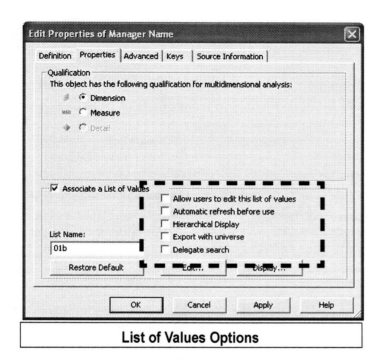

List of Values Options

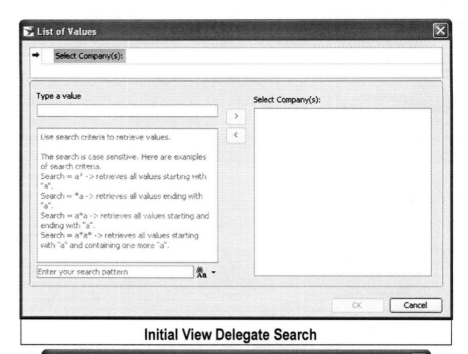

Initial View Delegate Search

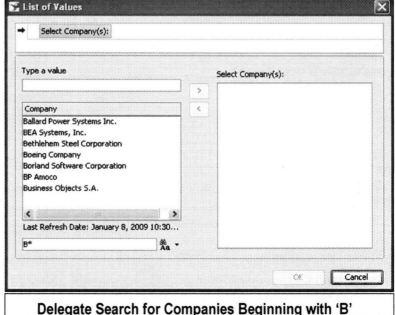

Delegate Search for Companies Beginning with 'B'

Allow Users to Edit This List of Values
Report Developers and Viewers can modify the query.
Automatic Refresh Before Use
List of Values will run query before list is displayed
Hiearchical Display
Works with Cascading Lists of Values
Export with Universe
Makes the custom List of Values available to other Report Developers
Delegate Search
Allows only text values that match an entered pattern to be returned to the list

List of Values Options

Universe Designers can set various options on the List of Values for an object.

Allow Users to Edit this List of Values: Report developers can modify the list of values for their local reports. This only works with local applications, such as Web Intelligence Rich Client. This option is selected by default.

Automatic Refresh before Each Use: This will run the query before displaying the list of values. At first this seems like a good idea, but in practice it is not, because some queries may take a long time. In addition, many lists are static, such as states in the USA.

Hierarchical Display: This is used to organize objects into classes. We will discuss this option later in this chapter.

Export with Universe: When we modify a List of Values, an LOV file is created on our harddrive. This file is available only on the machine that it is created on. Only local applications, such as Universe Designer, Desktop Intelligence, and Web Intelligence Rich Client can access the file. If we want other people to use our custom lists, than we select the Export with Universe option, which will export the list of values with the universe and make it available to other applications, such as Web Intelligence thin client.

Delegate Search: This is a new XIV3 feature. It allows only text data that matches an entered pattern to be returned to the list of values. This helps report refreshers limit the amount of values in the list. The prompt dialogs for this option are shown in the graphic. The initial view of the dialog displays instructions on how to use the search, which is case sensitive. Delegate search is available only for text objects.

Notes

Hierarchical Display (Desktop Intelligence)

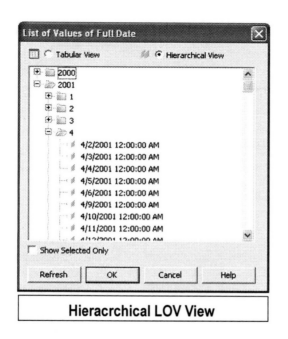

Hieracrhical LOV View

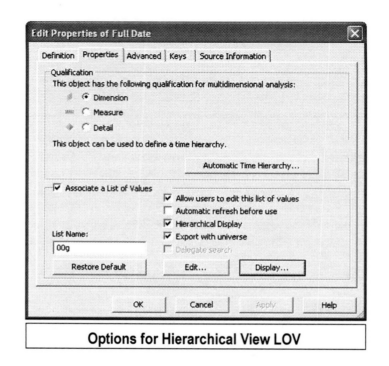

Options for Hierarchical View LOV

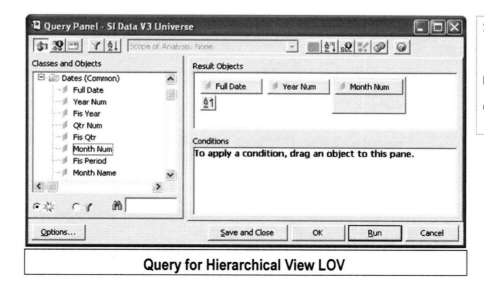

Query for Hierarchical View LOV

```
SELECT DISTINCT
  SIDATE.FULL_DATE,
  SIDATE.YEAR_NUM,
  SIDATE.MONTH_NUM
FROM
  SIDATE
ORDER BY
  1
```

Hierarchical Display (Desktop Intelligence)

The biggest complaint that I hear about Lists of Values is that the values are hard to find. In the previous example, we sorted the values to make it easier. Now, we are going to categorize the values in a hierarchical view. To create this type of view, all we need to do is add more objects to the LOV's query. The first object will always be the lowest level in the hierarchy. After the first object, the objects are arranged from most general to most detail. In the case of date, it may go Date, Year, and then Month, as shown in this example.

Hierarchies allow people to quickly traverse large amounts of values, because we can just hop category to category. This is especially important when there is no logical sort to the values.

After creating a hierarchical LOV, it is important to set the LOV options on the Properties tab for the object. The options Hierarchical View and Export with Universe should be selected.

- Hierarchical View will make sure that the values are displayed in a hierarchical fashion. If this option is not checked, then the values will presented as a tabular list, with the columns in the same order as the objects in the query for the LOV.
- Export with Universe causes the list to be exported with the universe. The list will be stored in the Document domain and available to the users of the universe.

Exercise: Create a Hierarchical List of Values

1. Locate the *Full Date* object, in the Universe section of the Designer, and double-click on it to display the Edit Properties dialog.
2. Click on the Properties tab to activate the tab.
3. Click the *Edit* button to display the Query Panel for the LOV.
4. Open the Date (Common) class in the Common folder of the Classes and Objects section.
5. Double-click on Year Num and Month Num.
   (Make sure that the order of objects in the Result Objects section is Full Date, Year Num, Month Name.)
6. Click on the Full Date object in the Result Objects section, and then click the A-Z button in the upper-left section of the dialog.
7. Click Run to execute the query.
8. Check the Hierarchical Display and Export with Universe options.
9. Click OK.

Notes

Cascading Lists of Values (Web Intelligence)

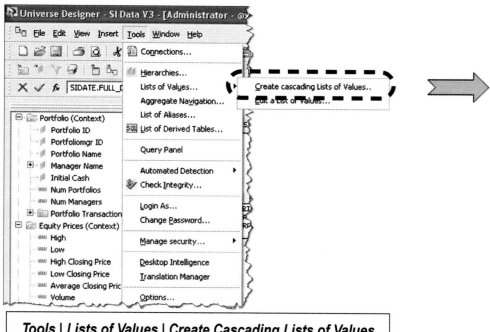

Tools | Lists of Values | Create Cascading Lists of Values

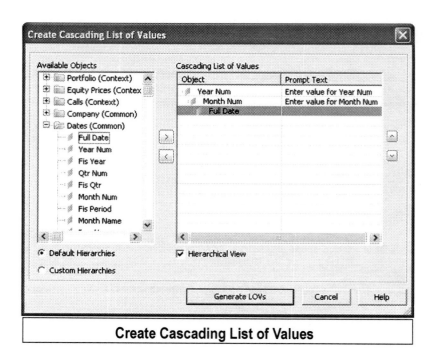

Create Cascading List of Values

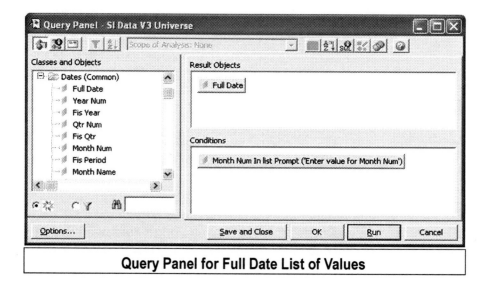

Query Panel for Full Date List of Values

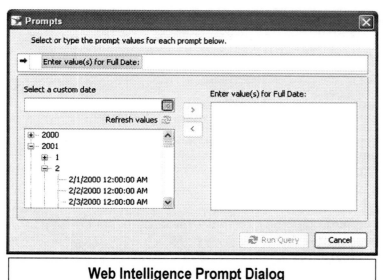

Web Intelligence Prompt Dialog

Cascading Lists of Values (Web Intelligence)

The Hierarchical view in Desktop Intelligence makes values in large lists much easier to locate. However, this technique will not work in Web Intelligence, where we must use Cascading Lists of Values to do the same thing. To create a cascading list of values, we select *Tools | Lists of Values | Create Cascading Lists of Values...* from the menu.

In the *Create Cascading Lists of Values* dialog, we create an object hierarchy by double-clicking on the Available (Dimension) Objects, which places the objects in the *Cascading List of Values* section. Once the hierarchy is defined, then click the *Generate LOV's* button to create the lists of values. Business Objects will create a list for each object in the hierarchy, except the last object. Each of the queries will be a select distinct on the object, plus a condition that prompts for the value of the later object in the list. For example, the Full Date LOV will prompt for Month Num, and Month Num will prompt for Year Num. This is why there is no need for the last object to have a LOV, because it needs no prompt. However, if the list is not sorted properly, then you will need to create a list of values for the last object and sort the values.

So what is the difference between the Desktop Intelligence and Web Intelligence versions, since they both display in similar views? The difference is that with the Desktop Intelligence method, all of the values are returned to the dialog and are just categorized into the different classes. In Web Intelligence, the Cascading List of Values only populates a folder when its contents is viewed. This keeps the number of values to a minimum and helps with the list of values performance.

Exercise: Create a Cascading List of Values

1. Select | *Tools | Lists of Values | Create Cascading Lists of Values* | from the menu.
2. Open the Dates (Common) class.
3. Double-click on Year Num, Month Num, and Full Date. This will place them in the *Cascading List of Values* list.
4. Click the *Generate LOV's* button.
5. Click *OK*.
   The Hierarchical Display and Export with Universe options will be checked in the Properties tab for Full Date and Month Num. There is no List of Values created for Year Num, since it is the last object in the list. If the Years are not sorted properly in the List of Values, then you will need to create a custom list that sorts Year Nums.

Notes

Index Awareness

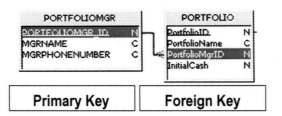

Primary Key | Foreign Key

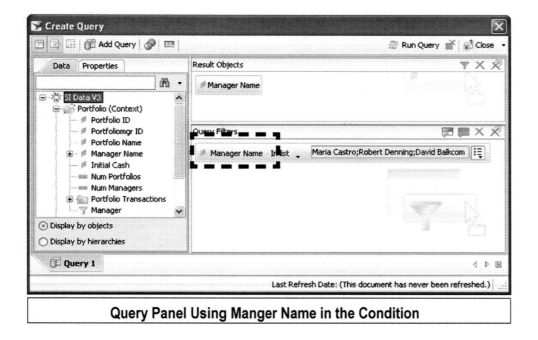

Query Panel Using Manger Name in the Condition

Keys Tab of Edit Properties Dialog

<u>**With Index Awareness**</u>

```
SELECT
  PORTFOLIOMGR.MGRNAME
FROM
  PORTFOLIOMGR
WHERE
  PORTFOLIOMGR.PORTFOLIOMGRID  IN  (2, 6)
```

<u>**Without Index Awareness**</u>

```
SELECT
  PORTFOLIOMGR.MGRNAME
FROM
  PORTFOLIOMGR
WHERE
  PORTFOLIOMGR.MGRNAME  IN  ('Maria Castro', 'David Balkcom')
```

Manager

@Select(Portfolio (Context)\Portfoliomgr ID) In @Prompt('Enter Manager Name(s)', 'A','Portfolio (Context)\Manager Name',multi,**primary_key**)

Index Awareness

We are usually interested in the non-indexed fields of a look-up table. This is the nature of look-up tables, since if we were interested in the keys, then we would just get them from the fact table or other joined tables. These non-indexed fields are usually some kind of descriptor, such as name, description, address, region name, and so forth. While we humans like to process information that is in text form, computers like the numeric id's much better. For example, a computer can search and find the value of 6, much faster than it can find the name David Balkcom. This is true, because numeric compares are much faster than text compares. For this reason, many database designers will only index numeric (and date) fields. Since this is true, it is much faster to use numeric fields in the conditions of queries.

Since humans like text and computers like numbers, Business Objects has added Index Awareness to Designer. Index Awareness allows us to list the primary and foreign keys for an object, on the Keys tab in the Edit Properties dialog. Then, Business Objects will use the key fields, instead of the text field, in the where condition of a query. This can be seen in the graphic.

In version XIV3, Business Objects added a new constant argument that is available for the @Prompt function - primary_key. It replaces free or constrained, and lets Business Objects know that there is Index awareness defined for this object. Notice that in the @Prompt, the object is the Primary Key (@Select(Portfolio (Context)\Portfoliomgr ID)) and not the text object, while the list of values is on the text object (Portfolio (Context)\Manager Name). However, in the Query Filters section of a query, the Manager Name Object is used to create the condition. This is very important to realize, because if the primary key object is not used in the @Prompt, then the @Prompt will fail. So, with prompts we use the primary key object and with constant operands, we use the object with the keys defined on the Keys tab.

Exercise: Define Index Awareness for Manager Name

1. Double-click on the Manager Name object to display the Edit Properties dialog for the object.
2. Click on the Keys tabs to activate the tab.
3. Click the *Insert* button to insert a new index definition.
4. Select Primary Key as the key type.
5. Enter PORTFOLIOMGR.PORTFOLIOMGR_ID in the Select field.
6. Click the *Insert* button to insert a new index definition.
7. Select Foreign Key as the key type.
8. Enter PORTFOLIO.PortfolioMgrID in the Select field.
9. Click OK to dismiss the dialog.
   Remember to use the primary_key constant to replace free/ constrained, and to use the Primary Key object when creating conditions with the @Prompt on Index Aware objects.

Notes

Hiding Items

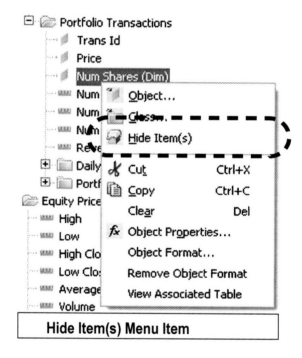

Hide Item(s) Menu Item

Hidden Objects in Universe

Hiding Items

There are times that we need objects for conditions and formulas, but do not want people using the universe to see these objects. There are other times when we should delete objects and/or classes, but think that we may need them later or we keep them around because they have some important formula that we do not want to lose. In these cases, it may be better to hide the object and/or class in the Universe section.

To hide an object, right-click on it, and then choose Hide Item(s) from the pop-up menu. The objects will then be invisible to anyone using the universe, but will still be available to universe designers to use in other objects. Hidden objects are italicized in the Universe section.

At this point, we should examine the objects Num Shares (Dim) and Num Shares (No Group By). These are special objects that perform special functions and probably should not be on the same level as Num Shares. The reason for this is that if someone tries to build a report with Num Shares (Dim), then that report would probably be not correct, because the values will behave as dimensions and not measures. The Num Shares (No Group By) will yield the correct results, but may return many more rows than necessary.

We can do one of two things with these objects. We could build a subclass called Portfolio Transactions - Advanced, and then move the objects into this folder. Then they would be available to people that are brave enough to enter into the Advanced folder - hopefully, the brave ones will understand how the objects work. The second option is to just hide them. I recommend that one of these options are taken, because it is very dangerous to leave a dimension object that should behave as a measure available to report developers

Notes

Access Restrictions

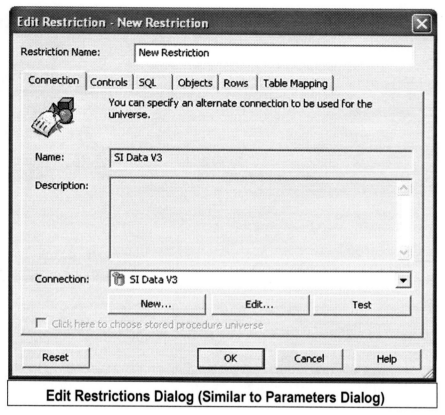

Edit Restrictions Dialog (Similar to Parameters Dialog)

Connection
Specifies different connection.

Controls
Modify the options on the Controls tab of the Parameters dialog.

SQL
Modify the selections on the SQL tab of the Parameters dialog.

Objects
Restricts objects from selected users and/or groups.

Rows
Allows for where clauses to be applied to SQL for restricted tables.

Table Mapping
Use a different table for selected users and/or groups.

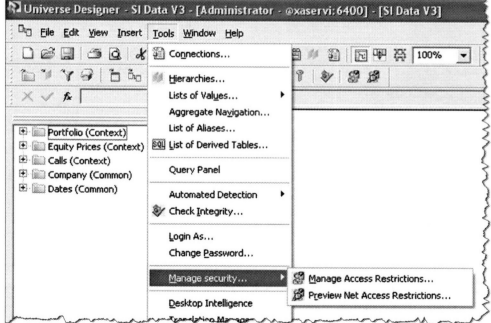

Access Restrictions

In this previous example, we decided to hide two objects that may be improperly used. At the time, one might ask why we created the objects, if we were just going to hide them. We created them, because they are useful to report developers that know how to correctly use the objects. However, we cannot release the universe to the entire population of report developers, where we will expose these objects to developers of varying skill levels. So, we just opted to hide the objects.

Access restrictions allow us to hide these objects from selected users or groups, which may be better than hiding the objects from all developers. With this feature, we can also change many other attributes of a universe. These attributes are listed in the graphic.

To access the Manage Access Restrictions dialog, select *Tools | Manage Security... | Manage Access Restrictions...* from the menu.

Notes

Manage Access Restrictions

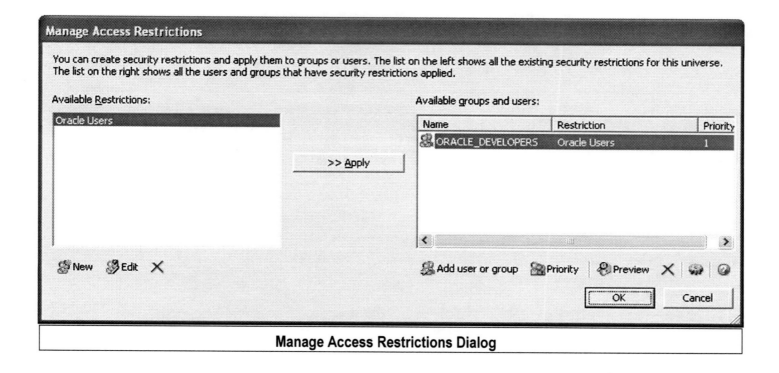

Manage Access Restrictions Dialog

Manage Access Restrictions

The Manage Access Restrictions dialog allows us to manage restrictions in the universe and the users and groups that the restrictions are applied to. The left side of the dialog allows us to manage the restriction definitions and the right side allows us to manage the users and groups with restrictions. In the graphic, there is a single restriction that overrides the number of rows that the universe can return. This option is on the Controls tab of the Edit Restriction dialog, hence the name: Control - 100,000 Rows. Universe Designers can name the restriction with any label. But, I like to include the tab and function in the name, as this helps me to identify the restriction, without having to edit it to see its definition.

On the Restriction side of the dialog, we can create new restrictions and edit and/or delete existing restrictions. When we click the New or Edit button, the Edit Restriction dialog is displayed. If we are editing an existing restriction, then the modified elements of the dialog will be in red font. This lets developers know that the option has been modified (overridden).

On the Available Groups and Users side of the dialog, we can ad users and groups to the list, set priorities to the groups, preview the net restriction for a user or group, remove users or groups from the list, and set combination options. This side allows us to manage how restrictions will apply and to see how the restrictions will apply to users that are in multiple groups.

Notes

Access Restrictions (Connection and Controls)

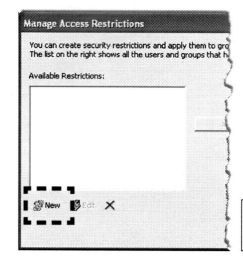

New Button in
Manage Access Dialog

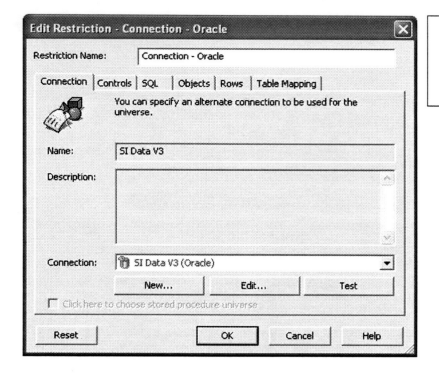

Can set the
Connection
or Modify
Query Conrls

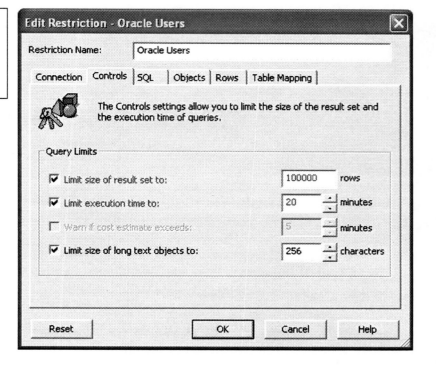

Access Restrictions (Connection and Controls)

To create a restriction, we click on the New... button in the Manage Access Restrictions dialog. Clicking the Add... button will launch the Edit Restriction dialog, which contains a few tabs that are very similar to some of the tabs in the Parameters dialog. To modify a restriction, we just change its setting in this dialog. All modified (overridden) restrictions will appear in red font.

To modify the connection, we just select or create a new connection on the Connection tab. This allows different connections with the same universe. We may override the connection for developers to use a development connection, while the default is for production. This will allow the same universe to be used for development and production. In the example, we modified our SQL Server connection to point to Oracle. Many companies also use localize connections, this allows one universe to be used throughout the world.

Many companies set query limits on their universes. The most common seems to be about 50,000 rows and 10 minutes. This works for a majority of developers, but there is always a few that need more rows or time. We can modify these controls with the Controls tab in the Edit Restrictions dialog.

Notes

Access Restrictions (SQL and Objects)

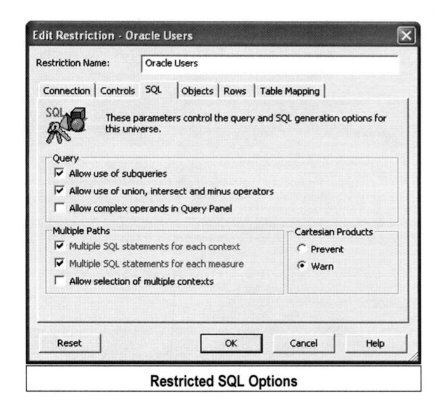

Restricted SQL Options

Restricted Objects

Access Restrictions (SQL and Objects)

Earlier, we discussed the ramifications of checking the Multiple SQL Statements for Each Measure and for Each Context. We taught that it makes the SQL behave differently, which may be difficult to manage in an enterprise environment. So, I explained that I usually don't check these options. However, there will always be a few people that need these options checked. Therefore, they are available in the Edit Restrictions dialog on the SQL tab.

In addition, we also discussed that we should hide objects that may be misinterpreted, because if they are misused, then the reports may be incorrect. However, these objects can be very useful, if used correctly. In a large organization, only a few developers will understand how to use objects, such as these (Num Shares (No Group By) and Num Shares (Dim)). So, we can leave them visible in the universe definition and then set the restrictions on the Objects tab of the Edit Restrictions dialog. In this manner, we can control who has access to these objects.

Notes

Access Restrictions (Rows)

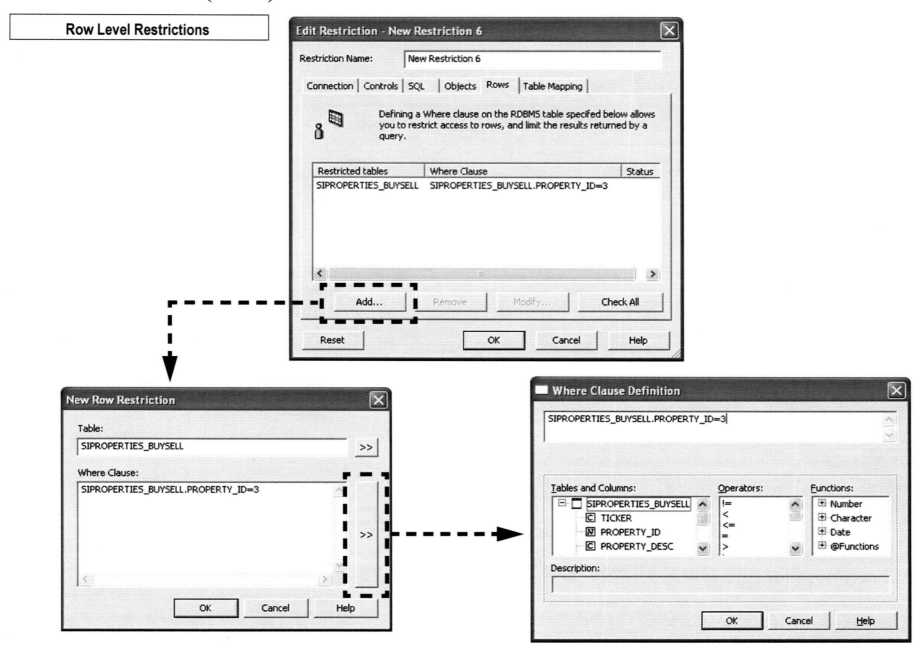

Access Restrictions (Rows)

People are always discussing Row Level Security, and you can find many different discussions on the internet, including many on www.forumtopics.com. They have these discussions, because Business Objects has changed the way Row Level Security is implemented with some of the versions. The current version XIV3, and probably later versions as well, has done a pretty good job, and it should eliminate the need for such discussions.

We can set row level security in the Edit Restrictions dialog on the Rows tab. This tab allows us to place where conditions on tables within the universe. Then, we can assign the restriction to Business Objects users or groups. So, now it is very easy to limit the data that can be viewed. For example, we can limit the Southeast Region's revenue to just the Southeast region's managers.

Another solution that this tab can provide is solving our Properties Chasm-Trap. Earlier, we discuss four different methods to solving this problem - Conditions on the objects, Conditions on the Joins, Conditions on the Derived Table Definition, and Views in the database. Well, here is another one. We can alias the table, such as SIPROPERTIES_BUYSELL and join the aliased table to COMPANY, just as we did before. However, this time don't put a self-join on the table to restrict the data to PROPERTY_ID = 3. Instead, create a restriction that will limit the data to PROPERTY_ID = 3, then apply this restriction to everybody. Chasm-trap solved, but this may not be a good solution, because it is not apparent that the chasm-trap has been solved and other Designers may try to fix it.

To create the Row Restriction, we click the *Add...* button on the Rows tab. This will launch the New Row Restriction dialog, where a restriction can be typed in. Instead of typing the restriction, the >> button can be clicked, which will launch the *Where Clause Definition* dialog. We can create a restriction in this dialog by selecting fields from tables and using the Operators and Functions that are available.

Notes

Access Restrictions (Table Mapping)

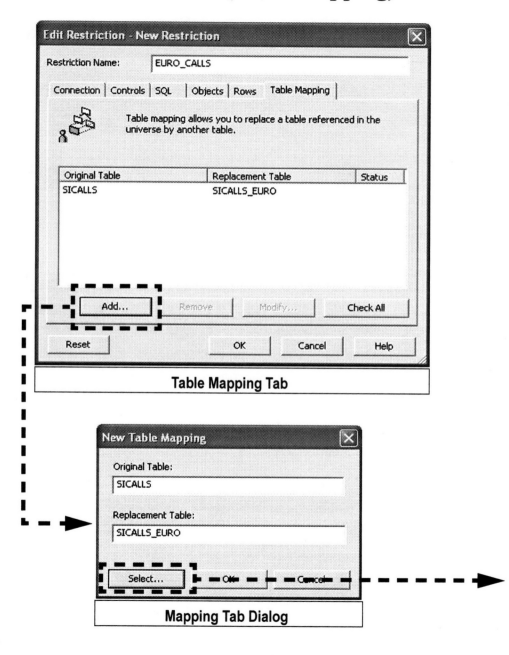

Table Mapping Tab

Mapping Tab Dialog

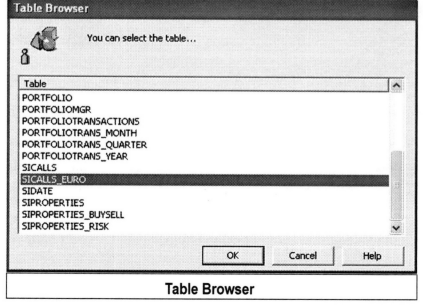

Table Browser

Access Restrictions (Table Mapping)

I once worked at a company that had three regions - Asia, Europe, and Americas. Each of these businesses shared the same customer list and other dimension tables, but they each had their own fact table. The way they implemented a solution for this, was to name the fact table with an @Prompt. The trick here was to type the prompt as a number and not text, then it could be used in the From clause of the SQL. When people refreshed reports with this universe, Business Objects would prompt for the name of the table, which would be one of the three table names.

The above solution worked well, but it allows people to view the data in regions other than their own. Table mapping replaces the table in the query based on which group the user is in. This is much more secure, because the report developer has no control as to which table the query will use. By the way, it is very important to disallow developers from modifying the SQL in these environments. This will prevent developers from simply replacing the table name in the SQL of the query.

Table mapping does not have to be just for security, it can also be for convenience. In the example in the graphic, we are replacing the SICALLS table with the SICALLS _EURO for the European users. This will allow two different groups of users to use the same universe.

Notes

Assigning Restrictions

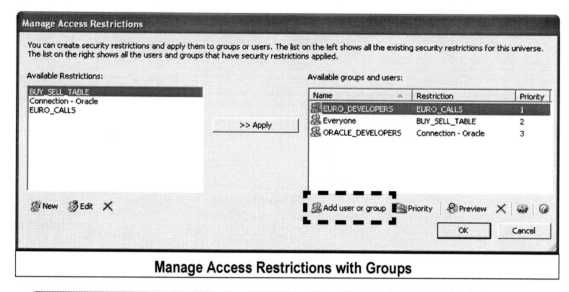

Manage Access Restrictions with Groups

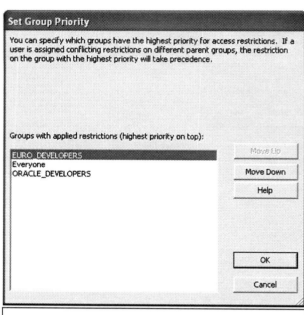

Set Group Priority Dialog

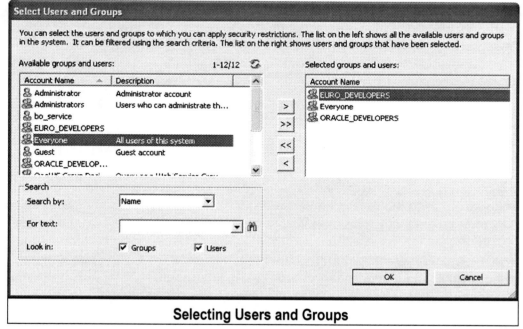

Selecting Users and Groups

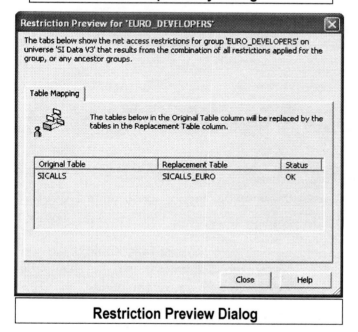

Restriction Preview Dialog

Assigning Restrictions

We created restrictions in the last few pages. Now, it is time to assign them to users and/or groups. To add users and/or groups to the Available Groups and Users list, click the *Add User or Group* button. This will launch the Select Users and Groups dialog. Simply move items from the Available Groups and Users list to the Selected Groups and Users list. Then click OK to return the selected items to the Manage Access Restrictions dialog.

When a group is first added, it will have <none> in the restrictions column, which means that there has not been a restriction assigned to the user and/or group. To assign the restriction, select the restriction, select the user or group, and then click the apply button. The restriction will be listed in the Restriction column after it has been applied.

Notice the Priority column on the right side of the Available Groups and Users list in the Manage Access Restrictions dialog. This column echoes the priority on the group. This is important if a user belongs to more than one group, because if conflicting restrictions is place on two different groups, of which a user is a member of both, then the group with the lowest priority number will have precedence. To change the priorities, click the *Priority* button, and then reorder the list of groups. The groups higher in the list have priority over groups lower in the list.

Click the *Preview* button to see the actual restrictions placed on a group. The restrictions will be shown in the Restriction Preview dialog, as shown in the graphic.

Notes

Between Joins

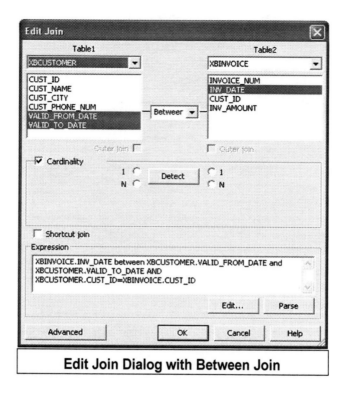

Edit Join Dialog with Between Join

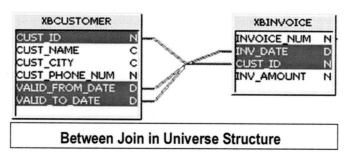

Between Join in Universe Structure

XBINVOICE.INV_DATE **BETWEEN**
XBCUSTOMER.VALID_FROM_DATE **AND**
XBCUSTOMER.VALID_TO_DATE AND
XBINVOICE.CUST_ID=XBCUSTOMERCST_ID

Between Joins

So far, we have only used equal joins, which are the most common type of join. However, there are other types of joins - Not Equal, Greater Than, Less Than,..., and Between. Basically, keys can be related with almost any logical operator - these joins are called Theta Joins. For example, suppose that you had a table of salaries and you wanted to know everybody who made more than the person on the current row, so basically you want a bunch of lists, in which each list states the employees that make more than the current record employee. You could use the Greater Than operator in the join to do this.

This could be done by aliasing the salary table and then joining on salary with the greater than operator. So, it would look something like:

Select Employee.Employee_ID, Employee.Salary, Employee_Aliased.Employee_ID,Employee_Aliased.Salary
From Employee
        Employee Employee_Aliased
Where Employee.Salary < Employee_Aliased.Salary

With Business Objects, we would simply alias the Employee table, and then join the salaries by dragging Salary from one table to the other. Then, double-click on the join and change the Equal sign (=) to a Greater Than sign (>).

Another theta join is the Between join. This works where one table has two keys that represent a range, and the other table has a key that points into the range. This can be seen with the Date Range Keys in XBCUSTOMER and the INV_DATE key in XBINVOICE. This type of join will return a row from XBCUSTOMER when the FROM_DATE is less than the INV_DATE and the TO_DATE is greater than the INV_DATE.

To create the Between join, simply drag one key on top of the FROM_DATE key. Then, double-click on the join, and then while holding the [Ctrl] key, click on the TO_DATE key. Notice that I also included CUST_ID = CUST_ID in the join expression. I believe it is best to have a single join expression, so I include CUST_ID in the expression, instead of dragging CUST_ID on top of CUST_ID and starting another join.

Notes

Advanced Join Properties

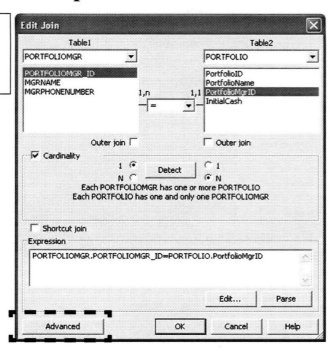

Advaned button in Edit Join Dialog

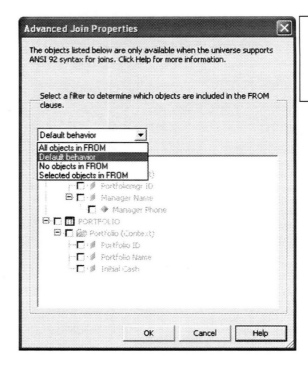

Advanced Join Properties Dialog

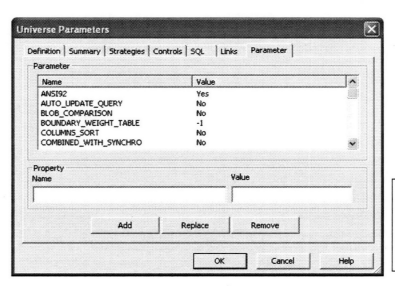

ANSI92 Option in the Universe Parameters Dialog

Advanced Join Properties

With the advent of ANSI92, fields can be in the From clause of a SQL statement. This may affect the joins' behavior when they are part of a larger query. With the Advanced Join Properties dialog, you can place none of the objects in the from clause, you can place all of the objects in the from clause, or you can select which objects are allowed in the from clause. There is also an option the just do the default behavior.

I usually just accept the default behavior, because I have found no real need (as of yet) to specify where the objects should be.

I once had a student contact me and he said that he ported his reports from a reporting system to Business Objects, and that he had a report that worked fine in the old system, but it didn't work well in Business Objects. He said that there was a condition in the where clause in the older system report that applied to the entire dataset, and then he said that in Business Objects, the condition had moved up into the From clause. This probably evolved because the older system was not ANSI 92.

After some discussion, we decided to use the Advanced Join Property to not allow this object in the From clause. He said that this forced the object into the Where clause and the query now worked fine.

Notes

Refreshing the Structure

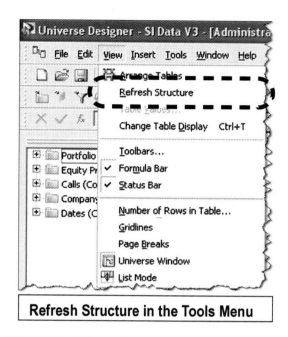

Refresh Structure in the Tools Menu

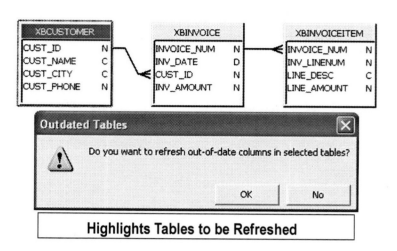

Highlights Tables to be Refreshed

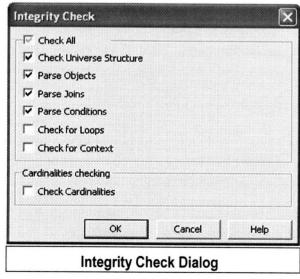

Integrity Check Dialog

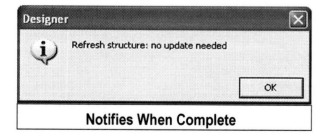

Notifies When Complete

Refreshing the Structure

Database tables often change, especially during development. We need the tables in our universes to exactly match the tables in the database - in both table name and columns. To update the tables in the universe, select | *View* | *Refresh Structure* | from the menu.

Be prepared to make changes to your universe, if some tables are updated. We will know which tables are updated, because Designer will highlight the changed tables. Some table updates won't hurt the existing structure, such as addition columns in a table. It is important to note these new columns and decide if there should be new objects to represent the columns in the universe. Some changes do hurt the universe, such as deleted and renamed columns and tables.

When a column or table name is modified, all of the objects that use these elements will be in error. The error could be one of the following: !Unknown.CUST_ID, CUSTOMER.!Unknown, @Select(*!Unknown\!Unknown*) or have no change at all, but in all cases the object will not work, because the definition points to a field or table that doesn't exist anymore.

After refreshing the structure, it is best to run an Integrity check. To display the Integrity Check dialog, select | *Tools* | *Check Integrity* | from the menu. We probably just need the *Parse Objects*, *Parse Joins* and *Parse Conditions* options selected. If a table has been deleted, then you will also want *Check Universe Structure* selected. When the check is complete, it will display a list of all of the selected errors in the universe. We can double-click on the error in the list and the Edit Properties dialog will be displayed for the object in error. Modify the object to make it correct and then double-click on the next error. Do this until all errors have been fixed.

Now, we can run the Integrity Check one more time and hopefully there are no errors. Well, at least errors that we don't want. Sometimes an object will display an error and work well in a query. We know that they work, because we test them in reports. We will talk about such an error in a few slides.

Notes

Arranging the Tables in the Structure

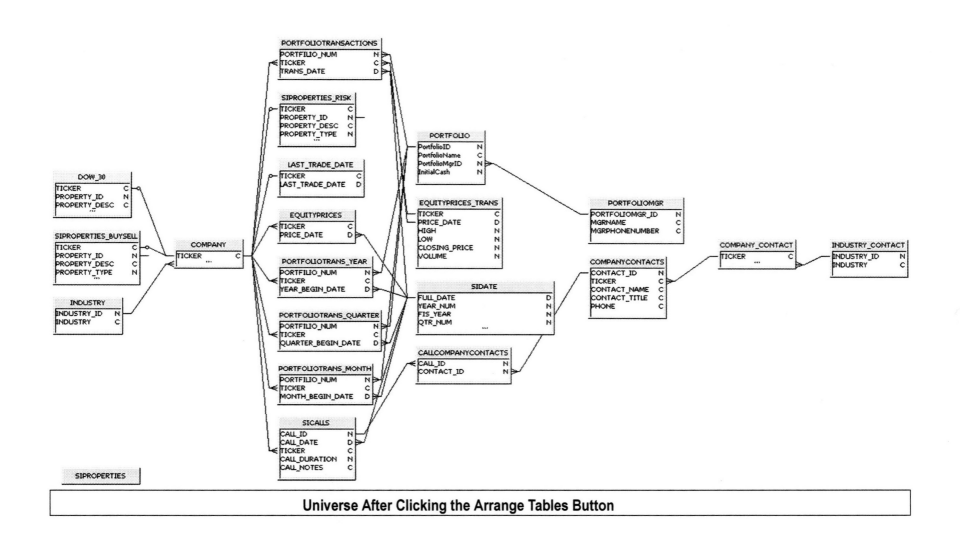

Universe After Clicking the Arrange Tables Button

Arranging the Tables in the Structure

One of the considerations when designing a universe is the table arrangement in the structure. It is very important that it is easy to read. We do this by grouping the tables into logical groups - Customer and supporting tables, Product and supporting tables, and so forth. We also make sure that as few as possible joins cross. It is very difficult to know which tables join to each other, when the joins cross like roads on a roadmap. We have GPS for roadmaps, but in the universe we are on our own.

In our universe, there is only one join that crosses. It is almost impossible to not cross this join, because there are other tables that need to be joined to the CallCompanyContacts table. However, the rest of the joins do not cross. This makes it easy for us to see the loops and possible contexts. It also helps us to see the relationship between the tables. It does something else that is very important... It shows others that we care enough to organize our structure. I have worked places where the universe is a hodge-podge of tables and joins. It is impossible to figure anything out and it makes me just want to turn around and leave, because I do not believe that they care about the universe or its purpose. However, I usually stay and straighten it out for them. Just doing this makes them think that I am a genius.

There is a quick method that usually works. You can select *Tools | Arrange Tables* from the menu. Be prepared to click the Undo button, because it may not work well. Of course, it may be better to tweak the results, rather than to undo.

Notes

Printing the Universe Definitions

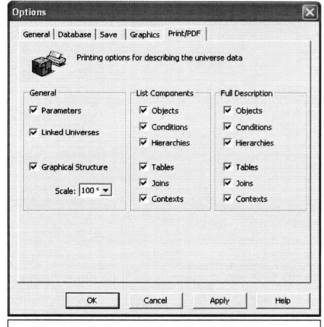

Set Print Options on the Print/PDF Tab

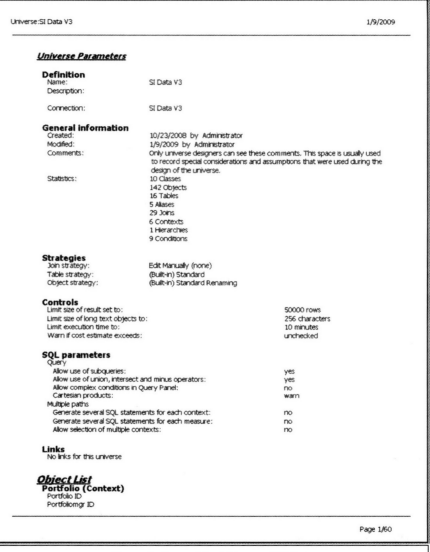

Sample from First Page of Print

Printing the Universe Definitions

There are times that we need to print the definitions of our universe. It is important for contingency plans, where we can use the print to recreate the universe. It is also important for documenting the universe.

Business Objects Designer does a good job of allowing us to select what aspects of our universe to print. We can print everything or just the parameters, as shown in the graphic. To print a universe, we simply select *File | Print...* from the main menu. There is also a convenient Print Preview option in the same menu.

To create a PDF, we select *File | Save As...* from the menu and select the *Portable Document Format* option in the *Save as Type* drop list. PDF's allow us to email and save the printed universe.

Note: The *Scale* control will allow you to shrink the universe to fit it in the Universe Report. However, it also shrinks it in the Workspace, even though the Zoom control on the toolbar says 100%. This confuses a lot of people, because they don't realize that the universe can be resized on the Print tab of the Options dialog. So, if you use the scale control to print a universe, then please set it back to 100%.

Exercise: Print Preview SI Equity - Designer Course

1. Select | *Tools* | *Options* | from the menu to display the Options dialog.
2. Click on the Print/PDF tab to activate it.
3. Check all options.
4. Click *OK*.
5. Select | *File* | *Print Preview...*| from the menu.
6. Browse through the preview.
   (Notice all of the work that we have done to make this universe.
   You should have a great sense of accomplishment, because you now know more than most people that call themselves Universe Designers.)

Notes

Stored Procedure Universe

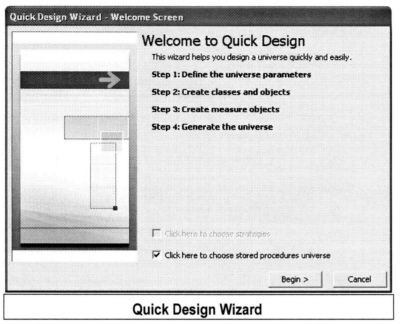

Quick Design Wizard

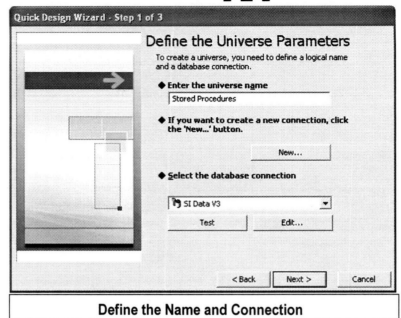

Define the Name and Connection

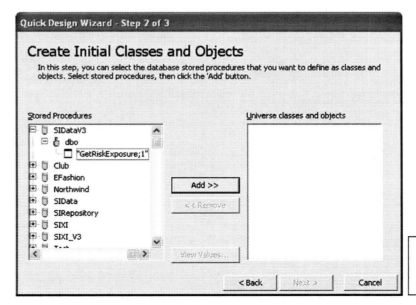

Select a Stored Procedure from the List of Database

Stored Procedure Universe

With Business Objects XI V3, you can now make Stored Procedure Universes. Back in the early 1990's, most reports were based on stored procedures. Stored procedures are just packaged SQL that returns a dataset, much the same way a SQL statement does. However, stored procedures can contain more than a simple SQL statement, which makes them much more powerful. They are also in convenient packages that we just call to return a set of data for a report. Many developers like stored procedures for these reasons, and, in addition, they are more easily secured than opening up an environment to a query tool.

So, why did we move away from stored procedures? I remember when I was working at DLJ in New York City. We were building a derivative calculator that needed database support and reports. So, we hired a new database person to do perform these tasks. About two months after hiring him, he had more than 400 stored procedures to perform various tasks and reporting functions. I remember thinking that if he quit, we would have to spend months trying to figure out what all those procedures did. Not only the quantity of stored procedures could be overwhelming, but the divergence within the procedures can be a great problem. Since procedures are individual packages, it is very difficult to enforce programming procedures. So, many managers are happy, when the stored procedures appear to be working. Only, to later find out that they are not.

So, Business Objects started a new method of creating reports using universes. This is what I have been teaching you throughout this book. Even though universes were a great solution, many developers still needed to use stored procedures for various reasons. Therefore, Business Objects now allows for Stored Procedure universes, which is really a collection of Stored Procedures and Derived tables.

To create a stored procedure universe, we use the Quick Design Wizard. To activate the wizard, click the *Quick Design Wizard* button on the Standard toolbar. On the first step of the wizard, select the *Click here to choose stored procedures universe* option. Then, click the *Next* button. In the next step of the wizard, we name our universe in the *Enter the Universe Name* field, and then we select a connection from the *Select the Database Connection* drop list. After clicking the Next button, a stored procedure can be selected from the list. Just click on the procedure to select it, and then click the *Add>>* button.

Notes

Adding the Stored Procedure

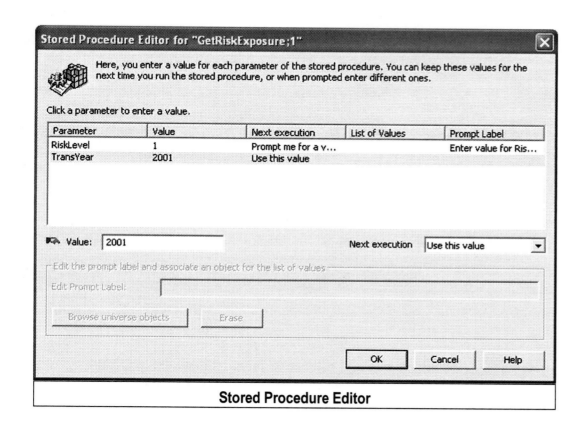

Stored Procedure Editor

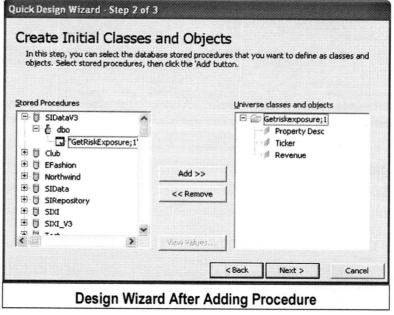

Design Wizard After Adding Procedure

Next Execution Options

Use this value

Prompt me for value

Adding the Stored Procedure

After the *Add>>* button is clicked, the Stored Procedure will move over to the *Universe Classes and Objects* side of the dialog. If the procedure accepts values through arguments, then the Stored Procedure Editor will be displayed, before the procedure is displayed. In this dialog, we assign values to the arguments.

We have to hardcode values for the creation of the Stored Procedure table, because Business Objects needs data to create the table. However, we have the option to tell Business Objects to use the hardcoded values every time the procedure is refreshed, or to prompt for new values. We do this by selecting one of the options from the Next Execution drop list. After clicking OK, a class and objects will be created for the stored procedure.

Notes

Working with Stored Procedures

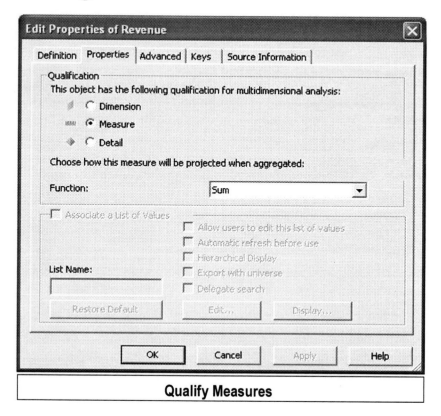

Qualify Measures

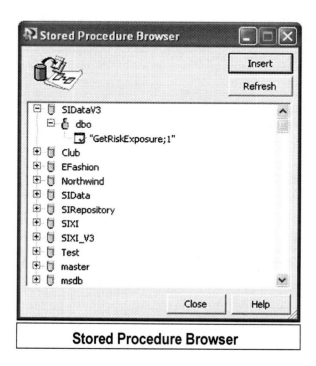

Stored Procedure Browser

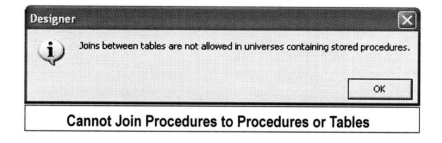

Cannot Join Procedures to Procedures or Tables

Working with Stored Procedures

After the stored procedure is inserted into the universe, then the objects must be properly qualified. For example, Revenue in our example should be a measure. Once the objects are properly qualified, then the stored procedure universe will behave as any other universe.

We can re-qualify objects by double-clicking on them in the Universe section and changing their qualification on the Properties tab of the Edit Properties dialog.

To report developers, the universe behaves as any other universe. However, it is not the same to a universe developer, because there are no joins allowed. The reason for this is that each stored procedure is a discrete package that returns a set of data. If these sets of data were joined, then there would be several considerations on how to actually link the data sets. If a report needs data from joined procedures, then the report developer can insert data sets from multiple procedures and derived tables, and then merge the dimensions to link the data sets. Remember, that if developers are doing this, then they would appreciate detail objects, if there are any candidates.

We can insert additional stored procedures by double-clicking on the white space in the workspace, or by selecting *Insert | Stored Procedures...* from the menu. This will display the Stored Procedure dialog, which is populated with procedures that the connection has rights to. We can also insert tables and derived tables, although, the tables cannot be joined, as mentioned in the previous paragraph. Therefore, the tables should be some sort of summary tables.

Notes

Chapter Summary

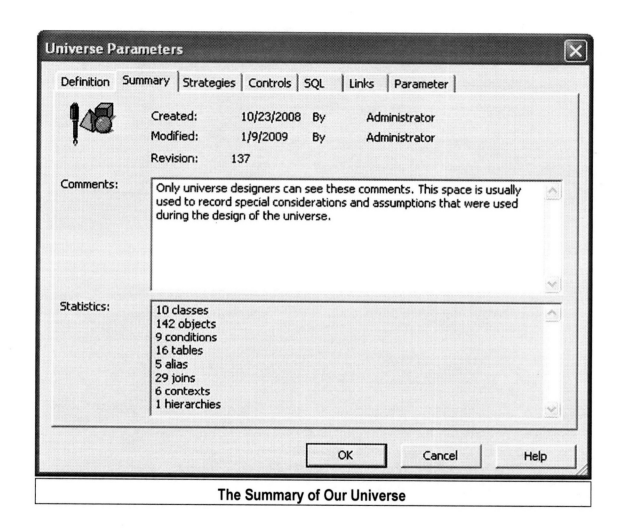

The Summary of Our Universe

Chapter Summary

In this chapter we discussed Lists of Values, Index awareness, and some other Business Objects features. It is important to have a List of Values strategy, as report refreshers will be presented with these lists.

Index awareness is also very important for database performance, as it allows keys to be used in conditions, rather than text fields. In small databases, this may be of little matter, but in large databases, this is very important to take advantage of.

Lastly, we discussed stored procedure universes. These are universes that allow us to access stored procedure through the already familiar universe interface. Stored procedure universes allow for a consistent interface for both procedures and related tables.

Notes

Course Summary

Congratulations. You have finished the course. In this chapter, I just offer some advice and thank you for trusting this manual to teach you how to create universes with Business Objects. This version of the manual contains a lot more than previous versions, and if you learned everything presented, then you will be a great universe designer.

Course Summary

This has been a very comprehensive and sometimes very creative course. We have learned how to create universes for our companies, which is a tremendous responsibility. Even though it is a large responsibility, I hope that you feel confident to take on this effort. I have seen too many smart people yield to others, because they feel that others could do a better job.

I have tried to put almost everything that can happen when creating universes into this course. So, if you feel confident with this course, then you should be able to handle almost any job. Just remember that there is almost always a fact table and supporting dimension tables. Just find and identify them and start joining. Create some objects and conditions and then make some reports. If the reports are correct, then you are doing a good job.

Always try to think like the people that will be using the universe. How will they like the objects organized? What conditions do they need? Do they want custom lists of values? I have worked at a few places where the universe designers absolutely refuse to create a report. If they do not create a report, then how can they know that their universes work? They did not know and many times the universes did not work. What a strain this was on everybody and how foolish were those IT managers that insisted that is not their job to test the universes.

My suggestion is to test all of your universes by creating documents and comparing the results to expected results. They should match exactly, unless the data or rules have changed from the older systems. I have seen many rookie designers explain every discrepancy with some kind of weird business rule that nobody knows about or understands. It has been my experience that not many older systems are inaccurate. Therefore, we should strive to get the same results out of our new systems.

One more piece of advice - *Keep a good relationship with both the database people and the business people*. Many times we work right in between these two groups and it is very important that we can freely communicate with them. Try to address all issues and keep reassuring your business people. Also, try to thank the database people as much as possible. They are often forgotten and you as the designer are often given the credit for the system. Remember that the database people make it possible for you to create great universes. I have never made a great universe on a bad database. It just doesn't work.

I hope that if you get stuck, you don't quit. There are too many quitters in this world and we will not add to this population. If you get stuck, please email me. You can get the address from my web site: www.schmidtink.com. There is also a great WEB site that has helped me many times. People call it BOB, I call it the best thing that ever happened to Business Objects. I guess calling it BOB is just more compact. Anyway, it is at this URL: http://www.forumtopics.com/busobj/index.php.

Thanks for Listening and Learning

Thanks for staying with this course and giving it your best. I appreciate your effort and hope that you are rewarded with a great career. I write these books for people just like you, and knowing that you will be able to enhance your career, and thus improving your life, is such motivation for me. As long as you all continue to read, I will continue to write. Thank you so much.

Best Regards,
Robert D. Schmidt
www.SchmidtInk.com

Notes